Societal Entrepreneurship

Positioning, Penetrating, Promoting

Edited by

Karin Berglund

Associate Professor and Centre Director, Stockholm School of Entrepreneurship, Stockholm University, Sweden

Bengt Johannisson

Professor Emeritus, Linnaeus University, Sweden

Birgitta Schwartz

Associate Professor and Senior Lecturer, Mälardalen University, Sweden

Edward Elgar
Cheltenham, UK • Northampton, MA, USA

Published by
Edward Elgar Publishing Limited
The Lypiatts
15 Lansdown Road
Cheltenham
Glos GL50 2JA
UK

Edward Elgar Publishing, Inc.
William Pratt House
9 Dewey Court
Northampton
Massachusetts 01060
USA

A catalogue record for this book
is available from the British Library

Library of Congress Control Number: 2012942064

ISBN 978 1 78100 632 0 (cased)

Typeset by Servis Filmsetting Ltd, Stockport, Cheshire
Printed and bound by MPG Books Group, UK

Contents

PART III PROMOTING SOCIETAL ENTREPRENEURSHIP
– AN EDUCATIONAL PERSPECTIVE

Figures

Tables

Contributors

Lena Andersson, PhD, holds a postdoctoral position in Business Administration at Linköping University. She is affiliated both to the Department of Management and Engineering and to the Institute for Research on Migration, Ethnicity and Society. Since 2004 she has been engaged in research concerning entrepreneurial organizing processes, mainly in and through the public sector. Her work puts focus on sensemaking in cross-sectoral initiatives such as intermediary organizations. In 2010 Lena defended her PhD thesis in which, by means of interactive methods, she portrays struggles involved in organizing between sectors. Currently, Lena is engaged in research regarding ethnic and gender dimensions in public-sector reorganizing.

Karin Berglund, PhD, is Associate Professor at Stockholm University School of Business and Centre Director of Stockholm School of Entrepreneurship. Previously she held a position at Mälardalen University. Her overarching research interest lies in visualizing the suppressed forms, groups and values of entrepreneurship. Karin has published in international journals covering different topics related to entrepreneurship such as gender, education, innovation, critical pedagogy, and regional development and now social/societal entrepreneurship. Her methodological interests lie within ethnography, discourse analysis, narrative research and participatory action research. Before entering academia Karin had a career in the private small business sector, and also took part in starting a new venture.

Carina A. Holmgren is a PhD student at the School of Innovation, Design and Technology at Mälardalen University, and CEO of PEER (Policy Entrepreneurship Evaluation Research). Carina has been engaged in research concerning initiatives in the small business and entrepreneurship policy area since 2003 and is specialized in entrepreneurship education. She has published reports and books concerning entrepreneurship education, competence development in micro firms, entrepreneurship and small business policy and interactive research methods. Her ongoing thesis project concerns the translation of the entrepreneurship concept from policy into Swedish primary and secondary school education practices.

Bengt Johannisson is Professor Emeritus of Entrepreneurship at Linnaeus University and at Jönköping International Business School in Sweden. Between 1998 and 2007 he was editor-in-chief of *Entrepreneurship and Regional Development* and he has published widely on entrepreneurship, personal networking, and family business, as well as on local and regional development. In the 1980s he published pioneering research in community entrepreneurship. More recently Bengt has propagated more responsible and interactive enquiries into entrepreneurship, including enactive research. He has initiated several inter-university networks on research and postgraduate studies in entrepreneurship in Sweden. For 15 years he co-directed the European Doctoral Programme in Entrepreneurship and Small Business Management. Bengt was the 2008 Winner of the Global Award for Entrepreneurship Research.

Anders W. Johansson has been Professor of Entrepreneurship at Linnaeus University since 2008 and Vice Dean of the School of Business and Economics 2010–2012. Previously he was Professor of Entrepreneurship at Mälardalen University. His publications cover core issues of entrepreneurship such as innovation, regional development, family business, advising small businesses, gender issues, narrative approach, and discourse analysis and interactive research methods. In these areas he has supervised a dozen PhD students. His research is based upon a broad view of entrepreneurship as a renewing power in society. Anders had a long career in the private sector as a small business consultant and has been working full time in the non-profit/voluntary sector for several years.

Erik Rosell is a PhD student in entrepreneurship at Linnaeus University. In his thesis he is working with interactive methods to produce close and detailed accounts of entrepreneurial processes as they emerge and develop in the non-profit/voluntary sector. His thesis is based upon a broad view of entrepreneurship that puts focus upon how change and renewal are performed in everyday actions and interactions.

Birgitta Schwartz, PhD, is Associate Professor in Business Administration at Mälardalen University. Her research is about company actions and strategies regarding sustainable development issues like environmental and social responsibility and how companies interplay with other organizations. She has published in the area of environmental strategies, CSR, standardization of environmental and social issues in organizations, Fair Trade, entrepreneurship and social entrepreneurship. She has supervised several doctoral students and is a member of the editorial board of the *Business Strategy and the Environment* journal.

Elisabeth Sundin, PhD, is Professor Emerita in Business Administration and Management at Linköping University. She is also one of the senior research leaders at HELIX VINN Excellence Centre on "Managing Mobility for Learning, Health and Innovation". Previously she was a professor at the National Institute of Working Life and at Jönköping International Business School. Her research fields and publications include different areas and are now focused on organizational change, especially public sector organizations, described and analysed from the perspectives of SMEs, entrepreneurship and gender. She is also interested in the methods and development of the social sciences.

Malin Tillmar, PhD, is Associate Professor in Business Administration and Deputy Director of HELIX VINN Excellence Centre at Linköping University. Her research focuses on less explored aspects of entrepreneurship, often with an interactive approach. In 2002 she defended her dissertation "Swedish Tribalism and Tanzanian Agency: Preconditions for Trust and Cooperation in a Small Business Context". Since then she has studied entrepreneurship in the era of public sector transformation and societal entrepreneurship. In 2005 she won the FSF-Nutek prize for young entrepreneurship researchers. Results have been published, for example in *Scandinavian Journal of Management, Entrepreneurship and Regional Development* and *International Journal of Gender and Entrepreneurship*.

Preface

Entrepreneurship is the outcome of a collective effort, and so is this book. It is of course up to our readers to judge if this anthology and the messages it communicates are innovative, but in the making of this book we have tried to practise creative organizing. Its contributors originate in an alliance between three Swedish universities; Linnaeus University (a recent merger of Växjö and Kalmar Universities), Linköping University and Mälardalen University. Together we submitted a research proposal when the Swedish Knowledge Foundation in 2008 invited applicants to their research programme on social entrepreneurship. The foundation's generous funding of the project – *Organizing Societal Entrepreneurship in Sweden (OSIS)* – made it possible to establish a research network including not only project members but also other Swedish researchers in the field.

Our staffing of the knowledge-creation process in OSIS also includes practitioners. Trading upon the well-established Scandinavian tradition of interactive research the Swedish Knowledge Foundation also financially supported four social enterprises and non-profit organizations that participated in dialogues with the researchers. Three of these co-producers of knowledge appear in this book, the Moon House, Oria and Social Entrepreneurship in Practice (SIP). Additional generous funding by Växjö University made it possible to also include the social enterprise Macken in the research process. We think that the dialogues with these social enterprises have been mutually appreciated by practitioners and researchers and have produced considerable added scientific value to this anthology.

This book and the research milieu that it has built originate in an earlier initiative by the Swedish Knowledge Foundation to mobilize research on social and societal entrepreneurship in Sweden. Part of those efforts was presented in the anthology *Entrepreneurship in the Name of Society*, published in 2009. The book and its many contributions from several disciplines and universities from all parts of Sweden were, in addition to Bengt Johannisson, edited by Malin Gawell and Mats Lundqvist. They both continued to support OSIS by participating in the different seminars that have been organized by the project over the years. Especially valuable was their critical review of the original drafts of the chapters making this book. We thank them and Friederike Welter at Jönköping International Business School, who also participated in the scrutinizing process.

The Swedish Knowledge Foundation has thus enabled us to create a learning context that, like societal entrepreneurship crossing boundaries between the private, public and non-profit/voluntary sectors, brings together researchers and practitioners from different academic and non-academic settings. We feel that we have appreciated this opportunity to practise some entrepreneurship ourselves and we hope that this feeling has materialized in words that make new sense to you, our readers.

Karin Berglund, Bengt Johannisson and Birgitta Schwartz
Stockholm, Växjö and Västerås, April 2012

1. Introduction: in the beginning was societal entrepreneurship

Karin Berglund and Bengt Johannisson

SETTING THE STAGE

We imagine that human beings in historical times were enterprising, climbing the ladder of evolution, inventing 'tools' (such as language or the ability to make fire), creating new ways to organize and working out new means to improve living conditions for themselves as well as for society at large. Entrepreneurship/Entrepreneuring we thus view as being as old as human beings' existence on earth, constituting practices that in many different ways have contributed to what is perceived today as progress. During the industrial era entrepreneurship as progress was associated with growth and material wealth-making. In present times enterprising people who are able to recreate societal structures that enforce sustainable development, environmentally, socially, ethically as well as financially, are much sought after.

Entrepreneurship as a societal phenomenon also has a long history, albeit often forgotten in the academic context. As early as the original 1911/12 German version of *Theory of Economic Development* (1934) Schumpeter put economic activity in a societal context, although the chapter that brought it up was 'lost in translation' in the English version. In modern times social issues were re-discovered when the aftermath of the oil crisis in the 1970s challenged the industrialized world. In Sweden the notion of 'societal' entrepreneurs was introduced to depict all the enthusiasts who took charge of organizing the needed local recovery processes in peripheral regions. When this research was published in English 'societal' was translated into 'community' (Johannisson and Nilsson 1989), re-establishing Gemeinschaft values and practices; compare Tönnies (1965). In this vein entrepreneurship scholars have stressed the importance of disconnecting entrepreneurship from the economic sphere (Hjorth 2003; Steyaert and Katz 2004), which has enhanced our ability to view entrepreneurship as a multi-dimensional phenomenon that occurs in society at large (see for example. Bill et al. 2010).

Referring to the writings of Gabriel Tarde, Johansson (2010) points out the importance of imitation in the crafting of new ventures. Chris Steyaert (see for example Steyaert 2004) associates entrepreneurship with prosaic and everyday 'entrepreneuring'. Johannisson proposes that children in their play reveal human beings as naturally born entrepreneurs and that entrepreneurship is a generically collective activity (Johannisson 2011). These views position entrepreneurship as genuinely associated with human activity, located in societies that adopt Gemeinschaft practices characterized by strong relationships and mutual concern, contrasting the dominating Gesellschaft orientation of market actors who were focused on by Schumpeter. While Gesellschaft principles can be described as directing entrepreneurship in a top-down way, Gemeinschaft principles mobilize entrepreneuring from the bottom up. Understanding entrepreneurship as a mobilizing force is thus vital.

However, we still know little about how the mobilization of everyday societal entrepreneuring is enacted. We need to know more about how the fine-grained details of everyday life form in new patterns and how human beings invent 'tools' and organize in new ways to solve problems and create opportunities on the many arenas that contemporary societies offer. This means that we struggle in trying to achieve, understand and appreciate the kind of entrepreneurship that does not only comply with the whims of the market with its rather arbitrary ideological agenda, but changes our understanding of entrepreneurship and its role in creating new and better worlds.

When concern for the societal dimension of entrepreneurship was re-invented by the global academic and non-academic communities in parallel, it was generally addressed as 'social' entrepreneurship (see for example Fayolle and Matlay (2010)). In an anthology presenting different understandings of entrepreneurship in (Swedish) society Gawell et al. (2009) stated that just contrasting social and traditional (commercial) entrepreneurship may hide important aspects of entrepreneurship as a societal phenomenon. The images of social and commercial are often juxtaposed, underpinning the notion of their differences, which often results in discussions of 'either or', rather than 'both and'. In the anthology *An Introduction to Social Entrepreneurship* this more nuanced view of social entrepreneurship is exposed by scholars who from different disciplines seek to voice social entrepreneurship, not only as juxtaposed to traditional entrepreneurship, but also from the perspective of history, sociology and cultural theory (Ziegler 2009). This addresses the struggles to create a sustainable modern society.

Likewise, in this book we take a point of departure in entrepreneurship as a struggle to create a sustainable society. Entrepreneurship is addressed in particular as a concern for all sectors in society, as truly 'societal'; commercial as well as social. This leads to a 'both and' perspective that also embraces the non-profit/voluntary (NPVO) sector and pays attention to movements between sectors. Consequently, viewing the field through the glasses of societal entrepreneurship, we wish to contribute with a 'both and' language, which includes many further appearances of the entrepreneurial phenomenon. Common to all forms of societal entrepreneurship is that they (1) mobilize initiatives, (2) provide an innovative force, and (3) channel a value creation power (see Gawell et al. 2009). While the notion of an 'innovative force that channels value creation' is part of the traditional entrepreneurship discourse, that of mobilizing initiatives is of particular interest to societal entrepreneurship.

At an individual level mobilizing emphasizes how men and women in everyday life become enrolled in entrepreneurial practices without viewing themselves as entrepreneurs in the first place (Holmquist and Sundin 2002; Sundin, 2004; Berglund and Wigren 2011). Berglund and Johansson (2007) further this reasoning by paying attention to dominant entrepreneurship discourses as excluding, reinforcing the image of the entrepreneur as a gender-biased and ethnocentrically determined figure. Drawing upon the ideas of the critical pedagogue Paolo Freire (1970), known for his emancipatory pedagogy, Berglund and Johansson conclude that contemporary entrepreneurship discourse, often considered to maintain agency and support action, works in the opposite direction. The reason is that it excludes the many people who do not relate to themselves as societal entrepreneurs, which prevents entrepreneurship from manifesting itself throughout society. Consequently, critical thinking is required to free us in the Western world context from an oppressive discourse and replace it with a view that acknowledges each and everyone's enterprising capacity in the contexts they are familiar with. Considering the bottom-up principle of mobilizing, it is of particular interest in relation to marginalized groups, to ideas that do not fit in with growth rhetoric, and to places that are not viewed as entrepreneurial, according to Gesellschaft principles.

The purpose of this anthology is thus to propose, and from different perspectives illuminate, the notion of 'societal entrepreneurship' as a concept that emphasizes the need for enterprising people in all sectors and corners of contemporary society. The view embraced is that societal entrepreneurship is a concept that spans from recognizing entrepreneuring in dull and mundane life to capturing global and pioneering movements and clarifying sweeping descriptions of how structures change. Our purpose also includes setting the agenda for entrepreneuring efforts that break with the practices that do not benefit the making of a sustainable society. Our understanding of societal entrepreneurship signals that the shape it takes is sensitively dependent upon context. This means that the ambition with this book can only be achieved through a close dialogue between emerging themes and an empirical reality, based in Sweden. Simply stated: context matters (see Welter 2011).

Our approach means that we do not have the capacity to provide an exhaustive review of the extant literature on societal entrepreneurship with its varying perspectives on the phenomenon. We rather confine ourselves to a discourse that analytically and empirically clarifies the meaning and implications of the perspective that we propose. This is done by *positioning* entrepreneurship in societal contexts, *penetrating* its bright and also its dark sides, as well as discussing how it can be *promoted*. Accordingly, the upcoming chapters are organized into these themes. In the concluding chapter we return to the notion of positioning, penetrating and promoting with the ambition of weaving together the three different themes with the conceptual and methodological strands that are brought up in this introductory chapter.

Recognizing societal entrepreneurship as a contextual phenomenon, the Swedish setting that accommodates it is here briefly presented. Thereafter, entrepreneurship is further discussed and more specifically put in relation to the three sectors: the for-profit/private, the government/public and the non-profit/voluntary (NPVO) sector. These concepts are needed to position our approach. We then discuss conceptual and methodological implications of approaching societal entrepreneurship, before a more elaborate introduction to the themes of positioning, penetrating and promoting concludes our exposé of societal entrepreneurship.

THE SWEDISH CONTEXT

Societal entrepreneurship is not exclusive to Sweden, but for a number of reasons we believe that Sweden is an especially interesting setting for demonstrating the interplay between context and the forms societal entrepreneurship takes. Sweden itself is a dense national context that is, not only because of its limited population, tightly embedded in an international setting. Sweden is a welfare state that has not been at war for over two centuries. Besides, during the first three quarters of this period it had a very homogenous population that has contributed significantly to the making of a society that has invited all three sectors. Strong popular movements, such as the labour unions, the sports associations, the free churches and the temperance movement have built a pervasive non-profit sector. In some places such as Gnosjö, an industrial district and entrepreneurial

Swedish context, these movements have carried out many public-sector functions (see for example Wigren 2003).

Sweden's relatively small domestic market has made the country very alert to global influences and open for social experiments, which makes Sweden a perfect testing ground for new ideas in general, and new technologies in particular. Entering Arlanda international airport in Stockholm, a range of famous Swedes on big posters welcome the visitor; from the well-known royal family, and the cultural icons Ingmar Bergman and Greta Garbo, to sports legends like Björn Borg (tennis), Annika Sörenstam (golf) and Ingemar Stenmark (downhill skiing). In the midst of them, a few entrepreneurs are visible. However, the business community is mainly associated with large industries and technological advancement, medical improvement and the support of research progress (the Nobel Prize). From an international viewpoint Sweden is also known for its neutrality as well as its efforts to be part of UN peace-making (Dag Hammarskjöld, Olof Palme and Jan Eliasson, the new UN Deputy Secretary General , to mention a few), and it has a long history with the Social Democratic party ruling the political agenda. This situation was however reversed in 2010 when the Conservative/Liberal alliance was re-elected for another period of four years. At present, the Social Democratic party faces severe internal and external problems and seems to go through some major challenges in remaking its politics for the future.

In the book *Is the Swede a Human Being?* Berggren and Trägårdh (2006) in a novel way capture Swedish culture as the context that embeds us. The ideas of solidarity and equal rights are reinterpreted. These ideas, the authors argue, are not only a leftover from the ruling Social Democratic party but are much more thoroughly grounded in Swedish culture. Understanding the complexity of 'Swedishness' and its historical roots, the authors end up with the thought-provoking claim that Swedes want – more than anything – to be left alone. But they also want to leave others alone. Instead of focusing on solidarity and equal rights, the mutual contract between individuals and the state is emphasized. This contract is labelled 'state individualism', with an advanced social welfare system guaranteeing each individual's independence from family, charity and other communities.

Consequently, all twentieth century reforms, except for parental leave insurance, enforce the state individualism principle. High Swedish incomes and company taxes make the social welfare system possible. One reform with implications for (women's) entrepreneurship is the childcare system. Ahl (2006: 607) maintains that, in comparison to the United States, Sweden offers a childcare system which creates opportunities for both men and women to work – and start companies – without the interruption of starting a family, whereas in the US the context of combining childcare from a home-based business is seen as an opportunity for women. The point is that the system creates conditions, albeit often invisible and taken for granted, which shape the need, possibilities and potential for how (societal) entrepreneurship can be staged. Reflecting on this example, taxes can be seen as the necessary evil that Swedes need to pay for their coveted independence.

Each person is thus seen to have the power to direct her or his own life, which indicates that a radical form of individualism prevails in Sweden (see also Hofstede's (1980) positioning of Sweden on his global map of work-related values). However, Swedes have not turned into the stereo-typically depicted quiet, cold and independent individuals because they have been subjugated by a dominant state, but because it suits the his-torically constructed Swedish mentality, grounded in direct relations with power institution (the Kingdom) instead of a feudal structure which was more prominent in continental Europe (Berggren and Trägårdh 2006). The autonomy of the financially strong Swedish municipalities and the highly developed welfare system thus makes individual freedom possible. Yet, over the last few decades it has been threatened by the strong neo-liberal currents that promote a belief in individualism, de-regulation, privatiza-tions and a free market. In our view, this awakens the need of societal entrepreneurship, not only as a research subject but as a movement that has grown important to Swedes. Here we will illustrate how people move in between sectors. The intermediaries in a municipality move in between local politicians, civil servants and small business owners (Chapter 5). The teachers involved in entrepreneurship education move in between educa-tional systems, interacting with consultants who want to be part of chan-ging the school and local organizations that are enthusiastic about the idea of introducing entrepreneurship into (public, private and non-profit) education; see Chapter 9. The social enterprise Macken (Chapter 3) can be seen as a hub in which the 'movers' from different sectors meet, working on current issues in the local community, only to move on in due course. These movements also cross national boundaries. The social entrepreneur building up a Fair Trade company moves in between customers well-initiated in the threat of consumerism, national fair-trade organizations and the Indian context; see Chapter 6.

Considering the continuous strong presence of the welfare system, with security being (still) best provided by the impersonal state, 'social' is in one sense left outside this equation. As will be illustrated here, however, 'the social' manifests itself in new ways among those who find a common interest in a topic or a will to change something, but also to prevent change from occurring. Social relations are thus necessary to ensure freedom.

From one perspective Sweden would do quite well in the process of the Western world where the family institution is severely threatened. Practices grown out of state individualism are more compatible with individualism as personal freedom than in nations where the contract is made between the individual and the family, as in the United States, or between the state and the family, as in Germany (Berggren and Trägårdh 2006). On the other hand, the emerging neo-liberal agenda does not always make cooperation easy. An example is given by Merle et al. (2003) in their study of the entrepreneurial transformation of the Swedish university system. In this case, 'entrepreneurial' was influenced by policy, emphasizing knowledge exploitation, pushing learning processes into the background. Their conclusion is that, when one aspect of a thing – in this case knowledge exploitation – is highlighted, the practices of knowledge exploration and creation that precede the desired output were hampered. In this case the role of policy was ambiguous in the sense that it created an entrepreneurial process only to make it limp. The role of entrepreneurship and innovation policy in supporting societal entrepreneurship may thus be ambiguous. Supporting one type of entrepreneurship does not mean supporting the processes that revitalize societal structures, which is discussed in this book in the case of intermediaries working in the public sector (see Chapter 5).

As indicated, Sweden is characterized by a financially very strong local and national public sector. In 2009, 29.5 per cent of the total working population, or 1,317,000 persons, were employed by the public sector, that is, local/regional municipalities and the state.[1] The remaining employment is primarily cared for by the private sector (including independent businesspeople), leaving a minor share to the non-profit/voluntary (NPVO) sector. However, we here ascribe an important intermediating or catalytic function in society to that sector. In a recent report by Statistics Sweden the 2009 scope of and contributions by Swedish civil society, that is the NPVO sector, are reported in detail (Statistics Sweden 2011). The study adopts the United Nations' International Classification of Non-Profit Organisations (ICNPO), which means that only self-governed voluntary, yet formal, organizations with no owners expecting a return are considered. The study states Swedish civil society includes 50,000 economically active organizations with an overall turnover of well over 200 billion SEK (in 2009 the exchange rate for a euro varied between 11.4 and 10.2 SEK). Approximately 61,000 people were employed full time (or the equivalent) and, in addition, almost one million Swedes made contributions as organized volunteers. Swedish civil society consists overall of 25 million memberships in voluntary organizations – the Swedish population being about nine million – and jointly they deliver almost as much labour as their employees (the equivalent of 53,000 full-time workers). While 6 million Swedes aged 16 or above are members of at least one organization and 3.9 million are union members, only 360,000 are actively involved, and even fewer are politically active. Voluntary work is especially common in the leisure and cultural area, and men are more active than women. The report reveals that the overall financial transfer from the public sector to the NPVO sector in return for its contributions in 2009 amounted to 36 billion SEK, about 45 per cent of which was provided by the state and the rest by the municipalities.

Reviewing changes in the Swedish NPVO sector/civil society at the turn of the millennium, Wijkström's (2011) point of departure is the increasingly blurred boundaries between the three sectors. The ideology of the private sector as the domicile of managerialism has not only influenced the public sector, through NPM (New Public Management), but the NPVO sector as well. Another re-orientation with further implications for how societal entrepreneurship appears in the Swedish context is that a great many organizations in the NPVO sector have changed from being a voice for different interests and ideas to become involved in hands-on social work. Adopting the terminology suggested by Knutsen and Brower (2010), there is a move from expressive to instrumental accountability among the organizations constituting the sector. See also Segnestam Larsson 2011.There is also a change in the input of work by paid staff and unpaid work by organization members and volunteers. While work by paid staff (in terms of the equivalence of full-time workers) only increased by 10 per cent over the 1992–2002 period, and the unpaid work done by organization members did not change at all, the contributions by volunteers increased by 150 per cent. Wijkström's conclusion is that not just social enterprises but also the majority of organizations belonging to the NPVO today appear as hybrid constructs.

FEATURING CROSS-SECTORAL ENTREPRENEURSHIP IN CONTEMPORARY SOCIETY

In order to understand the potential of entrepreneurship as a mobilizing social force the interplay between sectors has to be highlighted, as discussed by Sundin and Tillmar (2010) in *Handbook of Research of Social Entrepreneurship*. Already the notion of 'community' suggests that societal entrepreneurship calls for a holistic approach including all aspects of (a miniature) society. Putting the focus on how societies are organized, the activities and the governing of all its three sectors (the private, public and NPVO ones) have then to be considered. Rather than associating entrepreneurship with an individual, however bold and energetic, with strategic social measures in corporations, with caring public institutions or with contributions by the NPVO sector, we here consider the very bridging between the three sectors as the core of what we address as 'societal entrepreneurship'. Before presenting the characteristics of these sectors and their different logics and profiles in Swedish society, we need, however briefly, to comment upon how societal entrepreneurship relates to other notions of entrepreneurship, except the commercial aspect.

Modern society is characterized by a division of labour and responsibility between organizations and institutions. The latter contribute order, the 'rules of the game', while organizations use the regulated and protected space for structured goal-directed activities. Writings on 'social entrepreneurship' or commercial entrepreneurship usually take this division for granted. However, as will be elaborated below, societal entrepreneurship is closely related to institutions as an arena for entrepreneurship. Critically reviewing the notion of 'institutional entrepreneurship' Czarniawska (2009) identifies three groups of – individual or collective – institutional entrepreneurs: those who ignore or protest against the existing institutional order, those who institute a new practice hoping it will become institutionalized, and those who establish a formal organization with the intention to make it into an institution in its own right. As regards the first group we elsewhere address them as 'extreme entrepreneurs' (Johannisson and Wigren 2006), although we argue that protest does not have to mean that a new institution is established. As for the second group, Sundin and Tillmar (2008) provide examples of public employees in the Swedish context who change institutions by initiating new practices.

In most contemporary societies, in welfare states for certain, public human activities are clustered in three sectors: the for-profit/private, the public, and the non-profit/voluntary (NPVO) sectors (see also Tillmar 2009). The boundaries between the three sectors are continuously being re-negotiated, and thus become blurred. Times of turbulence have challenged the public sector and invited a private-sector vocabulary and venturing initiatives. Both these sectors consider the NPVO sector as either a backup or as an arena where new ways to deal with economic or social challenges can be tested, only to be later appropriated by the other sectors, which then contribute with new values and practices.

Societal entrepreneurship as value-creation processes across sector borders implies dealing with several institutional settings which are widely apart in structural respects. In the organization literature, both on management and on institutions, the notion of 'logic' is often referred to as a key concept when it comes to featuring operating characteristics. Prahalad

(2004: 172), a leading scholar in the (strategy) field, describes business logic as follows:

> [t]he dominant logic of the company is, in essence, the DNA of the organisation. It reflects how managers are socialised. It manifests itself often, in an implicit theory of competition and value creation. It is embedded in standard operating procedures, shaping not only how the members of the organisation act but also how they think. Because it is the source of the company's past success, it becomes *the lens* through which managers see all emerging opportunities (italics in original).

Companies responding to new expectations from the surrounding community are shown in Schwartz's (2009) study of how firms cope with environmental demands as primarily automorphic. This means that they repeat their earlier successful strategies and imitate their own history rather than imitating others. According to the *Handbook of Organizational Institutionalism*, institutional logic concerns 'the socially constructed, historical patterns of material practices, assumptions, values, beliefs, and rules by which individuals produce and reproduce their material subsistence, organize time and space, and provide meaning to their social reality' (Thornton and Ocasio 1999: 804; see also Thornton and Ocasio 2008). Obviously, logic both in a business and in an institutional setting relates to sense-making as well as to action, to practice, although not as explicitly as an ideology.

Rather than trying to 'translate' either of the proposed logics, or an amalgamated version of them, into comprehensive definitions of different 'sector logics' we here bring forward some aspects of such logic that draw upon the organization literature and that we think comes out differently in each sector. The ambition is not to provide a conclusive model of sector logics but rather use the concept of sector logics diagnostically in a way that invites an understanding of the differences and similarities between the three sectors that have implications for the way societal entrepreneurship is enacted. Accordingly, in Table 1.1 an overview of the aspects is provided with brief comments.

The features of the *institutional pillars* providing each sector with a basic order constitute the point of departure. There are (of course) many different understandings of institutions, but considering our concern for the micro/meso levels, that is societal entrepreneurship as an intra- and inter-organizational phenomenon in a national –Swedish – context, the framework provided by Scott (2008) is appropriate. Accordingly, institutions 'are comprised of regulative, normative and cultural-cognitive elements that, together with associated activities and resources, provide stability and meaning to social life' (ibid., p. 48). Certainly laws and regu-

Table 1.1   Aspects of sector logics

	Private Sector	Public Sector	NPVO Sector
Institutional pillars	Normative	Regulative	Cognitive/Cultural
Time perspective	Short-term	Long-term	Short- and long-term
Focal form of capital	Financial	Human	Social
Interaction rationale	Calculative	Ideational/ Calculative	Ideational/Genuine
Commitment	Voice/exit	Loyalty	Involvement
Control	Output	Process	Culture
Innovation	Advancing technologies	Ongoing reforming	Mobilizing human capacities
Outlook	Global	Local	Glocal

lations frame the activities in all three sectors but are obviously especially relevant in the public sector, since all actions there must be formally sanctioned. In the private sector shared norms, for example industry standards, and values, such as codes of conduct, are important in order to reduce transaction costs and build mutually binding expectations between actors. The NPVO sector rests on a pillar that is deeply founded in cognitive structures which in turn are embedded in multiple cultural layers. This signals inertia but also stable and common beliefs and responsibility for society.

In the private sector the *time perspective* of actors, organizational or individual, is a short-term perspective. Today ideas travel fast and so do resources, not least the financial ones. Taking and keeping the lead in the market is fundamental, whether we have management or traditional images of entrepreneurship in mind. Schumpeter's as well as Kirzner's theorizing were both about exploiting the temporary monopolies that innovativeness and alertness create. The public sector, in contrast, defends long-term perspectives. Only then is it possible to carry out reforms since in the name of democracy they first have to be carefully investigated, then presented and processed in the political system and finally furnished with a competent administration in order to be properly implemented. Organizations in the NPVO sector may apply either a long- or a short-time perspective depending on whether the issue concerned calls for immediate action or for solutions that are sustainable over time. As several cases in this volume will report, what time perspective is practised by NPVO organizations is very much contingent upon what needs are left to care for when the two other sectors have organized what they are able and willing to deal with.

Since the private sector is driven by economic values, financial *capital* dominates resourcing. Firms that are in their formative years, as well as those which stay entrepreneurial, however, use to a larger extent the other forms of capital to resource their operations (Johannisson 2008). The public sector organizations are of course dependent on (financial) funding of costs, but in that sector the core form of capital, that which makes a difference and quality, is professional knowledge, that is human capital. The NPVO sector stands out with its focus on social capital, both individual and collective (Esser 2008). The former is important to individual social enterprises since the personal and professional networks that constitute the social capital form bridges to further resources. Collective social capital is constituted as an asset of the members in a community, whether we have a nation or a small location in mind.

Studying different interaction rationales Sjöstrand (1992) identifies six 'institutions' or *interaction rationales.* In Sjöstrand's terminology, the private sector typically practises a calculative rationale, while the other two sectors develop, according to situation and context, a repertoire where two rationales dominate jointly. Public sector agents have thus on one hand to adhere to enacted norms in society in order to represent the citizens, and on the other they have to use the resources allocated so that instrumental efficiency is achieved. This is described as interaction combining a calculative and an ideational rationale. NPVO organizations are also guided by ideals with a deep concern for human values but in their practice, as carried out by individual members, genuine/personal relations strongly influence how they carry out their work, which is characterized by a combination of an ideational and a genuine rationale.

How people contribute to their organization, that is, to its efficiency and effectiveness or, alternatively, leave the organization, is reflected in their *commitment* to it when challenged. Hirschman (1977, 1982) (see also Stryjan 1987), provides a basic structuring of the construct: exit, voice, loyalty or involvement. The opposite of just leaving the organization ('exit') is deep commitment to its mission, which means creative and positive action on one's own initiative ('involvement'). Criticism may be negative but may also trigger creative change ('voice'), while staying passive just preserves the status quo ('loyalty'). In private sector organizations members either protest or criticize by taking their own action ('voice') or leave the organization ('exit') and maybe launch a hostile spinoff. In the public sector we expect employees to be loyal to the role of the sector and its contributions to creating welfare in general and their own place of work in particular. In NPVOs, where participation is either based on personal commitment or on associated voluntary engagement, involvement – literally indicating embodied and emotional movement – signifies identification with the organization and its social cause; see for example Wijkström 2011.

All organizations need to *control* their members, their behaviour and contributions to the common interest in order to provide proper government. In the organization literature three modes of control – output, process and culture control – are usually recognized (see for example Ouchi 1980). We then expect that private sector organizations will primarily be judged by what they achieve on the market, that is, their output. In the public sector where the quality and instrumentality of single operations are very much dependent on how related activities are run, process control occupies first place. Culture control presumably dominates organizations in the NPVO sector, considering that people join and contribute because they share the value basis and mission of the organization concerned.

Coping with *innovation* is crucial in all organizational life, and all entrepreneurial contexts in particular. As underlined above, we consider (social) innovation to be a pillar for any kind of societal entrepreneurship. Featuring innovation as an element constituting one of the sector logics, we associate innovation in the private sector as mainly technology-driven. Technology in this context is not just a physical feature but may, as for example in the experience industry, also include social technology, for example managing people's perceptions of reality. While such innovations in the private sector are often associated with radical change, innovations in the public sector often appear as reforms, as adjustments that are carefully negotiated among many stakeholders In the NPVO sector we consider innovation mainly as organizational ingenuity, finding (new) ways of making people recognize their unique capabilities and making them pattern into concerted action for the creation of social value.

What *outlook* organizations have is crucial, considering both that we are concerned with societal entrepreneurship and with the Swedish context where (physical) space is important. Here we then associate outlook with the dominant frame of reference, whose extension may vary in physical, social and mental spaces (Hernes 2003). As elaborated elsewhere (Johannisson and Lindholm Dahlstrand 2012), we associate a local outlook with a view where the three spaces coincide in the enacted environment. A global outlook, in contrast, only considers place (physical space) if it is instrumentally rational. This is also the outlook we ascribe to organizations in the private sector. In the public sector, in contrast, a local, here of course also including a regional, even a national, perspective rules. In our view, a unique feature of the NPVO sector is that its organizations and the members that inhabit them are involved in taking local action to do good both locally and globally, whether we have, for example, environmental protection or fair trade in mind.

To summarize and underline: the structuring of the contrasting features of sector logics in Table 1.1 should be looked upon rather as 'ideal' types in the Weberian sense than as empirically supported elements of (emerging) theoretical constructs. As such 'ideal' features we think that they can on one hand be used as an intellectual sounding board for the empirical accounts provided by the following chapters in this anthology, and on the other hand become substantiated by the illustrations that those reports provide.

CONCEPTUAL AND METHODOLOGICAL CHALLENGES

Initiatives that we identify as societal entrepreneurship are constructed for special purposes and settings. This has theoretical and methodological implications and calls for a contextual approach (see Welter 2011). Here it means that only by considering the historical, temporal, institutional and spatial settings will it be possible to get further insight into the societal entrepreneurship phenomenon. This enlightenment includes how the contexts enable, or obstruct, the initiatives taken by societal entrepreneurs, who often do not even view themselves as entrepreneurs but as activists, dedicated enthusiasts or change-makers (Berglund and Wigren 2011). Recognizing that the understanding of entrepreneurship is dependent on the context also challenges dominating understandings of entrepreneurship and the way they may be studied.

Social sciences in general and inquiry into societal entrepreneurship in particular for a number of reasons invite a broad range of methodologies, or modes of approaching the empirical world. Being embedded in Geertzian webs of meaning rather than based on natural laws social 'facts' on one hand remain stable due to institutionalization, and on the other hand, when the web bursts because of accumulated tensions, may become obsolete overnight. On the societal level we experienced in 2011 such turmoil in the Arab world, while on the micro level we experience that coincidences become institutionalized as a fashion (Czarniawska and Joerges 1996). Here we see a bridge between social innovations and entrepreneurship involving both the creation of new worlds and societal entrepreneurship as interactive, organizational efforts with a highly transformative potential. Spinosa et al. (1997) illustrate the general bridge between entrepreneurship and world-making and Gawell (2006) forestalls with her concept 'activist entrepreneurship' those processes which, amplified by social media, make social ruptures such as the Arab revolutions possible. Such radical changes do not only unfold themselves where they are most visible – close to war zones and revolutionary actions. More subtle changes, which may accumulate into social ruptures, also infiltrate into democratic, growth-oriented and individualized welfare societies.

Although chaos and complexity theories help us to make intelligible how microscopic and peripheral incidents may develop into a new institutional order and although contemporary ICTs help us to understand how such processes materialize, their embedding may both hinder and accelerate such changes. They do not just happen because of their ability to instantaneously mobilize attention, but because they rest on a force that has accumulated over a long time and is unleashed by some accidental incidence. The view of the entrepreneur as the most important ingredient in the process may thus be downplayed, favouring an understanding of context, situation, the unexpected, and timing. This implies that serendipity, that is, when somebody finds something that he or she was not expecting to find, and then acts on it, is vital to understanding entrepreneuring. Even if the role of the entrepreneur is downplayed, s/he can never be reduced to somebody insignificant. We now know that Fleming was not the first to discover that penicillin was a good bactericide. It had been known for decades, but nobody had really done anything with this knowledge until Fleming did.

Hence, when new ideas hit a prepared mind – or an emerging organization – mechanisms which are illustrated in the literature on 'absorptive capacity' (Cohen and Levinthal 1990) and on 'serendipity' (Dew 2009) explain how concerted entrepreneurial action may be triggered. Such non-linear development also characterizes the emergence of social forms of entrepreneurship itself, today apparently on everyone's tongue and turning into a major perspective on societal change and renewal. This recognition has developed in parallel in the academic and professional/practical communities, presumably because of the increased awareness of the limits to linear economic growth and the need for the building of a sustainable society, sometimes also with a focus on ecological, sustainable or ethical entrepreneurship. Staying within the academic community, social entrepreneurship as a research field has become institutionalized very quickly, especially considering that even entrepreneurship in general has only recently become recognized as an academic field of research. Indicators of such institutionalization are for example discussed in a number of scientific journals, handbooks, publications, conferences, networks and education programmes. Another explanation of the forceful creation of the new special field of entrepreneurship studies is that the widening of traditional entrepreneurship studies have increased the dialogue with other disciplines such as sociology and anthropology and fields of research such as development studies. Situating entrepreneurship in the midst of society, and at the core of social sciences, was highlighted by Swedberg (2000) over ten years ago, bringing together several disciplines to give a more holistic view of the entrepreneurship phenomenon.

In spite of its early institutionalization, social/societal entrepreneurship as a research field is still in its formative years. It is then reasonable that it can learn a great deal from the field's close relatives as regards applied methodologies. The history of empirical entrepreneurship research, apart from a number of important historical inspirations, only goes back to the 1980s. Until the turn of the millennium this research on one hand concerned increasingly ambitious surveys testing or developing formal models, on the other reported 'anecdotal evidence'. Over the last decade, inspired by European research, the latter qualitative insight has become upgraded as 'narrative' research. Learning from the arduous journey of general entrepreneurship studies we see no reason to repeat that detour via quantitative research when designing a research agenda for social/societal entrepreneurship as a contextually sensitive phenomenon. As will be elaborated upon below, we rather consider narrative, ethnography and more advanced qualitative research as fundamental when inquiring into societal entrepreneurship.

Further biases in previous research into entrepreneurship that we want to avoid include emphasizing spectacular, heroic and dramatic achievements and their structural features. Here we rather argue as a point of departure that everyday collective practices and their emergence in their social/societal setting is the proper basic setting for research into (any kind of) entrepreneurship. This is in line with Steyaert and Hjorth's (2006) proposition that entrepreneurship is about social change and Steyaert's (2007) argument that entrepreneuring, that is the verb, rightly presents the phenomenon as processual (see also Johannisson 2011). Accordingly, we argue that entrepreneurship, as a social/societal phenomenon, is especially dependent on qualitative research in general and interactive research in particular. Before elaborating upon this we need however to comment further on the context or embedding of social phenomena such as (societal) entrepreneurship.

Broadening entrepreneurship from an economic to a social phenomenon obviously does not just mean including variables beyond the economic ones in modelling the phenomenon. Identifying 'contingencies' or intervening variables (see Lawrence and Lorsch 1967 for a seminal study) or 'configurations' (see Miller 1983) will not do justice to what we associate with embedding. It is rather about recognizing entrepreneurship as a practice that in a number of respects is tied and knitted into broader social structures. This position provides the basic argument for staying within the national context of Sweden and take further contextualization of different empirical studies from there.

Spatial contextualization, especially, may even bring about 'over-embeddedness'; see for example Grabher (1993). When one is embedded in a context, it is difficult to perceive the relevance of a place in terms of its traditions, location, people and the conditions that come with it. They become blind spots, making it difficult to see its values and how it can be enacted in novel ways. However, societal entrepreneurship is embedded in various contexts, involving processes that move beyond starting up and running a company, often including people who are in unexpected ways invited to co-produce social values. In the sense of constituting a multi-sector phenomenon, societal entrepreneurship thus implies moving between contexts, and it can therefore be seen as an ongoing process from embeddedness through dis-embeddedness to becoming re-embedded. This can be approached from multi-sited ethnography, which implies to empirically follow how cultural processes unfold (for example Marcus 1995); see also Chapter 8 on tracing the entrepreneurial approach in the preschool context.

The cultural phenomenon we are interested in unfolding we label societal entrepreneurship. The multi-sited ethnographic approach thus benefits the study of actors from different spatial contexts, with diverse institutional solutions and constraints, bringing in various historical imprints and the way they enact upon common ideas. This kind of research process requires being within the landscape that changes and calls for tacit knowing, which can be achieved from dwelling for a long time in the context. The motto is then not to study 'the people', but to inhabit different contexts, following the unfolding of change, being subsumed by the process itself, and relating to the actors involved as participants in the research process. Through this process the 'embedded' knowledge can be contrasted, creatively transformed, and moved from the margins to the centre; being re-valued.

While Welter (2011) stresses the need for qualitative research, especially by case studies, she seems to maintain a strong belief in the direct comparability of different cases. The view bridges over to the Eisenhardt (1989) ambition to generate theory based on comparative case research. We, however, think that the academic community, especially when inquiring into complex phenomena such as social/societal entrepreneurship, has to focus its efforts on identifying the uniqueness of the event. The findings of such a case study can rather be used for associations, or for the drawing of analogies (see Johannisson 2011), as well as for 'creative imitation' (see Johansson 2010). 'Bisociation' (Koestler 1964) rather stimulates a creative act that uses the different mental maps that researchers draw – because of their contrasting private and professional/public embedding – to feed radically new interpretations. Among practitioners bisociation is of course broad as well, since we see societal entrepreneuring as an outcome of encounters between representatives from different sectors.

Thus, presenting different cases of societal entrepreneurship within the (same) national/spatial (Swedish) setting where cultural, social and institutional contexts are tightly intertwined makes it possible to disclose different aspects of the phenomenon with greater reflexivity. Ascribing holistic features to the context means that (qualitative) research can only add further understandings, or critically question existing images of societal entrepreneurship. As a social construct the context remains evasive, open for new interpretations and constructions. Accordingly, Richardson (1994) argues that qualitative research should be guided by the principle of 'crystallization' rather than triangulation. While the former keeps an open mind for alternative understandings, the latter use of different methods is guided by the belief that such an approach brings us closer to a definitive truth.

Referring to the title of this introductory chapter we also think that it is important to take the societal embedding as a point of departure for searching for new understandings of entrepreneurship. A society's/nation's (formal) institutions usually make the most distinct contribution to what is considered to constitute the unique features of a specific society. On the other hand we associate societal entrepreneurship with creative organizing that pays little respect to the boundaries between sectors. Having said this we want to underline that the focus on the three sectors and their formal institutions may restrict the intellectual potentiality of our research venture. Referring to Tönnies' ideal types of generic organizing, Gesellschaft and Gemeinschaft (see the introductory discussion), the former is dependent on formal structures to keep selfishness at bay, while the latter represents a structure based on mutual concerns and ongoing dialogues that do not need a formal structure to become and stay sustainable. Part of our mission is to find out how this works in practice.

While all chapters pay attention to the challenges that societal venturing experience at the interfaces between the different sectors, the methodological tactics used differ according to the various aspects on societal entrepreneurship brought up. Table 1.2 provides an overview. Since these issues vary from distant interpretations of political and institutional statements in discourse analysis to committed participation on the part of the researcher(s) themselves in the entrepreneurial processes, the methodologies adopted vary considerably. What is more, in some chapters – most obviously those by Andersson and Johansson (Chapter 5) and Berglund and Johansson (Chapter 7) the authors bravely combine widely different empirical accounts to make their case. Studying intermediaries as societal entrepreneurs Andersson and Johansson even have to cross the boundaries between national contexts in order to find the necessary arguments. Studying the curse of associating entrepreneuring with a (male) hero Berglund and Johansson rely both on a close-up interactive study and on published biographical material.

As already pointed out, social accounts are always partially a product of the researchers themselves. As regards research into societal entrepreneurship this is especially obvious, both because of the subject and because of the methods adopted. First, as societal entrepreneurship is about initiating and promoting new innovative ways of creating an economically, socially and ecologically sustainable world, it is a practice that concerns all of us as fellow global citizens. We will return to this in the concluding chapter. Secondly, since research, whether publicly or privately financed, is expected to help in meeting human needs, commitment is especially obvious in research on societal entrepreneurship. Thirdly, such research means getting involved with highly dedicated people providing an emotional context that attracts and seduces us as researchers. Accordingly, we consider all encounters between researchers and actors/interlocutors as taking place in an atmosphere characterized by mutual concern that moves us far beyond that of collecting information. This general embedding in responsibility and responsiveness to the everyday appearances of societal entrepreneurship is important to keep in mind considering that the field reports of several chapters in the book are based on focused dialogues or interviews, occasionally combined with secondary data.

In listening to the field – that of societal entrepreneurship – as well as to Scandinavian traditions in social research several chapters adopt action or interactive research. See for example Chapter 3 on the social enterprise Macken, the study of the fair trade company Oria (Chapter 6), or the longitudinal study on teachers by Holmgren (Chapter 9). While the action is especially concerned with making the research process open and available to those involved, see for example Reason and Bradbury 2001, interactive research is based on the belief that combining explicit/academic knowledge and tacit/personal knowledge creates a road to further insight, see for example Nielsen and Svensson 2006. Some further reasons for the use of interactive approaches in this book are listed below:

1. Considering that our understanding of entrepreneurship is associated with human interaction as reflected in everyday practices, only personal participation in these micro-practices will make it possible to identify where they originated and how they impacted the realization of the event. Some researchers, for example Johannisson (2011), argue

Table 1.2 Modes of inquiry for revealing societal entrepreneurship (SE) as a contextual multi-faceted phenomenon

Chapter/Case	Aim	Mode of inquiry	Revealed organizing features in societal entrepreneuring
Positioning			
2. Societal entrepreneurship in 4 municipalities	To empirically explore how sectoral intertwining interplays with societal entrepreneurship	30 interviews in 2 large and 2 small municipalities	Dimensions of sectoral intertwining in time and space contexts
3. Macken	Tracking the practices of societal entrepreneuring	In-depth interviewing, observant participation, shadowing, diary dialogue	Social bricolage spontaneously producing societal innovations
4. ALW	Tracking entrepreneurship over time and sector borders	Retrospective studies of archival (secondary) data	The making of societal entrepreneurship into an institution
Penetrating			
5. Intermediaries –Closer-to-Companies	Exploring societal promotion of small businesses organized as an intermediary	Organizational ethnography (participant observations, interviews, interactive workshops)	Enactment of societal entrepreneurship by means of intermediary activities with both dark and bright sides
6. Fair Trade	Featuring entrepreneurship across market and societal contexts	Ethnography, in-depth interviewing, shadowing, mentoring	Fair trading and standardization as contradictory practices in contrasting cultural and institutional (national) contexts

7. Moon House	Enactive research at a scene where societal entrepreneurship unfolds	Ethnography (interviewing, participation, interactive participation, shadowing, mail dialogues)	How the dark side of entrepreneuring positions the entrepreneur in particular ways may hinder enterprising of the endeavour to proceed
Promoting			
8. Entrepreneurship in pre-schools	Tracking how entrepreneurial approach is framed in a context where play is highlighted	Ethnography, in-depth interviewing, shadowing, participant observation, text analysis	Entrepreneurial approach in the pre-school context giving a deeper understanding of entrepreneuring
9. Implementing entrepreneurship throughout the school system	Following the translation of entrepreneurship education	Policy text analysis and case studies	An understanding that the practice of entrepreneuring does not always co-exist with the discursive development
10. SIP	Opportunizing social challenges	Unintended enactive research	A constantly emerging societal venture offers inspiration, creativity and learning

that the researcher needs to enact an entrepreneurial process her-/ himself in order to get close enough. It is also well known in social research that the critical features of a social system only appear when the system is changing, or forced to change.

2.   Keeping the youth of the research field in mind as well as the phenomenon's sensitivity to context, researchers and the interlocutors have to collaborate closely in a genuine dialoguing order to make sense out of shared experiences.

3.   Expanding on the Scandinavian traditions as regards creating meeting places between academics and reflecting practitioners, the funding organization – The Swedish Knowledge Foundation – of the research presented in this book conditioned their financial support by expecting practitioners to be co-financed and actively contributing to the process of creating knowledge about, for and in societal entrepreneurship. This meant that several of the projects reported have evolved in close collaboration between researchers and the societal entrepreneurs concerned.

Some projects/chapters stand out with respect to their adoption of an interactive research approach. Schwartz, in her study of the micro-organizing of fair trade, has accompanied the entrepreneur in her everyday venturing in both the Swedish and the Indian contexts in order to catch the fine-tuned measures that make the dynamics of such a bridging socioeconomic activity (see Chapter 6). Equally, Berglund in her study of the Moon House took part in an entrepreneurial process that was initiated, which subsumed and enabled her to take part in entrepreneuring (Chapter 7). She did not create a 'scene' for experiencing entrepreneurship, as illustrated by Johannisson (2011), but took the opportunity to enter an already existing arena, which made her struggle to get disembedded in order to create knowledge about the process. Shadowing and everyday dialogue are not enough; the researcher also has to embody the entrepreneurial activity. Johannisson in his study of a social enterprise for a period embedded his explicit creation of accounts in a daily digital dialogue with the entrepreneur by dwelling in the enterprise itself and hanging around in its spatial and social context, which directly and indirectly supports the enterprise being studied (Chapter 3). Rosell, as one of the writers on the interface between academic and extramural education concerning (social) entrepreneurship, is personally involved as a contributor to further projects organized by the networked social enterprise. These examples pinpoint that the interactive approach implies not only commitment to the project concerned but also to the different contexts that embed it.

PROPOSING THREE THEMES

As stated in the introductory part of this chapter we, in this book, organize our responses to our challenge to make sense out of societal entrepreneurship by organizing the chapters into three themes: *positioning, penetrating* and *promoting*. Bringing in a new concept that captures a phenomenon differently means a responsibility to analytically and empirically position it in relation to other understandings of an entrepreneurship that move beyond commercial activity. Since the field of entrepreneurship is generally in great need of critical inquiry we think it is important to critically penetrate in whatever way entrepreneurship presents itself as societal. The third theme empirically takes a point of departure in the educational setting with the ambition of presenting ideas about how societal entrepreneurship can be promoted in the making of a better world. These three themes are further elaborated on and connected to chapters in the introductions to the parts of the book which contain the various themes, as well as in the concluding chapter. Here we thus only briefly introduce the themes.

Positioning societal entrepreneurship as evading all three sectors and challenging their different logics that carry each sector consequently discusses how societal entrepreneurship differs from commercial and institutional entrepreneurship and how societal entrepreneurship can make up for institutional (and market) failure. It is especially interesting and important to reflect upon how societal entrepreneurship differs over different spatial as well as temporal settings with respect to how it organizes innovation and renewal. Besides, ascribing entrepreneurial capabilities to all three sectors and its representatives, it is reasonable and equally important to empirically study how the sectors take turns and/or are intertwined in entrepreneurial processes.

Penetrating societal entrepreneurship calls for a critical examination of its dark and bright sides. This means paying attention to obvious dark sides, but perhaps even more importantly, acknowledging that everything – including entrepreneurship – has another story to tell than the popular media version about success, fame, creation, impact and growth. Consequently, it is easy to be seduced by the successful versions of entrepreneurship, rejecting its dark sides. The point made is that one comes with the other. This is recognized in a core concept that entrepreneurship scholars seem to agree upon, namely creative destruction, which lays the ground for the theory proposed by Schumpeter (1934). With a societal entrepreneurship perspective we also notice how values – ethical, environmental, and social – are at stake. They may be reinforced or set aside in the entrepreneurship that is conditioned in present times. In this vein a historical perspective informs us that the rules of the game change over time and with them the scope of action for entrepreneurs to, at best, either contribute to society in a productive way, or reinforce the status quo in an unproductive or, even worse, in a destructive way (Baumol, 1990).

The third perspective on societal entrepreneurship applied in this anthology is *promoting*, which addresses how societal entrepreneurship could be endorsed. In this section three chapters delve into how entrepreneurship education has been framed and enacted; from a preschool context throughout the school system to the university level. Following how teachers at the different levels in the school system make sense of entrepreneurship, enact it and transform it to something completely different, unfolds societal entrepreneurship as a phenomenon that breaks with institutions, invites multi-sector cooperation and acknowledges history. The notion of promoting thus moves beyond education as a practice in the world of school. This perspective rather stresses the importance of processes that work against specialization and differentiation, separating sectors and actors from each other, making it difficult for common life spheres to emerge that cross boundaries and traditional subdivisions where each sector is occupied by its own rules, practices and language. Promoting societal entrepreneurship can instead be better described as a process where actors from different sectors act together, creating a common language and shared practices, laying the ground for a sphere that does not belong to one sector or the other, but is shared for all of those involved, irrespective of their sectorial residence.

NOTE

1.   According to information especially provided by Statistics Sweden in March 2012.

REFERENCES

Ahl, H. (2006), 'Why research on women entrepreneurs needs new directions', *Entrepreneurship Theory and Practice*, **30**(5), 595–621.

Baumol, W.J. (1990), 'Entrepreneurship: productive, unproductive, and destructive', *Journal of Political Economy*, **98**(5), 893–921.

Berggren, H. and Trägårdh, L. (2006), *Är svensken människa?: gemenskap och oberoende i det moderna Sverige* (Is the Swede a Human Being: on community and independence in modern Sweden), Stockholm: Norstedt.

Berglund, K. and A.W. Johansson (2007), 'Entrepreneurship, discourses and conscientization in processes of regional development', *Entrepreneurship and Regional Development*, **19**(6), 499–525.

Berglund, K. and C. Wigren (2011), 'Societal entrepreneurship – the shaping of a different story of entrepreneurship', *Tamara Journal of Critical Organization*, **10**(1), 9–22.

Bill, F., B. Bjerke and A.W. Johansson (eds) (2010), *(De)mobilizing Entrepreneurship – Exploring Entrepreneurial Thinking and Action*, Cheltenham, UK and Northampton, MA, USA: Edward Elgar Publishing.

Cohen, W.M. and D.A. Levinthal (1990), 'Absorptive capacity: A new perspective on learning and innovation', *Administrative Science Quarterly*, **35**, 128–152.

Czarniawska, B. (2009), 'Emerging institutions: pyramids or anthills?', *Organization Studies*, **30**(4), 423–441.

Czarniawska, B. and B. Joerges (1996), 'Travel of ideas', in B. Czarniawska and G. Sevón (eds), *Translating Organizational Change*, Berlin: de Gruyter, pp. 13–48.

Dew, N. (2009), 'Serendipity in entrepreneurship', *Organization Studies*, **30**(4), 735–753.

Eisenhardt, K. (1989), 'Building theories from case study research', *Academy of Management Review*, **14**(4), 532–550.

Esser, H. (2008), 'The two meanings of social capital', in D. Castiglione, J.W. van Deth and G. Wolleb (eds), *The Handbook of Social Capital*, Oxford, UK: Oxford University Press, pp. 22–49.

Fayolle, A. and H. Matlay (eds) (2010), *Handbook of Research on Social Entrepreneurship*, Cheltenham, UK and Northampton, MA, USA: Edward Elgar Publishing.

Freire, P. (1970/1996), *Pedagogy of the Oppressed*, London: Penguin Books.

Gawell, M. (2006), *Activist Entrepreneurship. Attac'ing Norms and Disclosing Stories*, Stockholm: Stockholm University.

Gawell, M., B. Johannisson and M. Lundqvist (2009), *Entrepreneurship in the Name of Society*, Stockholm: The Knowledge Foundation.

Grabher, G. (ed.) (1993), *The Embedded Firm. On the Socioeconomics of Industrial Networks*, London: Routledge.

Hernes, T. (2003), 'Organization as evolution of space', in B. Czarniawska and G. Sevón (eds), *Northern Lights – Organization Theory in Scandinavia*, Copenhagen: Liber/Abstract/Copenhagen Business School Press, pp. 267–290.

Hirschman, A.O. (1977), *The Passions and the Interests*, Princeton, NJ: Princeton University Press.

Hirschman, A.O. (1982), *Shifting Involvements*, Oxford: Martin Robertson.

Hjorth, D. (2003), *Rewriting Entrepreneurship*, Malmö: Liber.

Hofstede, G. (1980), *Culture's Consequences: International Differences in Work-related Values*, Beverly Hills, CA: Sage.

Holmquist, C. and Sundin, E. (eds) (2002), *Företagerskan: om kvinnor och entre-prenörskap* ('The Entrepreneuse': on women and entrepreneurship), Stockholm: SNS Publisher.

Johannisson, B. (2008), 'The social construction of the disabled and unfashionable family business', in V. Gupta, N. Levenburg, L.L. Moore, J. Motwani and T.V. Schwarz (eds), *Culturally-sensitive Models of Family Business in Nordic Europe: A Compendium Using the Globe Paradigm*, Hyjderabad, ICFAI University, pp. 125–144.

Johannisson, B. (2011), 'Towards a practice theory of entrepreneuring', *Small Business Economics*, **36**(2), 135–150.

Johannisson, B. and Å. Lindholm Dahlstrand (2012), *Enacting Entrepreneurship and Regional Development*, London: Routledge.

Johannisson, B. and A. Nilsson (1989), 'Community entrepreneurship – networking for local development', *Journal of Entrepreneurship and Regional Development*, **1**(1), 1–19.

Johannisson, B and C. Wigren (2006), 'Extreme entrepreneurs – challenging the institutional framework', in P.R. Christensen and F. Poulfeldt (eds), *Managing Complexity and Change in SMEs: Frontiers in European Research*, Cheltenham, UK and Northampton, MA, USA: Edward Elgar Publishing, pp. 156–179.

Johansson, A.W. (2010), 'Innovation, creativity and imitation', in F. Bill, B. Bjerke and A.W. Johansson (eds) (2010), *(De)mobilizing Entrepreneurship – Exploring Entrepreneurial Thinking and Action*, Cheltenham, UK and Northampton, MA, USA: Edward Elgar Publishing, pp. 123–139.

Knutsen, W.L. and R.S. Brower (2010), 'Managing expressive and instrumental accountabilities in nonprofit and voluntary organizations: a qualitative investigation', *Nonprofit and Voluntary Sector Quarterly*, **39**(4), 588–610.

Koestler, A. (1964), *The Act of Creation*, London: Hutchinson.

Lawrence, P.B. and J.W. Lorsch (1967), *Organization and Environment*, Boston, MA: Harvard University Press.

Marcus, G.E. (1995), 'Ethnography in/of the world system: The emergence of multi-sited ethnography', *Annual Review of Anthropology*, **24**, 97–117.

Merle. J., M. Lundqvist and H. Hellsmark (2003), 'Entrepreneurial transformations in the Swedish University system: the case of Chalmers University of Technology', *Research Policy*, **32**(9), 1555–1568.

Miller, D. (1983), 'The correlates of entrepreneurship in three types of firms', *Management Science*, **29**(7), 770–791.

Nielsen, K.A. and L. Svensson (eds) (2006), *Action and Interactive Research. Beyond Practice and Theory*, Maastricht: Shaker Publishing.

Ouchi, W.G. (1980), 'Markets, bureaucracies and clans', *Administrative Science Quarterly*, **25**, 129–141.

Prahalad, C.K. (2004), 'The blinders of dominant logic', *Long Range Planning*, **37**, 171–179.

Reason, P. and H. Bradbury (eds) (2001), *Handbook of Action Research. Participative Inquiry and Practice*, Thousand Oaks, CA: Sage.

Richardson, L. (1994), 'Writing. A method of inquiry', in N.K. Denzin and S. Lincoln (eds), *Handbook of Qualitative Research*, London: Sage, pp. 516–529.

Schumpeter, J.A. (1911/1934), *The Theory of Economic Development*, Oxford: Oxford University Press.

Schwartz, B (2009), 'Environmental strategies as automorphic patterns of behaviour', *Business Strategy and the Environment*, **18**(3), 192–206.

Scott, W.R. (2008), *Institutions and Organizations*, third edition, Thousand Oaks, CA: Sage.

Segnestam Larsson, O. (2011), *Standardizing Civil Society: Interpreting Organizational Development in the Tension Between Instrumentalism and Expressivism*, Dissertation. Åbo: Åbo Akademi.

Sjöstrand, S.-E. (1992), 'On the rationale behind "irrational" institutions', *Journal of Economic Issues*, **XXVI**(4), 1007–1039.

Spinosa, C., F. Flores and H. Dreyfus (1997), *Disclosing New Worlds, Entrepreneurship, Democratic Action, and the Cultivation of Solidarity*, Cambridge, MA: The MIT Press.

Statistics Sweden (2011), *The Civil Society – an Assignment from the Government with Surveys from Statistics Sweden*, Örebro: Statistics Sweden.

Steyaert, C. (2007), '"Entrepreneuring" as a conceptual attractor? A review of process theories in 20 years of entrepreneurship studies', *Entrepreneurship and Regional Development*, **19**(6), 453–477.

Steyaert, C. and D. Hjorth (eds) (2006), *Entrepreneurship as Social Change*, Cheltenham, UK and Northampton, MA, USA: Edward Elgar Publishing.

Steyaert, C. and J. Katz (2004), 'Reclaiming the space of entrepreneurship in society: geographical, discursive and social dimensions', *Entrepreneurship and Regional Development*, **16**(3), 179–196.

Stryjan, Y. (1987), *Impossible Organizations. On Self-management and Organizational Reproduction*, Department of Sociology. Uppsala: Uppsala University.

Sundin, E. (2004), *En porträttbok: Den offentliga sektorns entreprenörer*, Stockholm: Kommentus Förlag.

Sundin, E. and M. Tillmar (2008), 'A nurse and a civil servant changing institutions: entrepreneurial processes in public sector organizations', *Scandinavian Journal of Management – Special Issue on 'Recreating/Recontextualising Entrepreneurship'*, **24**, 113–124.

Sundin E. and M. Tillmar (2010), 'The intertwining of social, commercial and public entrepreneurship', in A. Fayolle and H. Matlay (eds) (2010), *Handbook of Research on Social Entrepreneurship*, Cheltenham, UK and Northampton, MA, USA: Edward Elgar Publishing, pp.142–156.

Swedberg, R. (2000), *Entrepreneurship: The Social Science View*, Oxford and New York: Oxford University Press.

Thornton, P.A. and W. Ocasio (1999), 'Institutional logics and the historical contingency of power in organizations', *American Journal of Sociology*, **105**(3), 801–843.

Thornton, P.A and W. Ocasio (2008), 'Institutional logics', in R. Greenwood, C. Oliver, R. Suddaby and K. Sahlin (eds), *The Sage Handbook of Organizational Institutionalism*, Los Angeles: Sage, pp. 99–129.

Tillmar, M. (2009), 'Societal entrepreneurs in the health sector – crossing the frontiers', *Social Enterprise Journal*, **5**(3), 282–298.

Tönnies, F. (1965), *Community and Association*, London: Routledge & Kegan Paul.

Welter, F. (2011), 'Contextualizing entrepreneurship – conceptual challenges and ways forward', *Entrepreneurship Theory and Practice*, **35**(1), 165–184.

Wigren, C. (2003), *The Spirit of Gnosjö. The Grand Narrative and Beyond*, Doctoral dissertation. Jönköping: Jönköping International Business School.

Wijkström, F. (2011), '"Charity speak and business talk". The on-going hybridization of civil society', in F. Wijkström and A. Zimmer (eds), *Nordic Civil Society at a Cross-Roads. Transforming the Popular Movement Tradition*, Baden-Baden: Nomos, pp. 27–54.

Ziegler, R. (ed.) (2009), *An Introduction to Social Entrepreneurship: Voices, Preconditions, Contexts*, Cheltenham, UK and Northampton, MA, USA: Edward Elgar Publishing.

PART I

Positioning societal entrepreneuring as a sector-spanning phenomenon

For reasons elaborated upon in the introductory chapter the unique features of societal entrepreneurship concern social venturing that mobilizes people and resources in all three sectors in society: the private sector, the public sector and the NPVO sector. Our point is that the evolving of such social venturing is intimately dependent upon the scope and further features of each sector and their joint embedding in the broader historical and cultural context, here the national Swedish setting. Proposing this modelling of non-economic venturing in the interest of a sustainable society, it is thus of great importance first, to thoroughly found this approach conceptually and empirically in the Swedish context and secondly, provide accounts that on one hand demonstrate the variety of societal entrepreneurship as reflected in concrete projects, on the other invite detailed scrutiny of the intricacies of societal venturing as an everyday practice.

In Chapter 2 – *Sectoral intertwining at the grass root level* – Malin Tillmar provides context-specific accounts of 30 (Swedish) social entrepreneurs and their ventures, which operate in four locations – two small and two medium-sized municipalities – in different regions in Sweden. Her point of departure is a model, originally presented in Sundin and Tillmar (2010), which elaborates on the general difference between the three sectors and varying modes of their intertwining. The social projects that the 30 entrepreneurs have initiated are analysed with respect to features such as their age, formal structure and funding as well as to their contrasting – urban versus rural – locations. In order to scrutinize in further detail how these social ventures bridge sector boundaries the story of one social venture is told that elaborates on how such boundary-crossing is enacted, especially between the private and public sectors. Summarizing that case with the use of the original model Tillmar adds further lessons that the survey and the case study jointly provide.

Considering that societal entrepreneurship – like any entrepreneurship – is about creative organizing, one important conclusion is that the role of the project leader is very demanding. Nevertheless, in rural areas the necessary sectoral intertwining remains the responsibility of key individuals ('individual intertwining'), while social venturing in urban locations practise what Tillmar addresses as 'organizational intertwining'. This means that the integration of the different sector logics and resources is carried out by the organization that runs the social project. Such an ability to institutionalize leadership appears as a condition for making an organization that aims at contributing to the making of a sustainable world, itself sustainable.

The two further chapters making up Part I add a time dimension to the sector-bridging perspective that characterizes societal entrepreneurship. This concern for the dynamics of the phenomenon calls for really close-up studies; each chapter elaborates in great depth on a case located in the Swedish context, one in a regional centre and one in a small town in a rural region. These chapters add to the excursions into social and mental spaces uncovered by societal entrepreneurship.

Chapter 3 – *Tracking the everyday practices of societal entrepreneuring* – inquiries into the everyday dynamics of the phenomenon as genuinely emerging through activities and interactivities which ruthlessly cross sectoral boundaries. The case focused on is Macken, a social enterprise located in a regional centre in southern Sweden. Macken was established in 2005 and has since then expanded into a multifunctional operation. The influence of all three sectors is very distinct: business angels epitomizing the private sector logic have volunteered to design an appropriate management model, one of the operations, a business centre, is run in close collaboration with the public sector (the municipality) and the board of the cooperative is dominated by volunteers. Providing some basic assumptions about social venturing, the author Bengt Johannisson, using interactive methods, reports in detail on how leading actors in Macken jointly enact societal entrepreneuring. The rich accounts of the processes are used to propose further features of the making of social ventures. Such process characteristics include 'social bricolaging', that is the ongoing re-arrangement of existing ambitions and resources and the relations that represent them; 'amplified immediacy', the rhythm in both individual projects and the joint organization where they are embedded being in a constant state of urgency; and 'dynamic involvement' implying that new commitments do not mean that existing ones are abandoned but continue to be cared for. The chapter concludes with reflections on the need for balancing instrumental and expressive accountabilities in any sustainable social enterprise. The findings suggest, in the context of current (Swedish) society, that many, even thick-skinned business angels, are captivated by the social values and processes that both condition and are the outcome of societal entrepreneuring. Although the formal social enterprise, in Macken's case incorporated as a cooperative, is but one of the many appearances of societal entrepreneuring that this book reveals, it highlights its core feature: creative organizing in the name of society.

In Chapter 4 – *Narrating Astrid Lindgren's World as societal entrepreneurship* – Bengt Johannisson and Elisabeth Sundin instead adopt a long-term perspective on societal entrepreneurship and the way it presents itself in different stages over three decades. Relying on archival data as well as interview accounts the authors tell the story about how the milieu and messages of the books by Astrid Lindgren – the world-famous author of children's literature – were turned into an event park, Astrid Lindgren's World (ALW) for children to immerse into. ALW is located in Vimmerby, a small rural municipality in southern Sweden. The iconic status of the author and the cultural and symbolic values that are associated with it made the author appear as an institution that closely regulated, that is, provided the rules that those running the park had to follow in detail. The author's control during the first two decades was very much hands-on, including, for example, the physical inspection of the commercial activities in the park. Initiated by some local families wanting to offer their children a playing ground, organizations originating in all three sectors have over the years been involved, taking turns as regards the ownership and management of ALW. A major contribution by the authors is their interpretation of the evolvement of ALW as societal entrepreneurship as being a product of the creative tensions between different sector interests. The dual concepts of instrumental and expressive accountability are used to untangle the complexity generated by the various incorporated interests running the park. Johannisson and Sundin also reflect upon the relation between ALW as an early representative of the emerging Swedish experience industry and the municipality of Vimmerby as a traditional rural town dominated by traditional industry and commerce. In the beginning the relation was characterized, if not by hostility, at least by indifference. Today, with Astrid Lindgren's heirs as the owners of ALW, the tensions between the event park and the municipality finally seem to have been turned into a constructive dialogue.

REFERENCE

Sundin, E. and M. Tillmar (2010), 'The intertwining of social, commercial and public entrepreneurship', in A. Fayolle and H. Matlay (eds), *Handbook of Research on Social Entrepreneurship*, Cheltenham, UK and Northampton, MA, USA: Edward Elgar Publishing, pp. 142–156.

2. Sectoral intertwining at the grass root level

Malin Tillmar

PROLOGUE

> When we moved to the village, it was 70 km/h when you drove through. And our kids were small. We asked: 'Did anyone talk to the municipal office about this speed limit?' And people said: 'No, it wouldn't make any difference', but me and my wife, we wrote a letter and then it was 50. I think that is entrepreneurship, doing what others say doesn't work.

The societal entrepreneur was born and bred in a business family in a rural area. He is currently CEO in the family's real estate company with about 1000 apartments and also engaged in the family's car firm. The evening before the interview he had been to a board meeting with the association for business owners; he is on the board of the game preservation area and the hunting and shooting club and, last but not least, he is the chairman of Puls, a social labour market organization. The aim of Puls is to rehabilitate and integrate people through activities and jobs. The social insurance agency and the county council are its main funders. He narrates the story:

> One day Lena from Puls called and asked if I could come and join the board of Puls, then they had planned that if I was there I wouldn't be able to say no to becoming chairman, and they were right. I have been privileged since birth and in this job I see so much. We have a lot of refugees in our apartments for example. Many people who can't afford their apartments. And then we have to be thick-skinned. But I think that is how this commitment was wakened. When you grow up, you think everyone is in the same situation. But there is another reality.

INTRODUCTION

Framing the contributions to this anthology, the introductory chapter states that societal entrepreneurship pervades the boundary areas between the private, public and NPVO sectors. Furthermore, these sectors are often intertwined (Christensen et al., 2005). What is public in one dimension (for example ownership, funding, regulation or organization) is often private in another, and vice versa. Previous studies within the OSIS research program have illustrated that social, commercial and public entrepreneurship may also be intertwined, and even intersectoral (Sundin and Tillmar, 2010). More knowledge is, however, still needed about the features of this sectoral intertwining that characterizes societal entrepreneurship, as well as about how the entrepreneurs perceive and reflect upon the intertwining.

The vast majority of empirical examples of societal entrepreneurship focus on 'great men' (Nicholls, 2006), such as the Grameen bank founder Mohammed Yunus, and on recent initiatives by people like Bill Gates and Percy Barnevik. While recognizing the contributions of these people and the research about them, we need more knowledge about societal entrepreneurship closer to the grass root level. In my interpretation, this is also what, for example, Steyaert and Katz (2004) and Parkinson and Howorth (2008) ask for when calling for studies on the 'everydayness' of entrepreneurship.

In this chapter I will empirically explore and illustrate how sectoral intertwining affects and is affected by societal entrepreneurship at the grass root level. Then I use the information from an exploratory interview study encompassing 30 societal entrepreneurs. Taking the legal form of organization as an indicator of sectoral belonging and the composition of sources of funding as an indicator of the intertwining of sectors I will study the impact of contexts such as space (urban/rural ventures), time (when the organization was founded) and operation type. After comparing the 30 societal entrepreneurial ventures covered by the study along these dimensions, I will go deeper into the processes and consequences of intertwining. In other words, I will describe a representative case, which offers particularly rich data with regard to the processes of intertwining. Concluding the chapter I identify two main processes leading to bridging between sectors: individual and organizational intertwining. I also provide suggestions for further research and outline some practical implications of the inquiry.

SECTORAL INTERTWINING IN PREVIOUS STUDIES

The recent *Handbook of Research on Social Entrepreneurship*[1] (Fayolle and Matlay, 2010) states that cutting edge studies have now moved beyond the phase of adding the NPVO sector to entrepreneurship research.

Simultaneously, a full understanding of societal entrepreneurship requires not only perspectives imported from traditional entrepreneurship theory, but also special social perspectives on the phenomenon. Otherwise, we risk achieving a hegemony of economic perspectives over social life, resulting in monolithic understanding. In the debate about entrepreneurship and social entrepreneurship sectors and their different features play an important part. However, in practice the differences between the sectors are less clear than in theory (Christensen et al., 2005). The distinction can be made along several dimensions, such as ownership, financing, and service delivery. The end result is a continuum (ibid.). As discussed in Chapter 1, the construction of sectors varies between nations both in quantitative and qualitative dimensions. In Esping-Anderson's (1996) terms, different nations represent different welfare regimes, which means that the distribution of responsibility for children, for the elderly and other vulnerable groups differs radically between these regimes. Here I wish to point out that the sectors of the economy are intertwined at the outset. Initiatives taken by societal entrepreneurs do often contribute to the process of further intertwining, as we shall see below.

As if the hybridity of private and public sectors was not enough, societal entrepreneurs find themselves in the middle of tensions between different perspectives on funding and profit. In effect, both these sectors include for-profit and not-for-profit activities and organizations (Sundin and Tillmar, 2010). If or when social ventures introduce earned income strategies, they often experience tensions within the organization related to issues such as 'who we will become', and a fear of losing social values, or losing donors (Smith and Barr, 2007). These tensions are related to organizational identity, institutional form or risk. Institutional form tensions relate to legitimacy among different kinds of stakeholders. While actors on the market demand of the organization to give information in economic terms, donors and target groups oblige the organization to communicate in social terms, which poses a challenge (ibid.). The authors argue that these organizations also face risk-related tensions in the sense that they need to balance social and economic measurements of success, and avoid jeopardizing social values when taking economic risks in order to make an income. Organizational identity tensions involve the issues of 'who we are' and 'who we wish to become' and 'what should we engage in'.

The organizational landscape, in which societal entrepreneurs operate, is thus far from clear-cut. Currently, the ongoing changes of sectoral borders and the increase of hybrid organizational forms are to a large extent due to the transformation of the public sector and the implementation of New Public Management (NPM). Western European societies currently find themselves in different phases of this implementation (Hood, 1991; Christensen et al., 2005). As noted by Defourny (2010: 60): 'Western European countries are moving from a welfare state to a new welfare mix, where new bases are to be found for the sharing of responsibility among public authorities, private for-profit providers and third sector organizations.' In the Swedish context we have seen private sector logic (management principles, profit-units, outsourcing and so on) being introduced into the public sector (Forssell and Jansson, 2000) as well as increased outsourcing to so-called alternative providers, first through public procurement procedures and now increasingly through customer-choice models.

As we have seen in previous studies (see Tillmar, 2009; Sundin and Tillmar, 2010b), this process of reframing welfare production heavily alters the 'rules of the game' (North, 1990), or the institutional context, for entrepreneurship in these societies. Naturally, this holds true for societal entrepreneurship as well. Societal entrepreneurship is thus an example of the 'paradox of embedded agency' (Battilana, 2006), stemming from the fact that entrepreneurs both create and are created by their institutional environment. Expressed differently, Steyaert and Hjorth (2006: 1) write that there is a 'double sociality of entrepreneurship', implying that social (and societal, author's comment) entrepreneurship is affected by changes at the societal level, while simultaneously changing society.

Organizational and industrial processes are commonly divided into those occurring within organizations (that is, intra-organizational processes) and those taking place in inter-organizational relationships (IOR). Several processes of societal entrepreneurship encountered throughout the OSIS-research project have taken place in an inter-organizational context; (compare Tillmar, 2009 and Andersson and Johansson in Chapter 5). The importance of inter-organizational relationships for entrepreneurship has previously been recognized, particularly in the Swedish context (Johannisson, 2009). Entrepreneurial processes emerging from inter-organizational relationships have been termed inter-preneurship (Andersson, 2008). Continuing in this vein I illustrate that societal entrepreneurship is often not only inter-organizational, but inter-sectoral as well.

Sundin and Tillmar (2010) challenge the question posed by Austin et al. (2006) in 'Social and commercial entrepreneurship: same, different or both?'; whether commercial, social, or public, different forms of entrepreneurship may not be easy to distinguish, and trying to do so may be misleading. Entrepreneurial processes are often, for example, both social and commercial, or both public and social. In the typology below we have categorized the entrepreneurial processes into those taking place within organizations as intra-organizational and those occurring in interaction

Sector and orientation / Kind of process		Public sector		Private sector	
		Profit	Non-profit	Profit	Non-profit
Intra-organizational					
Inter-organizational	Intra-sector				
	Inter-sector				

Source: Sundin and Tillmar (2010), p. 153, table 8.2.

Figure 2.1   Dimensions of sectoral intertwining in societal entrepreneurship

between organizations as inter-organizational. In order to highlight the dynamics and complexity of societal entrepreneurship inter-organizational processes are divided into those that remain within one sector and those that cut across sectors (inter-sectoral entrepreneurial processes). Furthermore, we wished to challenge the idea of relating for-profits only to the private sector and non-profits to the two other sectors. The argument is that empirically we find profit organizations and even limited companies owned by the public sector, while many privately owned businesses (not the least small businesses) are oriented towards non-profit goals. The typology outlined was aimed to guide further studies on social and societal entrepreneurship, and is presented in Figure 2.1. In the case that I elaborate on below, the typology will be used to structure our understanding.

The active form *intertwining* is here used to denote that I ultimately wish to explore and discuss how this is done in practice, which in the next chapter is elaborated upon by Johannisson. Sectors become intertwined not the least through ongoing processes of entrepreneuring (compare with Steyaert, 2007; Johannisson, 2011). The processes of societal entrepreneuring and sectoral intertwining are closely connected. However, to understand these processes, they need to be contextualized. A common distinction between dimensions of context is that of Whetten (1989, 2009) between *Who, Where* and *When*. Many studies have focused on the 'Who dimension', that is, studying 'Who is the entrepreneur' (compare with Gartner, 1989). I will in the categorizations below pay special attention to the Where (space and operations of the social venturing) and When (time period for its initiation) dimensions. Welter (2011) highlights the Where dimension and its components: the business, social, spatial and institutional contexts.

THE INTERVIEW STUDY

Methods Used

The empirical inquiry reported here was originally initiated through collaboration between two middle-sized (Linköping and Botkyrka) and two small (Lycksele and Högsby) municipalities in Sweden. These municipalities took part in a network[2] aimed at stimulating and exploring the phenomenon of societal entrepreneurship. Linköping (with 143,000 inhabitants) and Botkyrka (with 80,000 inhabitants) represent urban areas, while the small municipalities Lycksele (with 12,000 inhabitants) and Högsby (with 6000 inhabitants) are located in rural regions.

The selection of interviewees was made in two steps. The first step was to identify between ten and twenty societal entrepreneurs from each municipality, through dialogues with civil servants from the business, recreation, and social departments. These officers in turn made use of their contacts with organizations such as Coompanion, Jobs and Society, Almi and the governmental employment services.[3] The second step was to select cases for further inquiry. This process included discussions guided by both a tentative definition of societal entrepreneurship and by the interests of the leading politician, the mayor. The tentative definition of societal entrepreneurship[4] was worked out by the municipal representatives in collaboration with the Knowledge Foundation and the research team. The municipal chairmen were interested in gaining knowledge about societal entrepreneurship but had a variety of purposes and operational goals. The relevant types of operation were defined by the municipalities as social work, local development, culture, integration, sports and economic growth. A selection of seven or eight interviewees per municipality was thus made to achieve this variety of cases in each municipality.

The 30 societal entrepreneurs selected were subsequently interviewed personally by a research assistant. The semi-structured interviews were all taped and transcribed. The study took place in the spring of 2010, and an empirically oriented report directed towards the funders was delivered in the autumn of 2010. For reasons of this chapter, the empirical raw material has since been re-visited by me in my capacity as project manager.

An overview of the 30 initiatives represented by the societal entrepreneurs interviewed is presented in the Appendix. When exploring intertwining between sectors, sole proprietorships and limited companies are regarded as organizations operating mainly in the private sector, while associations, cooperatives and foundations are regarded as organizations belonging to the NPVO sector.

A MULTITUDE OF SOCIETAL ENTREPRENEURING

When we compiled information on the 30 societal initiatives in the four municipalities we were struck by the variety of operations, purposes, organizational and legal forms and sources of funding. A systematic analysis was thus needed. At first, and even second, glance it was not easy to detect any patterns. In this section I will provide the reader with the categorizations that were finally made, exploring the relationships between legal form, context in terms of rural/urban setting, area of operations, source of funding and age of the organization. The Appendix presents a complete table of the initiatives, outlining name, area of operations, the municipality where it is situated as well as the legal form and sources of funding. On an overall level the pattern shows clearly that the majority of the organizations are associations and that the primary source of funding is the public sector.

Legal Form – Primarily Associations

Out of the 30 organizations, four are limited companies, while three are run as sole proprietorships. A total of 23 organizations are thus not-for-profit organizations, of which 18 are associations, three are cooperatives, one is a foundation and one is a unit of a church. They cover a broad range of activities. Some of them are sports clubs and others are civil society organizations which have existed and served their societal purpose for a very long time. Others again are newly registered with the purpose of serving a recently identified societal need and/or taking advantage of a new opportunity. The importance of the time and space contexts for organizational form will be further discussed below.

Funding – Primarily from the Public Sector

In one way or another most societal entrepreneurship at the grass root level is to some extent funded by the public sector, according to the interview study. Only three out of the 30 initiatives fund their operations solely through business activities, and another three are financed by public grants only. Among the other initiatives the degree of public funding varies, as do the types of grant and/or subsidy used. A mixture of different sorts of public funding is common. Table 2.1 lists the major types of funding that occur, as well as examples appearing among the social ventures.

The dominance and dependence of decreasing public funding of different kinds is clear in the empirical material. The public funding comes from the EU level (both the social and structural funds), the central government

Table 2.1   Sources of funding of the social initiatives

Public funding	Private funding
Central government[1] *The social insurance system* • Project – e.g. Verdandi, KoopS, Puls, Verdandi, Aboda Café, Cirkus Cirkör	*Gifts and donations* 'Mind and Body', Philadelfia Pentecostal et al.
The Regional Council[2] *such as* • Project – e.g. Bestorp Village	*Membership fees* from persons from affiliated organizations
County Administrative Board[3] • Project – e.g. Bestorp Village Norrgränden Heritage, Hulta Ecological Group	*Man-hours* • Project – IK Östria, 4Fathers, Norrgränden Heritage, Linköping Motor Club etc.
County Concil[4] • Project – e.g. Puls, KoopS, Cirkus Cirkör	*Sponsorships* Unconditional Project – Ruda Community, 4Fathers Linked to counter-performance
Municipality funding[5] • Project – e.g. KoopS, Cirkus Cirkör, Puls, Ruskele, Norrgränden, Hulta Ecological Group, Southside, Kristineberg Leisure, Aros Sports Club, Theatre and Culture, Ruda Community Association	*Commercial income generating* Selling care-services, Org. Elderly Care Housing • Project – e.g. Arne Svensson, Hulta Ecological Group Organizing events • Project – e.g. Cirkus Cirkör, The Pharaohs Organizing activities for the area inhabitants
EU grants European Social Fund Council (ESF)[6] Projects – e.g. Ruda Community Association • EU Structural Funds, Leader[7] Project – e.g. Bestorp Village, Norrgränden, Hulta Ecological Group Sources of funding for organizations that run social enterprises[8] • Project – e.g. Cirkus Cirkör Other grants which can be applies for in various foundations[9] • Project – e.g. Norrgränden Heritage, Hulta Ecological Group	• Project – e.g. Norrgränden Heritage Selling goods or services • Project – e.g. KoopS, Puls, Norrgränden Heritage Facilitating public service • Project – e.g. Högsby Network Exchange of services between organizations 4Fathers

Table 2.1   (continued)

Notes:
1. The central government responsible for the social security system, such as the Swedish Public Employment Service (Arbetsförmedlingen) and the Regional Social Insurance (Försäkringskassan).
2. Politically controlled organizations, which deal with growth and development issues. Owned by the municipalities in each county. The main tasks of Regional Councils (Regionförbunden) are – Municipal coordination, Government assignments, such as responsibility for the Regional Development Programme, RUP, which is also a steering document for the Regional Council. The organizations' target groups are public actors, trade and industry, non-profit organizations and residents of the county. They offer networks, coordination and financial support in order to achieve concrete goals that are beneficial to regional development, fostering innovation and entrepreneurship.
3. Particular initiatives for female and immigrant entrepreneurship, support for commercial services in rural areas. Rural allowance awarded by the The Regional Council (Länsstyrelsen) in cooperation with the Regional Council. Allowances also from its own funds.
4. The Public Health Care (Landstinget), also research, education, strategic health work.
5. Municipality funding such as operating grants, and practical support in the form of granting the use of premises and local government guarantee, social services.
6. Funds from ESF aim at promoting labour market integration of unemployed and disadvantaged population, primarily through support from training activities. www.esf.se.
7. Funds for creating a Leader area can be applied for from the County Administrative Board. Projects that are supported through Leader must belong to one of the three areas of the Rural Development Programme: improving the competitiveness of agriculture and forestry, improving the environment and countryside as well as the quality of life, enhancing entrepreneurship and favouring the development of the economy of the countryside.
8. Swedish Research Council, The Knowledge Foundation.
9. For instance, Banks, EcoBank, Saving banks.

level (primarily through the social insurance system and labour market initiatives) and the municipal level (primarily as grants to sports clubs and cultural activities). However, due to the scarce availability of public funding, private sources are also emerging. Sports clubs receive their incomes from membership fees, while gifts and donations seem more common among religious organizations. To judge from the interviews, commercial income-generating activities are increasing in importance. Sources of funding for different organizations are discussed in more detail below.

Societal Entrepreneurship in Time and Space

In Sweden the social economy moved higher on the political and policy agenda during the 1990s. The phenomenon became increasingly recognized, and gradually, during the first decade of the new millennium, funding possibilities increased.

The majority of the organizations in this study that were founded before the 1990s are associations. Engaging in popular-movement associations, like sports clubs, has long been a common way of pursuing and expressing one's societal commitment in the Swedish context. Among organizations founded after 1990 there are cooperatives and a larger number of sole proprietorship and limited companies. Thus, the multitude of legal forms is more apparent among initiatives started at a time when the social economy, and subsequently societal entrepreneurship, was open to public debate. A reflection is that entrepreneurs with societal commitment may currently, due to the changing discourse, be presented with a larger variety of legal forms of organization to choose from. Note, however, that funding still primarily comes from public sources, as discussed above.

The spatial dimension of context concerns the rural/urban divide and how it influences the processes of entrepreneurship and sectoral intertwining. One issue to explore is for example whether the embeddedness of entrepreneurship (Granovetter, 1985; Wigren, 2003) takes different forms depending on the context. Consequently, the entrepreneurs interviewed have been analysed with regard to whether they operate in rural contexts (the small municipalities), in an urban municipality within a rural region, or in urban contexts (the middle-sized municipalities). However, on the basis of the current study no clear patterns have been observed regarding the relationship between the legal form of organization and the situation of the organization in an urban or a rural context. If anything, the material suggests that there is a larger variety in the rural context. In the urban setting most organizations are either associations or limited companies, that is, clearly belonging to the NPVO or the private sector, according to my classification. To attain a deeper understanding, let us also explore how different sources of funding vary with the type of operation.

Sources of Funding and Type of Operation

Looking more closely at how the operations are funded, the sources of public and private funding according to Table 2.1 are further divided. Public sources include EU funds, central government funds and municipal funds. The private sector funding has been separated into commercial activities and private grants and/or membership fees. Operations focused on by societal entrepreneurs were grouped into social development and integration, local development and leisure (including sports) and culture. The legal forms were divided into associations (non-profit organizations), cooperatives (economic activities with no profit purposes), other non-profit organizations (foundations and churches), sole proprietorships, and limited companies.

A multitude of sources of funding as well as legal forms characterizes both social development/integration and local development. The
intertwining along the dimensions, sources of funding and legal form of
organization is striking. No limited company in this study is funded from
the EU, and none of the associations receive central government subsidies.
Otherwise there are many creative and intertwined combinations of legal
form and source of funding represented in the material.

As many as 12 of the associations included in the study deal with leisure
and culture. Many of them are sports clubs and the like. The majority of
these, as is common in the Swedish context, are funded through municipal
grants in combination with membership fees and income-generating activities such as selling for example clothes, candy, coffee and lottery tickets.

The importance of receiving an income from commercial activities to
fund leisure and sports clubs is brought out by the societal entrepreneurs,
mainly in the rural municipalities. To mention a few examples: representatives of Högsby IK (a sports association), Lycksele Art Society,
Theatre and Culture in Lycksele, and Kristineberg Leisure bear witness
to municipal cutbacks and the failure to meet the needs of the population
without commercial side activities and sponsors. The transformation of
the public sector and the restructuring of the economy are thus evident
among the associations as well. Hence, the current time context, which
implies a transformation of the public sectors and an intertwining of
sectors, clearly contributes to the ongoing sectoral intertwining of societal
entrepreneurship. This is especially salient among associations and in the
rural context.

Sources of Funding and Rural/Urban Context

By exploring the rural/urban dimension and its impact on the legal form
and source of funding this analysis also reveals a multitude of legal forms
and sources of funding in both rural and urban contexts. Very few clear
patterns are identifiable. The difference that is highlighted is that more
societal entrepreneurship takes place within associations in the rural
context than is the case in the urban context. In the latter societal entrepreneurship through limited companies was relatively more common. Yet,
there is variety also in the urban contexts.

Independently of the context, few entrepreneurial ventures stand out
as 'sectoral intertwiners' due to their ability to intertwine all three sectors
in their struggles to fund the operations that they are committed to. In
the urban municipality these cases include IK-Östria (personified by the
entrepreneur Nader), Cirkus Cirkör and KoopS. In the rural municipality the most obvious cases are Franklin Real Estate and Puls (see the

prologue). Arne Svensson, the real estate owner in a rural part of an urban municipality, is yet another case in point. The majority of these organizations focus their work on social integration. Using available sources of funding from different politically focused areas at different times in different places, these entrepreneurs seize the funding opportunities available to them. In areas where rural development support is given, this is applied for. In areas where funds are allotted to the social integration of new Swedes, these are applied for. In times when the so-called 'phase 3'[5] subsidies are provided for employees, these are applied for, and so on; however, the social purpose of the organizations remains. Due to the difficulties in attracting funds for social issues, taking advantage of funding opportunities is perhaps a more important cornerstone in societal entrepreneurship than in traditional entrepreneurship with commercial goals. However, as demonstrated by Johannisson (2008), even among high-growth traditional family businesses social and human capital may be considered more important than financial capital.

In these cases, just as in the case of commercial entrepreneurship, it is common for the individual entrepreneur and the organization to be closely tied together. The social, work and spatial spheres are often tightly connected, as for example previously noted in a study of a Swedish rural industrial district (Wigren, 2003). This fact makes the categorization into legal forms far from clear-cut. Business owners are also engaged in associations and act both as societal entrepreneurs and sponsors. When the same people are acting from positions in more than one sector, individual intertwining takes place. The analysis of the empirical material shows that individual intertwining is a more common process in the rural contexts. The most pronounced examples of such processes in this study are the cases of the social cooperative Puls, of Karl-Erik Törner at Lycksele Art Society and Lycksele Theatre and Culture and of Arne Svensson at the real estate business in Ulrika, as well as Franklin Real Estate Limited. Narrating their stories in detail is beyond the scope of this chapter. A representative quote from the empirical material is however that 'you need to be able to cajole people. Then if you have a high position in a company, or have a friend who has, that is how things work in neighbourhoods like this.' It is my contention that, among the spatial contexts involved in the study, the northern rural municipality of Lycksele is a place where individual intertwining plays a major role. Social context seems to play an important role in this municipality, in the sense that 'everyone knows practically everyone' from different areas of life. Social, political and commercial spheres thus overlap and are tightly interlinked for most of the interviewees. It would not be far-fetched to suspect that this may be a common pattern in rural areas.

Issues for Further Analysis

Societal entrepreneurship on grass root level thus shows a high degree of sectoral intertwining. On an overall level, the processes of sectoral intertwining evolve in two directions. First, as discussed and illustrated above, associations like sports clubs are increasingly forced to create funds from commercial activities. Secondly, societal entrepreneurship is organized not only in cooperatives but also as sole proprietorships and limited companies drawing upon, and depending on, public funding from municipalities, central government and the EU. Not the least, there are many involved in societal entrepreneuring in Sweden today who take advantage of the so-called 'phase 3' funds[6] on the labour market.

However, the overview also gives rise to questions such as: How are available sources of funding combined? How does the intertwining process unfold at grass root level, and what are its organizational consequences? To what extent is societal entrepreneurship affected by tensions between sectoral logics, as presented in the introductory chapter? These questions anyway call for a close-up study, so let us begin exploring them by narrating the case of KoopS. It is a cooperative that has managed to combine many sources of funding. It is also one of the cases from which I have a particularly rich empirical material that can be used to describe intertwining processes as the core of societal entrepreneurship.

A CLOSER LOOK AT KOOPS IN LINKÖPING

The KoopS cooperative started in 2006 as an informal group of five dedicated people with the ambition to reduce unemployment and social exclusion in the area of Skäggetorp in Linköping 200 km south of Stockholm. These five persons represented very different organizations, all involved in Skäggetorp, and were all affected by the social problems in the neighbourhood. They were *Staffan*, the local priest, *Thomas*, the principal of Bona Folk High School with a branch in Skäggetorp, *Dan*, the CEO of Communicante (running the local shopping centre), *Helene* from the Swedish Union of Tenants and *Nader*, a societal entrepreneur committed to integration through the IK Östria football club. Their first joint action was to contact the municipality to ask it to outsource some maintenance jobs to unemployed people in the neighbourhood of Skäggetorp. During 2008 the group formed a cooperative. To constitute the board they recruited a project manager, Malena Storm, who started her job in January 2009. The central government made a decision in 2008 to support areas with a great deal of segregation and unemployment.

Five areas were selected and Skäggetorp was one of them. Using these funds, the local government in cooperation with Coompanion created a position as 'District Developer',[7] now held by the societal entrepreneur Nader (mentioned above), and started a job-coaching project managed by Coompanion.

Apart from Malena, the KoopS cooperative employs a joiner and a painter on a long-term basis. They both receive wage supplements, the joiner from the Galaxy organization (see below) and the painter from the Public Employment Service's local office. In its first financial year, the organization's turnover was two million SEK and it grew to such an extent that it became cramped for space. The local unemployed people who are given jobs through KoopS sign a contract for short periods linked to specific tasks. Normally, KoopS receives wage supplements for these people as well as for apprentices. During a period in the summer of 2009 nineteen people were active at the cooperative.

A Head Start

Malena came to an empty office. Yet, she gave KoopS a head start, with active marketing and networking as her first measures. She invited a broad variety of organizations to dialogues. For example, she contacted the local government, the Public Employment Service (AF), the local public insurance office and all housing companies in the neighbourhood. KoopS was then immediately commissioned by Communicante (running the local shopping mall) to redecorate the shopping mall (Skäggetorp Centre). Three people from the Coompanion project worked together with the painter to get practical experience. Subsequently they were commissioned to do jobs such as painting fronts, doing joinery, digging foundations and redecorating an amusement park.

Not Only for Men

The jobs given to KoopS in this first phase were mainly of the kind often considered 'masculine'. However, Malena wanted KoopS to do something for the women living in Skäggetorp. Many of them were new Swedes who were illiterate and had not been to school, but they were skilled in tasks such as sewing and baking. Hence, KoopS placed a bid to run Café Malfors, situated near the popular tourist attraction Göta Canal and owned by the Göta Canal Company. KoopS won the contract and nine women were employed for the summer. Cleaning facilities for tourists were part of the contract. When the canal company conducted spot checks, it turned out that these women had done the best job of the cafés along the canal. The Café Malfors contract was such a success that the Göta Canal Company decided not to charge any rent for the premises.

In the autumn the Swedish Association of Tenants and Stångåstaden (a municipal housing company) cooperated to start a local café in Skäggetorp in order to provide employment for the women during the winter. It was called Café 65 and served bread and biscuits made with fair-trade ingredients. Out of this, the activities and operations of KoopS grew larger. These women and Malena started activities for children (with crafts once a week), a sewing cottage and a workshop for repairing of clothes.

A few women were also able to attend leadership training courses, through cooperation between KoopS and ABF. Other women have attended courses in hand hygiene to be able to work in a kitchen. An agreement has been made between the local school canteen and KoopS that makes the canteen kitchen available to the women after school hours.

Handling Complex Social Issues

Everyday business as a project manager of KoopS thus means searching for and creating jobs and funds as well as coordinating and mediating between the organizations involved (including contractors, funders and other local interest organizations). However, it also concerns working actively with the men and women who receive work through the organization. The idea is to give coaching to the people involved, aiming at integrating them into Swedish society. Doing this, Malena uses her training and experience as a therapist. Democracy and solidarity are key words in this profession. It is not an easy job considering the complex social problems. This is how she expresses it: 'To be here is to be in the middle of reality . . . It can be terribly exhausting and then you have to turn to yourself and think about . . . What can I do and am I satisfied with what I can do? You can never expect to get back what you give.'

Malena described a particular situation which she remembered very well when two women started fighting so badly that she had to call both the police and the ambulance. Eventually she found out that the women shared the same 'husband'/man, but were living at separate addresses. Both had a very tight economic situation, and the matter was about which address the social allowances should be sent to.

Linked Initiatives and Collaboration

KoopS is far from unique; among the societal entrepreneurial initiatives included in this study Puls in Lycksele, for example, represents a similar initiative. Even in Linköping there is a similar cooperative in another neighbourhood with many social problems, called 'Active Ryd' AKR. In another neighbourhood the 'Orangeriet' cooperative is focused on working with creativity and art. In Vadstena, a nearby city, there is a cooperative called KoopM specializing in people with psychiatric diagnoses. These cooperatives and organizations are familiar with each other and exchange ideas, advice and at times resources. As an example of the latter, KoopS has been given both tools and job opportunities from another NGO (Verdandi), which shut down its operations in Skäggetorp.

For the future Malena and Nader and a third person have made a project proposal for an activity centre in Skäggetorp. Five local government committees are willing to support the project and KoopS has been asked to manage it. The municipal department that owns the building is going to reduce the rent. The café activities are to move there, as well as a dressmaker's and a joiner's workshops.

However, towards the end of the interview with Malena, she revealed that she had resigned from the job as project manager of KoopS. She encountered a great many very tough social problems through her work with KoopS, primarily meeting people who were outside the labour market, and she worked a lot with organizing activities, as described above. As a trained stress and health consultant Malena had the ambition and desire to work more with individuals in order to see them grow. In her job at KoopS there was lack of time for that kind of work. The five dedicated people who started the cooperative and make up its board were, at the time of the interview, searching for Malena's successor.

Sectoral Intertwining at KoopS

As we have seen, KoopS is primarily a publicly funded non-government and cooperative organization, selling both goods and services on the market. We need not look closely to realize that the private, the public and the NPVO sectors are intimately intertwined in the operations of KoopS. More specifically, looking back at Figure 2.1, KoopS is clearly an example of inter-sectoral societal entrepreneurship. The cooperative is composed of its membership organizations, but there are also other organizations providing funding or job opportunities. The view taken here is that these organizations, by their involvement, are also part of the societal entrepreneuring through sectoral intertwining. In Figure 2.2 the contributing organizations as well as KoopS itself have been inserted into the theoretical model in order to illustrate which kinds of organization are intertwined.

The organizations involved all contribute to the enactment of societal

		Public sector		Private sector	
		Profit	Non-profit	Profit	Non-profit
Intra-organizational		Stångåstaden	AF, Public Insurance, Bona folk high school	Communicante Göta Canal Corporation	ABF, Verdandi, Nader, Swedish Union of Tenants, The Galaxy
Inter-organizational	Intra-sector				
	Inter-sector		KoopS Board and Management		

Figure 2.2   KoopS and its intertwined organizations

entrepreneurship. They belong to all four categories in the horizontal dimension of the figure, that is, public for-profit organizations and public non-profit as well as private for-profit organizations and private non-profit. Of the public organizations involved, the real estate company Stångåstaden operates for profit. Non-profit public organizations are for example AF, the public insurance organization, Coompanion, and Bona Folk High School. A special position in between the public and the private is held by the Swedish Church, which until recently was a state church. Other private non-profits involved in KoopS are ABF,[8] the Swedish Union of Tenants, the employees' association 'the Galaxy', Verdandi, and the entrepreneur Nader. The for-profit private organizations contributing to KoopS include, for example, the Göta Canal Corporation (see above) and Communicante (owner of the local shopping centre).

Some of these organizations were engaged already at the instigation of KoopS. Others have been linked to KoopS though the proactive management exercised by Malena. Looking at the functions of the organizations, the funds involved in the form of subsidies, grants and allowances come from the public non-profit organizations. The for-profit organizations, both public and private, are the customers who provide the jobs. That is, Stångåstaden, Communicante and the Göta Canal Corporation outsource some of their operations to KoopS and its workers on contract. KoopS is of course paid for its services, but not enough to cover the costs. The private non-profit organizations serve different functions, among which are to provide knowledge, enthusiasm and networks, but also funds and legitimacy.

Coordination, that is, the intertwining in the organizations' everyday activities, is handled by its CEOs. The approach is pragmatic, a feature of societal entrepreneurship that is elaborated on in Chapter 3. However, the board also serves an important function in the intertwining coordination process. In contrast to the *individual intertwining* discussed above, this process takes place on the organizational level and is thus addressed as *organizational intertwining.*

Consequences of Intertwining on Different Levels

Obviously, sectoral intertwining in organizing societal initiatives comes both with strengths, weaknesses, opportunities and threats.

A strength in an organization such as KoopS is of course the commitment of people from a variety of organizations. The board members of such an organization together access a lot of resources though their networks and also guarantee legitimacy in a broad spectrum of both private and public institutions. The resources and efforts required to coordinate this multitude of organizations is, however, a weakness in this organizational form. Attracting funds from different sources, negotiating contracts and mediating between very diverse stakeholders are demanding tasks for project managers. Malena, the project manager, also had to work actively with social integration tasks, which was the actual aim of the organization. The tensions of organizational identity and risk-taking were also to a large extent handled by Malena. Such a situation puts double, or even triple, requirements on a project manager. There is thus a risk of the development that happened in KoopS, where the project manager Malena eventually resigned. This is especially the case with organizational intertwining.

The main strength of sectoral intertwining of both organizational and individual kinds seems to be the opportunity to attract resources from a variety of sources. This regards financial as well as social and human capital. A non-profit organization can access grants not given to private or public organizations, while also accessing public project-funding, as well as selling goods and services on the market. Using the right sources at the right time and in the right place may be facilitated by individual intertwining. Major threats constitute the other side of the same coin. As we know, the availability of funds to apply for varies in unpredictable ways. This hampers the possibilities for long-term planning in the organizations. On the markets, not least the public markets for social services, competition from large international corporations is very tough (compare with Sundin and Tillmar, 2010b). Cooperatives of the described kind are dependent on smaller contracts, often below the limits for public procurement.

CONCLUSIONS AND IMPLICATIONS

The study reported here illustrates that societal entrepreneurs are both affected by and affect the processes of intertwining in their struggle to fulfil their social and societal goals. On an overall level, the processes of sectoral intertwining communicate two lessons. First, as discussed and illustrated above, associations like sports clubs are increasingly forced to generate funds from commercial activities. Secondly, societal entrepreneurship whether organized as cooperatives or as sole proprietorships or limited companies draw on, and depend on, public funding from municipalities, the central government and the EU.

One conclusion from the empirical material is that intertwining funding from all three sectors provides a cornerstone of societal entrepreneuring. Finding social issues which need to be dealt with is not a problem, and neither is the availability of ideas of ways to go about it. The problem is identifying, and taking advantage of, a variety of sources of funding. A few of the studied entrepreneurs succeed in doing so, either individually, as in the case of Franklin or in groups, as in the described KoopS case. In this process, these entrepreneurs simultaneously, and unintendedly, act as *sectoral intertwiners* (for a discussion on intentional mediation between organizations, see also Andersson and Johansson, Chapter 5).

Here I have thus empirically identified two different kinds of processes implying sectoral intertwining. First, the intertwining occurring when the same people are active in several sectors and link their grass root activities in the different sectors to each other. Such processes I address as *individual intertwining*. In comparing the rural and the urban contexts the individual intertwining seems to be more common in the rural context. The functions in society are there dependent on fewer people, and on the notion that 'everyone knows everyone'. Perhaps this pattern also connects to a Gemeinschaft orientation in these areas; see Chapter 1.

Second, the sectoral intertwining occurs through coordination within the association, cooperative, or enterprise, that is, when different kinds of organizations are interlinked. In KoopS, the case described, the employed manager's main working task was to deal with organizations such as funders, customers, collaborators and other stakeholders. Through her mediating role, aiming for the societal goals of her organization, she also engaged in a process of sectoral intertwining. Here I term this kind of intertwining *organizational intertwining*. Presumably, such intertwining is more typical for Gesellschaft-oriented contexts where formal relations are needed to supplement weak ties.

Even though institutional form tensions of intertwining may decrease over time, the issue of risk-taking tensions remains, as does the organizational identity tension. The long-term consequences of sectoral intertwining and the intertwining between sectoral logics and social and economic values are yet to be seen.

Further studies into the prerequisites for societal entrepreneurship at the grass root level are needed, with the focus on sectoral intertwining. Do the different formal and informal 'rules of the game' or logics in the sectors of the economy come into conflict with each other? Or, perhaps rather, when, where, how and why does this happen? What are the major tensions, and how do they differ in various contexts of time and space? How does the choice of legal form affect the organization, its operations, its organizing and hence the entrepreneuring? Funding from a particular source often comes with requirements and duties. How does the source of funding affect the processes of entrepreneuring and the linked processes of sectoral intertwining and societal entrepreneuring? Will economic values, that is, earned income, be used to attain social purposes? Or may social purposes at times be used to attain economic values? Work-integrating cooperatives operating as labour market intermediaries could, for example, be fruitful to analyse from the perspectives mentioned. See the discussion on these issues in Chapter 3.

What is it that we are witnessing now in the NPVO sector and in inter-sectoral cooperation with this sector? Is it a strengthening of this sector and of the entrepreneurs within it, or is it a kind of New NPVO Sector Management? Which logics, in terms of institutional pillars, focal form of capital and interaction rationale (compare with Berglund and Johannisson, Chapter 1 of this volume), will in the long run become dominating and perceived as being worth striving for?

Since almost all the societal entrepreneurs at grass root level interviewed for this study are dependent on public funding, this needs to be kept in mind by supporters of the initiatives. Although building on voluntary work, societal entrepreneurship also requires considerable resources from the other sectors. Some activities, such as perhaps activating and rehabilitating people in long-term unemployment, require inter-organizational initiatives. The inter-organizational and inter-sectoral approach that grass root level societal entrepreneurship represents has been fruitful to practise. Policy-makers may find other areas where such integration will be beneficial, while being aware of the threats and weaknesses discussed above.

NOTES

1. This chapter adheres to the same distinction between social and societal entrepreneurship as discussed in the introductory chapter. However, I also in some instances draw on and refer to relevant literature focusing on social entrepreneurship.
2. The network was funded by the Knowledge Foundation. Apart from the Knowledge Foundation, the mapping was funded by SALAR (Swedish Association of Local Authorities and Regions) and the participating municipalities.

3. Coompanion is an NGO giving free business development advice to cooperative enterprises. Jobs and Society is a foundation with numerous local offices giving free advice to start-ups. Almi is a state-owned limited company providing advisory services and credits to SMEs with growth potential.
4. Social entrepreneurship concerns initiatives aiming at improving what is missing or not functioning in the social structure. New solutions shaping a sustainable society: economically, socially and ecologically.
5. An unemployment programme came into force in July 2007. The Parliament adopted new regulations for health insurance, which affect everyone who has received sickness benefit or time-limited sickness compensation for the maximum period. The programme consists of three stages. Stage 1, max 150 days, consists mainly of mapping/surveying activities for job tracking, coaching and preparatory efforts. Stage 2, moreover, consists of practice and work training. Stage 3, the last, occurs after 450 days in the programme. Those who are still unemployed will be occupied by a so-called organizer appointed by the Public Employment Service. Each period in Stage 3/Phase 3, may last two years at the most. Source: http://www.arbetsformedlingen.se/For-arbetssokande/Stod-och-service/Fa-extra-stod/Arbetslos-lange/Jobb--och-utvecklingsgarantin/Fragor-och-svar-om-fas-3.html (accessed 24 January 2012).
6. An unemployment programme came to force in July 2007. The Parliament adopted new regulations for health insurance, which affect everyone who has received sickness benefit or time-limited sickness compensation for the maximum period. The programme consists of three stages: Stage 1, a maximum of 150 days, consists mainly of mapping/surveying activities for job tracking, coaching and preparatory efforts; Stage 2 consists of practice and work training; and Stage 3 occurs after 450 days in the programme. Those who still are unemployed are occupied by a so called 'organizer' appointed by the Public Employment Service. Each period in Stage 3, may last two years at the most. Source: http://www.arbetsformedlingen.se/For-arbetssokande/Stod-och-service/Fa-extra-stod/Arbetslos-lange/Jobb--och-utvecklingsgarantin/Fragor-och-svar-om-fas-3.html (accessed 24 January 2012).
7. District development/urban development is part of the work for sustainable development. The sustainable society is a society, where economic development, social welfare and solidarity are united with a good environment. It is a society imbued with democratic values and respect for human rights. Source: http://www.linkoping.se/sv/Om-kommunen/Utveckling-och-samverkan/Stadsdelsutveckling--Urban-utveckling (accessed 24 January 2012).
8. The Workers' Educational Association.

REFERENCES

Andersson, L. (2008), 'Intraprenörskap – Ett Företagsnära entreprenörskap i det offentligas regi', in Lundström and Sundin (eds), *Perspektiv på förnyelse och entreprenörskap i offentlig verksamhet*, Örebro, FSF.

Austin, J., H. Stevenson and J. Wei-Skillern (2006), 'Social and commercial entrepreneurship: Same, different, or both?', *Entrepreneurship Theory and Practice*, **30** (1), 1–22.

Battilana, J. (2006), 'Agency and institution – the enabling role of individuals' social position', *Organization*, **13** (5), 653–676.

Christensen, T., P. Lægreid, P.G. Roness and K.A. Røvik (2005), *Organisationsteori för Offentlig Sektor*, Malmö: Liber.

Defourny, J. (2010), 'Concepts and realities of social enterprise: a European perspective', in A. Fayolle and H. Matlay (eds), *Handbook of Research on Social*

Entrepreneurship, Cheltenham, UK and Northampton, MA, USA: Edward Elgar Publishing, pp. 57–87.

Esping-Anderson, G. (1996), *Welfare States in Transition: National Adaptations in Global Economics*, London: Sage.

Fayolle, A. and H. Matlay (2010) (eds), *Handbook of Research on Social Entrepreneurship*, Cheltenham, UK and Northampton, MA, USA: Edward Elgar Publishing.

Forssell, A. and D. Jansson (2000), *Idéer som fängslar: recept för en offentlig reformation*, Malmö: Liber.

Gartner, W. (1989), 'Who is an entrepreneur? is the wrong question', *Entrepreneurship Theory and Practice*, **11** (3), 47–68.

Granovetter M. (1985), 'Economic action and social structure: the problem of embeddedness', *American Journal of Sociology*, **91** (3), 481–510.

Hjorth, D. (2010), 'On provocation, education and entrepreneurship', *Entrepreneurship & Regional Development*, **23** (1–2), 49–63.

Hood, C. (1991), 'A public management for all seasons?', *Public Administration*, **69** (1), 3–19.

Johannisson, B. (2008), 'The social construction of the disabled and unfashionable family business', in V. Gupta, N. Levenburg, L.L. Moore, J. Motwani and T.V. Schwarz (eds), *Culturally-sensitive Models of Family Business in Nordic Europe: A Compendium Using the Globe Paradigm*, Hyderabad: ICFAI University, pp. 125–144.

Johannisson, B. (2009), 'Industrial districts in Scandinavia', in G. Becattini, M. Bellandi and L. De Propris (eds), *A Handbook of Industrial Districts*, Cheltenham, UK and Northampton, MA, USA: Edgar Elgar Publishing, pp. 521–534.

Johannisson, B. (2011), 'Towards a practice theory of entrepreneuring', *Small Business Economics*, **36** (2), 135–150.

Nicholls, A. (ed.) (2006), *Social Entrepreneurship: New Models of Sustainable Social Change*, New York: Oxford University Press.

North, D.C. (1990), *Institutions, Institutional Change and Economic Performance*, Cambridge: Cambridge University Press

Parkinson, C. and C. Howorth (2008), 'The language of social entrepreneurs', *Entrepreneurship & Regional Development*, **20** (3), 285–309.

Smith, B. and T. Barr (2007), 'Reducing poverty through social entrepreneurship: The case of Edun', in J. Stonerand and C. Wankel (eds), *Innovative Approaches to Reducing Global Poverty*, Charlotte, NC: Information Age Publishing, pp. 27–42.

Steyaert, C. (2007), '"Entrepreneuring" as a conceptual attractor? A review of process theories in 20 years of entrepreneurship studies', Special Issue: Pioneering New Fields of Entrepreneurship, *Entrepreneurship and Regional Development*, **19** (6), 453–477.

Steyaert, C. and D. Hjorth (2006), 'Introduction: What is social in social entrepreneurship?', in C. Steyaert and D. Hjorth (eds), *Entrepreneurship & Regional Development*, **16** (3), 179–196.

Steyaert, C. and J. Katz (2004), 'Reclaiming the space of entrepreneurship in society: Geographical, discursive and social dimensions', *Entrepreneurship & Regional Development*, **16** (3), 179–196.

Sundin E. and M. Tillmar (2010), 'The intertwining of social, commercial and public entrepreneurship', in A. Fayolle and H. Matlay (eds), *Handbook of*

Research on Social Entrepreneurship, Cheltenham, UK and Northampton, MA, USA: Edward Elgar Publishing, pp. 142–156.

Sundin, E. and M. Tillmar (2010b), 'The masculinization of the elderly care sector: Local-level studies of public sector outsourcing', *International Journal of Gender and Entrepreneurship*, **2** (1) 49–67.

Tillmar, M. (2009), 'Societal entrepreneurs in the health sector – crossing the frontiers, *Social Enterprise Journal*, **5** (3), 282–298.

Valeau, P. (2010), 'Social entrepreneurs in non-profit organizations: innovation and dilemmas', in A. Fayolle and H. Matlay (eds), *Handbook of Research on Social Entrepreneurship*, Cheltenham, UK and Northampton, MA, USA: Edward Elgar Publishing, pp. 205–231.

Welter, F. (2011), 'Contextualizing entrepreneurship: Conceptual challenges and ways forward', *Entrepreneurship Theory and Practice*, **35** (1), 165–184.

Whetten, D.A. (1989), 'What constitutes a theoretical contribution?', *Academy of Management Review*, **14** (4), 490–495.

Whetten, D.A. (2009), 'An examination of the interface between context and theory applied to the study of Chinese organizations', *Management and Organization Review*, **5** (1), 29–55.

Wigren, C. (2003), *The Spirit of Gnosjö: The Grand Narrative and Beyond,* Diss., Jönköping: Jönköping International Business School.

APPENDIX

Table A2.1 Overview of the initiatives involved in the study

Main area of operations	Municipality	Start	Name	Non-profit org.	Type of organization	Sources of funding
Integration	Linköping	1981	IK Östria	Yes	Association	Local government grants, membership fees, income-generating activities, EU grants.
Leisure	Linköping	1964	Linköping Motor Club	Yes	Association	Competitions, food services, local government grants for sports, local government guarantee
Local development	Linköping	1995	Hulta Ecological Group	Yes	Association	Local government grants
Sports, Leisure	Högsby	1900	Högsby IK	Yes	Association	Supplementary business activities, sponsors, local government operating grants, membership fees
Sports, Leisure	Lycksele	1970	Aros Sports Club	Yes	Association	Membership fees
Leisure	Lycksele	1991	The Pharaohs, Motor Club	Yes	Association	Membership fees, profit from racing events, project applications, sponsors
Leisure Local development	Högsby	1995	Allgunnen Fishing Area	Yes	Association	Selling fishing licenses
Social work	Botkyrka	1980	Mind and Body Church of Sweden, three Free Churches, the Salvation Army	Yes	Association	Gifts and donations, the Public Employment Service's Phase 3 grants

Field	Municipality	Year	Organization		Legal form	Funding sources
Social work, Leisure	Högsby	1977	Ruda Community Association	Yes	Association	Membership fees, Local government grants, sponsors
Culture	Högsby	1968	Norrgränden Heritage	Yes	Association	Business activities, operating grants, local government rural allowance
Social work	Botkyrka	1896	Verdandi	Yes	Association	The Public Employment Service's Phase 3 grants
Local development, Social work	Botkyrka	2007	Young Alliance	Yes	Association	Associated Companies, membership fees, selling Young Entrepreneurs' services to schools, local government support
Leisure	Botkyrka	1907	Southside Youth recreation centre	Yes	Association	Municipal grants
Leisure	Botkyrka	2000	4Fathers	Yes	Association	Sponsors, new non-financial forms of cooperation
Culture	Lycksele	1981	Lycksele Art Society	Yes	Association	Membership fees, local government grants, certain supplementary business activities
Culture	Lycksele	1967	Theatre and Culture in Lycksele	Yes	Association	Membership fees, local government grants, sponsors
Culture, Local development	Botkyrka	1995	Cirkus Cirkör	Yes	Association, which owns a limited company	Business, central and local government grants, county council grants
Social work, Leisure	Lycksele	1998	Puls	Yes	Association, which owns a limited company	Employment support from social insurance system/business actors

Table A2.1 (continued)

Main area of operations	Municipality	Start	Name	Non-profit org.	Type of organization	Sources of funding
Local development	Linköping	1999	Bestorp Village Community, Östergötlands Foods, East-Swedish Tourism Council	Yes	Association Co-operative	Membership fees, EU Grants
Social work	Linköping	2009	KoopS	Yes	Co-operative	Grants from different social insurance systems/business actors
Local development	Lycksele	2003	Kristineberg Leisure	Yes	Co-operative	Membership fees, local government grants, business
Rural development Local development	Lycksele	1989	Ruskele Village Community, Ruskele Hus (Housing Foundation)	Yes	Foundation	Membership fees, local government guarantee and operating grants
Social work	Högsby	1955	Philadelphia Pentecostal Church and the Mission Covenant Church of Sweden	Yes	Units of Church of Sweden	Grants, gifts

Sector	Location	Year	Name		Legal form	Type	Funding
Local development	Linköping	1980	Arne Svensson	No Yes	Sole Proprietorship Social entrepreneurship, active in associations		Local government grants, income-generating activities, EU grants
Tourism, Growth	Högsby	2000	Fågelfors Hat Shop	No	Sole proprietorship	Business	
Tourism Local development	Högsby	2002	Aboda Café	No	Sole proprietorship	Business	
Health Local development	Linköping	2003	Yoga Power	No	Limited company	Business	
Social work	Botkyrka	2001	Fittja Operation and Maintenance	No	Limited Company	Business	
Local development	Högsby	2003	Högsby Network	No	Limited company	Business	
Social work Leisure Local development	Lycksele	1965	Calle Franklin	No Yes	Franklin Real Estate Ltd Social entrepreneurship, active in associations	Business	Membership fees, grants from different social insurance system actors, local government grants, business

3. Tracking the everyday practices of societal entrepreneuring

Bengt Johannisson

PROLOGUE

Christer, the business angel, and I are sitting in his glazed-in veranda at the waterside on a sunny day in May (2010), talking about his first encounter with the social entrepreneur Fredrik Bergman:

> I am in my car, on my way home, he calls me – this kind of call I get twice a month, sometimes a week, someone who calls and discreetly asks about something, often it is a damned salesman. So I was actually quite brief and said that now you really have to summarize what you want, I haven't got all the time in the world. As you know Fredrik is a bit of a roundabout so I said that maybe it is better if I tell you how I work and you can line up. – If I am going to invest there are three things that I have a look at: head, heart and wallet. The head says that I have to understand what you are going for and see the logic and the business opportunities. The heart says that I have to sympathize with not just the key concept but also with you and your key affiliates. Because that is what I focus upon, the persons. Third, I am no . . . philanthropist but I want to invest, I want to join in and take responsibility for the decision that I make and that is best done by putting in some own money. Then you become a bit more careful using them. Already there a problem appeared because Fredrik said that is impossible. So you are one of those . . . egoists who do not want a partner in your company? No, Fredrik said, it is a cooperative you know. Cooperative! Cooperative, what the hell is that? Is it a co-op store and similar stuff! Fredrik said: Have you ever heard of Macken. For sure I have heard of Macken, I said, I love Macken. I have tried to support it, I have bought bikes there. I think it is the most beautiful idea. Recycling bikes and working with immigrants, all that. Fantastic! So I said, if it is about Macken, I am willing to join in.

THE CALL FOR A PRACTICE APPROACH

Once upon a time when social and societal aspects of entrepreneurship were in their infancy, such images mainly concerned rural contexts where entrepreneurship dressed as 'community entrepreneurship' was assumed to bring attention to what was physically located in the periphery (see Johannisson and Nilsson 1989; Johannisson 1990). Besides, not too long ago, irrational and myopic thinking and a trivial and unreflected practice were ascribed to small-scale business operations, initiated and organized by family owner-managers or cooperatives. Large markets and public corporations, in contrast, were, and still are, presented as rational and systematic structures guided by long-term objectives and enacted through advanced plans and routines. Today we know better. Marginality not only in physical but also in social and mental space has triggered social and societal entrepreneurship, and digital times have reformed the logic that guides the organizing of human endeavours. The very practice of venturing, whether commercial or social, receives much more respect. Accordingly, I here propose a practice approach to social/societal entrepreneurship that supplements discursive approaches, whether the reflective view provided by Dey and Steyaert (2010) or the analytical dichotomization proposed by Nicholls (2010).

The present concern for practice in organization studies in general (see for example Schatzki 2001, 2005; Chia and MacKay 2007) has also incorporated entrepreneurship research (see Johannisson 2011). General definitions of practice either concern general human activities, for example Schatzki (2005), or discursive/symbolic issues, for example Wenger (1998: 5): 'Practice: a way of talking about the shared historical and social resources, frameworks, and perspectives that can sustain mutual engagement in action.' Both these definitions have to be qualified. First, in contrast to Schatzki, I think that interactivity, rather than 'just' activity, should be focused on. Besides, people respond to artefacts, not only to people. Second, in contrast to Wenger I claim that tension and conflict are neither possible nor desirable to avoid since they energize organizations and keep them alert (Normann 1977; Grabher 2001). Third, considering entrepreneurship in general as creative organizing, practices as bundles of interactions are expected to permeate formal boundaries such as the one between the organization and the environment. As stated in the introductory chapter, societal entrepreneurship concerns processes that cross the boundaries between sectors in society.

The purpose of this chapter is to outline a conceptual roadmap for empirical journeys into the practices of societal entrepreneurship. The ambition is to track emergent patterns concerning the way societal entrepreneurship is enacted as creative organizing. This calls for an approach that recognizes the uniqueness of any social event but also contextualizes it in order to make it possible to position it empirically and conceptually. Exploring the unique features of societal organizing on the micro-level I have designed and enacted a close-up study of the social enterprise Macken.

Macken is located in Växjö, a university town in southern Sweden and the centre of quite a small region/county with 160 thousand inhabitants, half of them living in urban Växjö. It is (inter)nationally recognized as a 'green city' that in addition presents itself as a multicultural town. Many of the new Swedes, though, live in a special residential area with its own private and public service centres, including schools – and Macken. Several other social enterprises operate in Växjö but all of them organize a considerably narrower range of activities than Macken. This social venture was launched in 2005 by Fredrik Bergman, a journalist and Folk High School teacher, a former syndicalist and environment activist. He initiated a local debate on the importance of recycling that intrigued a local politician. Her involvement triggered the unique political decision stating that Bergman and the emergent cooperative were allowed to screen everything that was brought to the local dump. Everything that was possible to recycle/recondition, for example furniture, bikes or textile fabric, could be taken away. User-value is thus recreated by reconditioning such items in 'language workshops' staffed by teams consisting of physically disabled or socially marginalized native Swedes and not yet integrated new Swedes. This arrangement makes both groups gain considerably in terms of increased self-respect. The new Swedes are introduced to a new language in a working context that is familiar to them and the native Swedes can use their knowledge about the trade and Sweden in a constructive way. Macken's products are distributed through its two own second-hand outlets. Macken also provides services such as courses in Swedish and in how to run your own company in collaboration with public organizations and institutions and offers private sector business companies services such as maintenance services.

In the next section I provide some conceptual thoughts which have guided my inquiry into Macken's practices. After presenting and reflecting upon my way of doing research in Macken I deliver a quite detailed report on Macken and how it has enacted its vision. Out of a dialogue between proposed concepts and the empirical accounts some generic features of the practice of societal entrepreneurship are generated. In the final section I comment on how we can and should govern the forces associated with societal entrepreneuring.

ORGANIZING SOCIETAL ENTREPRENEURSHIP – SOME BASIC ASSUMPTIONS

As early as 1973 Henry Mintzberg in his seminal text 'Managers at Work' demonstrated that management is about a messy everyday coping

(Mintzberg 1973). In those days March and Olsen (1976) also presented organizations as 'organized anarchies', proposing that coincidence, rather than plans, rules everyday life (in the public sector). A chaos perspective – see for example Stacey (1996) – was proposed as a framework to capture the need for instant action in coping with the surprises that the environment incessantly produces. In such a perspective planning is just a waste of time. Recent (European) research has come to the paradoxical conclusion that even the constant change produced by everyday life with all its myopic concerns, spontaneity and improvizations must be accepted as a routine (see for example Chia and MacKay 2007). Having said this, it is of course a challenge to find out how social ventures, presumably considerably less structured and professionally run than public and corporate bureaucracies, are able to cope in an inter-sectoral environment. The prologue narrating the encounter between Christer, a business angel with (then) a naked management ideology, and Fredrik, the social entrepreneur driven by emotions and ideals, signals the need to inquire into the everyday practices of societal entrepreneurship in order grasp how the contrasting logics of the sectors, summarized in Chapter 1, are dealt with.

Elsewhere I argue that a practice approach for good reasons puts the searchlight on the hands-on way new ventures emerge, that is, how they come into being as organized events. (Johannisson 2011). This approach to entrepreneurship definitely redirects the attention from both personal/ individual features and from the dramatized aura that surrounds entrepreneurship when associated with radical innovation and heroism to rather concern mundane activities (see also Chapter 7 by Berglund and Johansson). In line with a practice approach I associate entrepreneurship with initiative and organizing in everyday life; see Hjorth et al. 2003 and Steyaert 2004, where the authors relate entrepreneurship to creative and persistent imitation as much as to rational innovation (see also Johansson 2010). The challenges associated with viewing entrepreneurship, or better entrepreneuring (Steyaert 2007; Johannisson 2011), as ongoing social projecting and practicing only become amplified when adapted to societal entrepreneurship. Such challenges will be briefly commented upon and subsequently furnished with some empirical accounts from Macken. I thus argue that sustainable societal entrepreneuring is associated with a number of capabilities:

- The capacity to address instrumental as well as expressive accountabilities by monitoring stakeholders and their different, sometimes even contrasting, contexts. Organizations involved with social entrepreneuring are especially challenged since they have to be able to both demonstrate efficiency/expediency in the use of resources for a variety of purposes and the ability to stand up for basic social values in a society dominated by economic forces (Knutsen and Brower 2010; Segnestam Larsson 2011).

- The courage to resist the pressure towards the routinization of operations. Increasingly standardized private and public sectors in contemporary society call for initiatives involving the NPVO sector that are able to fill the many gaps in the social context that the two other sectors leave when practising their standards. Caring for needy people with personal needs calls for extreme concern for details and flexibility, which in combination with constant resource scarcity makes improvization and social bricolage (Johannisson and Olaison 2007; Didomenico et al. 2010) into a rule (sic!). The call for versatility puts strong pressure on the staff and supporting volunteers of the social enterprise to practise 'street smartness', that is, to make use of actionable knowledge.
- The ability to balance the need for uniqueness and legitimacy in the context concerned. Every organization, including social ventures, has to be able, on one hand, to stand out, make a difference, and on the other hand, to achieve legitimacy (De Clercq and Voronov 2009). Although legitimacy currently, when societal entrepreneurship is generally recognized, is easily achieved, there is an ongoing competition as regards acquiring resources as well as drawing attention between different social enterprises. Readiness to take on new challenges and get involved in dialogues with different stakeholders then appears as a road to both uniqueness and legitimacy.
- The power to mobilize commitment in creating and maintaining the organization by attracting and tapping internal and external competencies: By involving the many, also those labelled as socially, mentally or physically disabled, that is by making visible and integrating all 'slices of genius' (Hill et al. 2010), they jointly can create a sustainable context for societal entrepreneuring. Such commitment must go beyond 'voice' and 'loyalty' (Hirschman 1974) to encompass 'involvement' that also takes its own initiatives and accepts responsibilities that benefit the organization (Hirschman 1982; Stryjan 1987).

When societal entrepreneuring becomes incorporated, all people involved appear as both the ends and the means of the enterprise's operations. On one hand this means that the organization has to meet the unique needs of each individual, on the other that the organization has access to the distinctive human and social resources carried by those involved, clients as well as staff and volunteers. Only by recognizing, that is, making use of, marginalized people's competencies will the objective to increase their self-confidence in order to facilitate their (re)entrance into Swedish society be attained. This puts pressure on social projecting. Market-oriented entrepreneurship can select among potential new ventures by separating ends and means and applying simplistic economic choice criteria. In contrast, a social enterprise constantly has to enact new ways of involving people and all sorts of challenges into social opportunities. In order to capture the practice of such venturing a study of the social enterprise Macken was initiated.

INQUIRING INTO THE PRACTICE OF SOCIETAL ENTREPRENEURING

Conceptual and empirical research into societal entrepreneurship as a practice is limited. In the introductory chapter we argued that only close-up studies can host the needed intense dialogue between conceptual constructs and empirical accounts. In a practice approach to entrepreneuring it is especially crucial to find ways to capture the local or the situated, the specific and the unique, the concrete and the detailed (Johannisson 2011). Theorizing on practice must be concerned with *how* activities/relations are established and work rather than with what they contain. There is thus a concern for the creation of 'actionable knowledge' (Jarzabkowski and Wilson 2006), that is for understanding what insight is appropriate for 'getting things done' in a particular context. This focus on relevant and situated knowledge explains why alertness to practices associated with, for example, spontaneity/intuition (Bourdieu 1977; Dalton 2004; Chia and MacKay 2007), creative imitation (Johansson 2010) and the use of analogy (Johannisson 2011) are so important when inquiring into all kinds of entrepreneuring, including societal entrepreneuring. These practices materialize as, for example, improvization, bricolage, as well as the use of multiple forms of capital (Davidsson and Honig 2003) and financial bootstrapping (Winborg 2000).

An adequate point of departure for searching for an appropriate method is the understanding of the phenomenon. Thus, first, inspired by Weick (1969/1979, 1995), I see societal entrepreneurship as an organizing endeavour aiming at sense-making and the subsequent hands-on enactment of ventures in ambiguous settings. Elsewhere I propose that venturing that aims at creating (new) economic or social value sediments out of the personal network of the individual and that continued networking crafts the further emergence of the venture (Johannisson 2000, see also the notion of 'effectuation' proposed by Sarasvathy (2001)). Secondly, the boundary between the venture and the (enacted) environment remains fuzzy throughout the venturing process. A third basic assumption is that entrepreneuring as the orchestration of embodied practices is an existential challenge that occupies everyday life, thus dissolving the boundary between private and public spheres.

Theorizing on practice Pierre Bourdieu reflects upon the gap between academic, formal/codified knowledge on one hand and the kind of knowledge that is acquired through the practice itself on the other (see for example Bourdieu 1977). This gap widens when change processes are targeted. There are two ways to get access to the personal experience of those involved. The first is self-reporting/reflection on the part of the practitioner, here the initiator/entrepreneur of the social enterprise. The second road to insight is considerably more radical in an academic context: self-reporting by a researcher who her-/himself launches a venture and builds insight by combining auto-ethnography and hands-on enactment. My own experience from such 'enactive' research is reported elsewhere (Johannisson 2005, 2011).

However, using auto-ethnography for theorizing practice has major general drawbacks. As regards the interlocutor's self-reporting as a practitioner s/he usually has little time for reflection, especially when being involved in creative, entrepreneurial processes where change is incessant. New events, behaviours and interactions are constantly emerging, calling for alertness and appropriate measures. Further, even if there is time for reflection, the committed actor will have difficulties in experiencing the evolving process, as s/he, just as the fish that does not know of the water, is unaware of the context. This reveals a paradox since such 'dwelling' in the world is also needed to practise improvization (Barrett 1998), trust one's intuition and give way to spontaneity; see Chia and MacKay 2007. These are all capabilities which are especially relevant to the practice of societal entrepreneurship. The alternative approach, where the researcher becomes the enactor, that is, temporarily takes on the identity of a practitioner, will only be productive if the researcher is already well acquainted with, has delved into, the setting where the evolving venturing takes place. If the research lacks such an experiential background the research will nurture 'introvert reflexivity' (compare Alvesson and Sköldberg 2000) and remain an island in the researcher's mind (compare Johannisson 2011).

Considering these drawbacks of auto-ethnography I here adopt a dialogue or interaction mode to gain the needed insight into the practices of societal entrepreneurship. In the present study of Macken this means that I draw upon three kinds of empirical accounts. Qualitative interviews, *conversations*, with key actors provide the first set of accounts. These include Fredrik Bergman and two more leaders in the organization (Plemka, the administrator, and Peder, the production manager who resigned in 2011) as well as one of the two business angels involved (Christer – the other one being 'Betan'). The second set of accounts consists of two *emailed daily dialogues* between Fredrik and myself for one month in 2010 (October) and for one week in 2011 (March/April). While the dialogue during the first period may be characterized as a reflective conversation about the conditions for running Macken, the spring dialogue reported Fredrik's everyday doings, which were only briefly commented upon by me. The third set of accounts reflects *my dwelling* in Macken and its spatial and social context. Part of that 'hanging around' experience directly concerned (and still concerns) the social enterprise and includes participant observation/observing participation in a number of formal and casual meetings with (part of) the organization members during 2009–2011 (and continuing as a member of a supportive network ('Macken's Friends') and as a coach for nascent entrepreneurs in 2012). Further dwelling experience is also gained by associating with further people, projects and organizations that are in turn linked to the social enterprise Macken at its location.

The story told in this chapter will mainly cover, in addition to Fredrik, the social entrepreneur, the role of the (two collaborating) business angels. As is stated in Chapter 1, the logic that carries the private sector, here epitomized by the business angels, increasingly colonizes the two other sectors. Accordingly, it is important in any inquiry into societal entrepreneurship to find out how such interventions materialize and are dealt with in practice. The prologue here offers a taste. In addition to the conversation with one of the two business angels (Christer) I reflected as an observant participant on their behaviour in formal and informal meetings with further representatives of the social enterprise.

THE COOPERATIVE MACKEN – FROM DUMP TO DIVINITY

To Structure or not to Structure

Under the formal umbrella of Macken as a cooperative new social ventures are constantly launched as an outcome of the interplay between the current needs of marginalized and excluded people on one hand, and financial, human and social resources which are available or mobilized on the other. In 2012 the operations thus include for example 'language workshops' for textile, furniture, cycle repairing and IT, cafés/restaurants, second-hand outlets and estate management. Macken is also trying to upgrade its services and products. For example, a professional designer has been contracted to not only refurbish used furniture but also aesthetically upgrade them into high-profile items. Over the years this new-venturing practice has produced a 'social' incubator where people are offered the opportunity to test their own business ideas. If these ventures turn out to be profitable the nascent entrepreneur may spin out and establish his or her own business.

Besides a salaried staff of about 30 persons Macken (as of autumn 2011) has engaged ten volunteers in different activities. In 2010 Macken's turnover was 680,000 euros. Slightly less than one third of that amount concerned the cooperative's own retail sales of second-hand goods as well as services. Twelve per cent of the turnover was support from a public foundation, while the remaining financial resources originated in EU funds and national/municipal authorities and organizations as compensation for different services provided by Macken, mainly targeting disabled people and new Swedes.

The Macken cooperative has 20 (individual) members, about half being employees, some board members and some external people (like myself). The board has altogether nine members who represent significant stakeholders as well as the staff. Recently (spring 2012) the board as well as the executive team of Macken were restructured. The latter consists of five people, including the chairperson, the top executive team (Fredrik, Plemka and the new CEO (Bisse)), the previous CEO and board member (Tina) and Lena, the board chairperson. Recently (2011) Fredrik stepped down as chair of the board and the chief executive at Macken to take charge of the new-venture development at the business centre. As a joint venture with the municipality of Växjö the social incubator was upgraded in 2011 into this business centre, which in addition offers administrative services and start-up training programmes (including coaching, an activity that, as indicated, includes external people like me as a resource).

Macken also has an advisory board – 'Macken's Friends' – staffed by resourceful people in the local context. It mainly operates as a sounding board. Macken and the majority of the other local social enterprises are members of a network administered by the regional branch of a national organization supporting cooperatives (Coompanion – where at the time of the study I was a board member for a period). Further overlapping membership in the different professional and social networks that embed Macken both provide a resource bank and access into different organizations in the private, public and NPVO sectors. Jointly they on one hand reflect the fuzzy borderland between the social enterprise and its enacted support-providing environment, on the other the intertwining of sectors elaborated upon in Chapters 1 and 2.

In spite of these formal structures Macken was run very informally in

2010 with Fredrik involved in almost every activity. We recognize this owner/leader dominance and involvement from traditional family businesses. Recent research into strategy-making presents it as integrated in everyday activities, as 'strategizing' (see for example Chia and Holt 2006; Johnson et al. 2007). However, as indicated, in a social enterprise this everyday dealing with strategic issues becomes multiplied. – in our joint diary Fredrik reported one day in his life (29 March 2011) as follows:

Finishing my column for *Smålandsposten* (a local newspaper) at about 5.30 in the morning. Go over to Macken at eight, fix a substitute job for Helen in Åseda tomorrow. Have a little chat with Frank who also worked in the bicycle repair shop. He has felt lost since we locked the door. But Frank and I take care of the bicycle service for municipal employees together on Friday morning, and until then he can renovate our cart, which is to be used for the kolkhoz.

At 8.30 I have an establishment talk with a guy from Somalia. A very nice guy. We have now met four times. The establishment talks are a panic. More and more people choose us as establishment pilots, while at the same time our pilots have quit one after the other. For various reasons – illness, moving, they're not allowed by their boss to work with this, or they're called in for extra to work somewhere else. I'm all on my own now with a whole pile of establishment talks. If you don't keep up with your four talks a month with the clients you are liable to pay damages to the Labour Exchange. So right now it is high time to find more pilots. At about nine I have a meeting with Pelle at Macken about the new Job Guarantee course for young people, a course run by the People's High School and Macken in collaboration, which addresses young unemployed who didn't get into upper secondary. It's a lot of fun to have these students at Macken. They're getting on well with our immigrants. Many of them go on to people's high school later. Macken will be a soft first term in people's high school studies.

Around 10 I empty the mailbox at our localities in Alvesta. I look into Göran, owner of the big ICA food market in Alvesta, and go on negotiating with him about letting Kerim set up his falafel cart outside ICA. Kerim is one of those we help in the business centre. ICA in Alvesta seems quite positive. We'll keep in touch next week.

At 10.30 I attend psychotherapy in Alvesta. I had a health check-up in Växjö a month ago and explained that my life doesn't function so well; I can't quite stand things. Besides, I had got high blood pressure. I explained to the doctor that there's something mentally wrong in my head, since I always feel that I do a poor job and that I should do more. But there are no more hours to spend. And I don't want to go on living in this strange way. The doctor referred me to a psychotherapist in Alvesta, something I was entirely positive about.

It's now the second time I visit her. A complex picture is beginning to emerge. For one thing, I suppose I'm a workaholic, who has got used to filling the whole calendar – and sort of got stuck in that rhythm. A real addiction, equivalent to alcohol or sweets. In addition, I suppose I'm extremely hooked on action by my upbringing. You are supposed to perform and prove yourself to the world. And for another thing, I might have a touch of ADHD, who knows. Anyway, this life style does me no good, so I'm highly motivated when I go to see the psychotherapist. I look at it as some minor research into who you are and why, an interesting and important examination that I hope will lead to a change.

Just before 12 I look up a guy for an establishment talk, but he's not around. At 12 I have lunch in the Macken restaurant at the Social Insurance Agency, chatting on about the future and strategies with Marta, who is in charge of the restaurant. She's a very nice and competent person.

At 12.45 I'm with Anders Meyer at the County Administrative Board to talk to him and Karin Borgenvall, who is Director of our School of Agriculture. We want to start (a training programme) right away even though the class is not quite full. Anders gives the OK.

At 1.30 p.m. Lars Apelmo and I are sitting in his old hairdressing salon, Salong Cocette, putting together an application for Macken Design. We're going to apply for money from both the Swedish Agency for Economic and Regional Growth, the State Inheritance Fund and the European Social Fund.

At 3.30 p.m. I attend a meeting with a girl from the people's high school, whose teacher has referred her to me. They want me to help her fix a job. For various reasons it's very important for her to get a job. I like the student very much, but it makes me sour in no time. Why should I help her? Can't the people's high school do this themselves? I ought to set boundaries.

At 4 o'clock I have an establishment talk with two newly arrived Iraqis.

At 5 there's a meeting in the library with the Macken business centre. Right now there are quite a few people we help, with varying results of course.

At 6 I'm supposed to be home cooking, even though Ann-Sofie has already started on it. Doesn't feel good. Today was my turn.

At 8.30 I drop into a farewell party for Pernilla, a wonderful teacher of Swedish for Immigrants, who is now leaving Macken.

At 9.30 I help my son Adam cramming before a social studies test.

At 10 Ann-Sofie and I are watching a film.

At 11.30 we [Fredrik and his wife] are asleep.

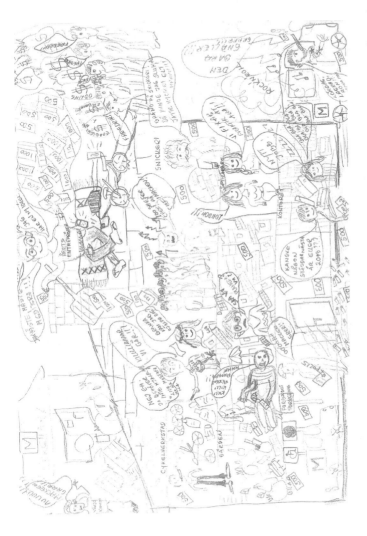

Note: I am grateful to Plemka Pavlovic, Macken's accountant, for making her dramatizing drawings of major events and everyday life in Macken available to me.

Figure 3.1   *Keep smiling – messy Macken with the social entrepreneur Fredrik in the middle and at the top*

71

The drawing in Figure 3.1 illustrates how messy Macken's daily operations appeared even to Plemka, the well-informed accountant, producing an escalating mess over the first five years after the incorporation of
Macken. The complexity and turbulence even seem to be beyond that of
organized anarchy, considering that there was only a minimum of internal
formal structure to balance untamed spontaneity, enacted not the least
by Fredrik Bergman. With only fuzzy boundaries between the cooperative and the environment new social ventures incessantly enter the scene.
Fredrik at the top of the drawing, designed as a Godfather, nevertheless
keeps smiling, obviously being happy with the unruly social operations
and himself communicating hope and faith. Others were not as enthusiastic, one of them being Plemka, since there was no time for even structuring
the operations. She and Fredrik had to deal hands on with the problems
as they appeared, and Plemka comments:

> We have been criticized for how we deal with Norremark (the dump), that we
> do not empty our container properly. We were close to losing our station there.
> Then Fredrik personally went there to clear up around it. Every time there is a
> crisis and we are about to lose a contract Fredrik goes to bring things into order
> again. I think it is really unfair to him.

Plemka argued in the autumn of 2010 that there had to be some minimum
order – in the administrative systems, in the operating procedures, on the
premises, both at the reception at the dump and in Macken's other build-
ings – or she would have to leave Macken. This is why the two business
angels Christer and Betan were brought in during October 2011. This is
how Christer clarifies his and his colleague's contribution to Macken:

> We were sitting here last week pushing for our views once more because this is
> important. Yet we tried not to be overly rational. It is not about being business-
> like and making money but about providing the key people who run this with
> a working place that functions and finding the right persons to do the work.
> There are far too many people who have got a free ride because of Fredrik's
> kindness.

The restructuring of the top echelon in Macken presented above was part
of a general administrative make-over in 2011 led by the other business
angel, Betan. His and Christer's ambition was and is to create a number
of profit-centres – or 'barrels' as they are called in Macken language after
Betan's drawing of the new emerging organization chart. The ongoing
activities were structured into different fields of activity, such as language
workshops, second-hand outlets and design. The administrative system
was adapted to support this new organization. Betan and Christer also
proposed that some of these 'barrels', for example the one organizing

design activities, might become so economically successful that they should be spun off as independent business units. This spinning-off strategy has caused a lot of anxiety in Macken since it confirmed the introduction of a different rationale, the private-sector logic. It made visible, even institutionalized, a divide between on one hand Macken's operations with a commercial potential, and on the other those driven because of their social-value creation.

No sooner was the new regime implemented than Plemka became worried. She realized what price she would have to pay in order to install a structure that was administratively feasible. After all, the previous messy system had created the overview that made it possible to be involved in all the facets of Macken as a social enterprise. Figure 3.2 accordingly illustrates how Plemka imagined the emerging hierarchical and unambiguous structure in Macken but with the 'barrels' rolling down the slope of the hierarchy and out of control of Fredrik and herself, both being obviously equally sad and confused. Plemka perceived the business angels as both the devil's henchmen promoting resource efficiency and 'cold' relations and as acting like 'real' angels with good intentions and warm relations.

Conversations about Macken's Practices

In order to communicate the constant and challenging call for creative organizing in Macken as enacted entrepreneurial practices, two micro-conversations (original statement and continued dialogue response) between Fredrik (Bergman), the social entrepreneur, and the researcher Bengt (Johannisson) were thus staged. One of these dialogues concerned the tensions of everyday life within Macken, the other the everyday private and public life of Fredrik. – on 21 October 2010 Fredrik emailed:

Oh. Today we had a really tough staff meeting at Macken. We have talked a lot about being straight to each other . . . Today, though, it was almost too good. If you are at a large staff meeting and speak out your disappointment with a person on the team who is present it becomes, to put it mildly, tense. Many of those working at Macken are, as you know, disabled and because of this presumably rather sensitive. Even with healthy people a meeting like the one we had would have been tough. Now it becomes almost unbearable. There is a need for rules about how to behave . . . It came out like running the gauntlet.

Macken may make me feel exhausted. Almost all our talk, everything that we bring up at board meetings and other meetings is about the workshops, about how difficult it is to make them work. We almost never talk about the operations that work well: teaching new Swedes Swedish, the social incubator, our branch operation, the estate management, the course at the Folk High School. It is as if those well-functioning operations did not exist. Parts of the organization where so called 'healthy' people work.

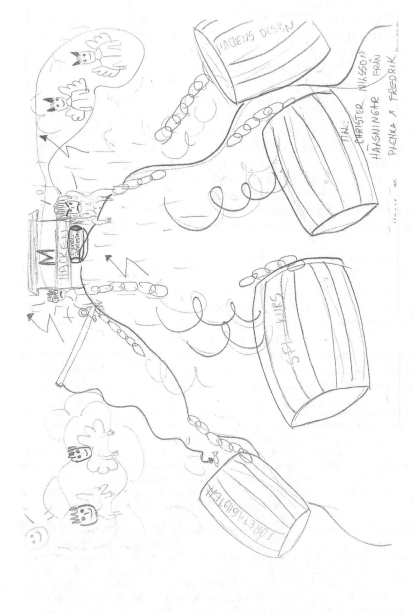

Figure 3.2   Business angels or social devils? – from committed chaos into a managerial iron cage

A broken sewing machine in the textile workshop or a missing drawer in the second-hand shop easily becomes a huge issue, almost immense. It ends up by straining at a gnat and swallowing a camel. It is totally out of all proportion, perhaps not in a human perspective but for sure if we put it in the perspective of our overall operations and definitely if we have the financial consequences in mind. The workshops are really difficult to work with and will remain so as long as many of their members' salaries are subsidized.

The next day (22 October) Bengt responds:

There must be a lot of frustration and tension in an organization that so much is dependent on involvement, where everything that is done must be meaningful to people who often at the same time struggle with their own identities. This obviously contrasts expressing discontent, generally or with one's relation to somebody else, in an organization where everyone feels safe in her/his role, in themselves and are well paid. However, I think that discussing only problems and seldom what works well is a more general organizational problem. This may reflect a collective self-observation that mere survival calls for problem solving.

In every organization details are important ... Perhaps conversations concerning such details as a lost piece of furniture should be allowed to take their time so that we can work out together what they are a symptom of. What is more, experience and chaos theory tell us that small things may make big ones happen.

I assume that it is in the workshops where the disabled people are expected to be active and participate hands-on. Then there should be no surprise that tensions appear. If they were expected to suddenly be as well-functioning as healthy people neither the workshops nor Macken at large would be needed.

Can the reason for your feeling uncomfortable at the staff meeting be your Swedishness and/or that you feel embarrassed considering that you are expected to [externally] present Macken as a well-functioning operation independently of how many the worries back home are.

The very same day, 22 October, the dialogue continues with Fredrik writing:

Exciting idea to first have worries coming up to the surface and be dealt with and then try to find out what they may indicate. This is an attitude that is emerging this autumn, however not without help from Christer and you.

Why is Fredrik so anxious about organizing? Well, one week earlier, on 15 October, Fredrik reflected on the first encounter with Christer Nilsson, the business angel who reported about the same incident as the one narrated in the prologue:

At the last meeting of the board there was a discussion about the need to approach a clever capitalist for support. Analysing the operations that we already are running, to see whether they could be made safer and more robust. I was told a person to call, an experienced entrepreneur who had built two empires before the age of 45 and who was now operating as a business angel. I called Christer Nilsson, that is his full name, two weeks ago and asked if he could pass by and have a chat with us.

He immediately told us that he had read about Macken and that it would a real pleasure to help us without any claim on remuneration. He had bought bikes at Macken and was fascinated by our business. He had never been in touch with a cooperative.

On Friday the same week we met for the first time. Christer then told me that the night before he had been to a birthday party, together with a number of regional business leaders, some of them retired. He had told them that he was going to meet with us. Then several further business leaders had told him that they wanted to join in and develop Macken. So now he showed up and told us that, if we wished, we could get an advisory board of experienced business leaders for free. 'People very much believe in your idea and see a great potential' he explained to us. 'They want to help out getting Macken going. Just because it is fun.'

The next day (16 October) Bengt's emailed response is:

Perhaps Christer's offer is TOO generous!? He may mainly be concerned with getting something out of it for himself. Just as I get a lot out of being close to Macken: excitement, a rewarding dialogue with you, and extremely interesting research material on an exceptionally topical issue. Christer may of course be motivated by genuine altruism but also by being aware that societal entrepreneurship is on everybody's lips and that he can use his involvement instrumentally in his business operations. The Good Capitalist . . .

Christer wants Macken's operations to be professionalized and financially upgraded. That sounds fine. However, the question is if that does not mean that the social responsibility and the rationality carried by care that has characterized Macken will vanish. Instead you will become a corporate structure with subsidiaries in for example design, recycling and social care or a kind of staffing company. Such a development calls for a risk analysis in order to stop Macken from becoming colonized by the management ideology [managerialism] that dominates society.

The same day Fredrik mails back:

I respond immediately. You are of course right, we have to be on our guard as regards people we don't know yet. Had Christer been an active capitalist I would have been more afraid. Now he is an ex-businessman. But of course, we don't need more action in Macken, the only thing that we need get going is the finances. That's why the board decided that we should talk to a capitalist. I completely agree with you that this means a risk that we get lost in managerialism and that the economy should never be given priority before people. That is why it is so difficult. You want to listen as well as reflect, try everything, and present it to the board before we take action.

Both accounts, Fredrik's and my dialogue, and joint learning and Fredrik's straightforward report on his doing that spring day presented above, reveal the complexity and dynamism of societal entrepreneuring. Obviously it is about a flow of actions and interactions that to an outsider appears as being totally out of control, as far away as possible from ideals that normative theories on management and institutional order preach. It seems impossible to foresee the eventing of the change process and even imagine the implications of individual events before another event emerges that calls for attention. This means that every event has to be dealt with hands-on prematurely. Only retrospectively may any kind of pattern be identified in the flow of (inter)activity and its implications tested in further (inter)action/experimenting so that appropriate coping practices may be outlined and possibly end up in a proposed routine. Alternatively it may be argued that this constant toe-dancing is what societal entepreneuring is all about. Elsewhere we propose that entrepreneurship is about considering change as a natural state (Hjorth et al. 2003), a view that fits into Chia's and Holt's (2006) image of reality as becoming. Fredrik's and my conversation and the further accounts provided above invite more specific interpretations of the practices of societal entrepreneuring.

CONCEPTUALIZING SOCIETAL ENTERPRENEURING – LESSONS FROM MACKEN

A common theme in the entrepreneurship literature is to map and conceptualize how new ventures become enacted; see for example Gartner 1985, Bouwen and Steyaert 1990, Aldrich 1999 and Sarasvathy 2001. Before contributing to such conceptualizing as regards societal entrepreneuring I want to summarize my lessons from the Macken story using conventional vocabulary. First, my visits backstage Macken show that societal entrepreneurship invites to a multitude of 'open spaces' that weak, and needy, strong and resourceful people seem to be equally attracted to. The former are empowered, through the daily encounters that make the practice of societal entrepreneuring, as they have the possibility to not only bring their problems but also inform others about the 'solutions' that they can offer to their problems. New citizens, for example, can expose the capabilities they bring from their countries of origin. Resourceful people are intrigued by the contrast between on one hand the 'free' play that personal commitment to social venturing invites to, on the other the designed role play in formal structures that they once inhabited or still do. This is how boundaries between the sectors dissolve. In the Macken case representatives of both the public sector (the municipality and regionalized state agencies) and the private sector (the business angels) (at least partially) submitted to the logic of the NPVO sector. Thus the business angels Christer and Betan subsequently have turned into 'social angels' with a dedication to 'doing good', because they realized that this is more challenging than using money to make more money. Even public officials who want to 'act outside the box' are provided an arena not too far away from home when contributing to the making of social enterprises in ways which are not formally regulated. Sometimes their involvement was enforced for nostalgic reasons. For example, two members of Macken's Friends with a considerable cultural and symbolic capital and with resourceful networks once themselves worked in (the same) social enterprise.

A second lesson is that the need for change is taken for granted just as in Macken people's presence as well as their interrelations are non-institutionalized. Instead organizing is ephemeral, that is relations are established, maintained and closed in an atmosphere of transcendence. Those involved practise an entrepreneurial approach; compare the contributions to Part III of this book. This does not only include client/customer participants but also the staff, whose majority only engages for a year or two or even less. However, there is a core of people at Macken including employees such as Fredrik and Plemka but also the business angels, and some of the employees and volunteers who epitomize stability and responsibility, which make them care for all those things that fall between two stools. The diary report by Fredrik from a spring day in 2011, above, illustrates this commitment well. Macken can then be considered as a transitional space that offers security and thus also invites play (compare Winnicott 1971)

As mentioned, Fredrik has withdrawn from the position as Macken's CEO in order to focus on new social venture development. In April 2011 he was temporarily replaced by Nina, member of the board ever since Macken's incorporation and an active social-venture activist as well as a media professional. In February 2012 she was succeeded by Bisse who is also acquainted with the management of social enterprises. Plemka remains in charge of accounting, while Nina is now a board member and an informal controller. Lena Tidblom, who before retiring founded and led a leading Swedish language institute for training new Swedes, is a volunteer and chairman of the board. Figure 3.3 illustrates how these four highly strong and competent women use their joint forces to try to keep the social entrepreneur Fredrik close to the 'real' world when with the help

Figure 3.3   Letting go and grasping firmly – trying to keep the social entrepreneur on earth

of a balloon he is (again) trying to vanish into skies that do not impose any limits to his dreams about new social ventures, this time concerning keeping sheep downtown Växjö. The drawing illustrates the ongoing competition between change and stability that appears in all ventures but seems to be amplified in societal venturing.

Third, the Macken story also demonstrates that dissolving the boundaries between sectors makes ventures emerge and become resourced sometimes by necessity – problems just have to be solved because the need is so obvious – and sometimes by believing in serendipity – coincidences that can be turned into opportunities. The field research also shows that for many persons the boundary between the private and public spheres of life is torn down as well – only to be re-built in order to avoid personal burnout; see above. Fredrik's diary reports that his involvement is existentially founded and an integrated part of ongoing identity crafting. Again, this feeling of belonging and contributing, of making a community, goes as well for the needy outsiders as for the resourceful insiders in Swedish society.

The inquiry into the practices of societal entrepreneurship as appearing in Macken stresses three features which reveal as much about sentiments as about (inter)action. First, the ongoing arranging of embodied needs and resources, people and relations, which I associate with the core of entrepreneuring as a process and with 'bricolage' as a particular kind of organizing, see Baker and Nelson 2005. Second, temporal features of the social-venturing process, that is regularities and disturbances in the flow of activities that produces a certain rhythm in societal entrepreneuring. Third, emotional and moral commitments that reflect a special kind of involvement among contributors to social enterprises. These features call for further elaboration and associated conceptualization.

There are three major reasons, building on the notion of 'bricolage' as presented by Levy Strauss (1962/1966), to qualify the notion of '*social bricolage*' in the context of social venturing that brings it beyond recycling artefacts at hand to new patterns; compare Didomenico et al. 2010. First, it is about an ongoing process, and thus bricolag*ing* in accordance with our understanding of entrepreneuring in general. Second, the aim of bricolaging – 'making do' – is not just to instrumentally solve a problem involving artefacts or, as elaborated upon by Sarasvathy (2001), to enter a journey with unclear ends and means (but with optional routes) to cover individual needs. It is social, even societal, bricolaging, because it is about social value production. Third, it is social, because it is about bringing people into new constellations (and across sectoral boundaries). The situation needs action and whoever is available is expected to contribute with his/her time and competencies, just as those involved are expected to offer mutual help to make those competencies visible and activated. This is an organizational challenge that is as far as one can get from relying on standards and routines.

Here I want to take the notion of social bricolage one step further. The increasing standardization and routinization in the private and public sectors accelerate the importance of social bricolage as an organizing device inherently associated with societal venturing. Such ventures can offer such organizing that ventures belonging to the private or public sector cannot. Social bricolage as a building block of entrepreneuring also includes a dynamic dimension where one 'thing', resource or opportunity, follows upon the other. Thus, for example, in Macken a textile workshop was carefully planned and enacted in order to facilitate the integration of female new Swedes, but out of that project also came an art exhibition when it turned out that one of the participants was also an artist. The similar social ambition made a woman in a neighbouring small community, who was a trained florist, volunteer to organize immigrant women in a workshop in her field of interest. Some of these operations are triggered in a very direct but casual way. For example, visitors to the local dump who met with Macken's people asked for help with transportation, and that triggered the establishment of a special logistic unit in Macken.

As a concept capturing the genuinely processual, dynamic features of social entrepreneuring as reflected in the doings and interactions in Macken I propose the notion of *amplified immediacy*. The stabilizing and institutionalized forces in the environment of the social enterprise generate together a dynamic tension which in turn produces what I associate with the basic rhythm of social entrepreneuring. This immediacy can be further qualified in five respects. First, as a temporal feature linked to spontaneity, which is based on the belief that every moment is or can be made into the 'right' one, a feature that is related to kairos and synchronicity, that is, to different aspects of timing (in contrast to chronological time). Second, immediacy communicates that a sensation does not have to pass any filter of time-consuming reflection in the cognitive space, which often makes the feeling of the 'right moment' disappear. Reflection rather happens in or after action (see Schön 1983). Third, since action, experimenting, is instantly triggered, inconvenient routes forward can quickly be excluded, creating space for trying out new, possibly more appropriate, options. Fourth, the inspired actor spontaneously searches partners in an existing personal network with the proper attitude and resources who can make an enactment take off. Fifth, immediacy itself mobilizes intense involvement, a feeling of ownership and a perceived responsibility to complete what has been initiated.

Involvement in societal entrepreneuring may be egoistic, as in many theories on entrepreneurship, or collective. If collective, it may be centripetal or centrifugal. Being centripetal, or selective, as in family businesses and local communities the concern is just about a closed group of people; compare for example Kanter (1972) and Johannisson and Wigren (2006). Centrifugal involvement is expansive, searching new arenas where a general social concern can be practised. In Macken, as epitomized by its core members, Fredrik and Plemka for example demonstrate deep involvement that appears as both centripetal and centrifugal. On one hand they show a deep concern for those people already being taken care of, on the other an equally dedicated openness to and responsibility for taking on new social challenges. What is more, this dual involvement in Macken increasingly reflects expressive and not instrumental accountabilities. Fredrik and Plemka often state that things just had to be done while the business angels Christer and Betan now more often argue that they are involved in Macken because of the fun of it. In practice this means that the latter advocate the mission of Macken as often as they preach the need for plans and routines. Accordingly, in both cases I label the commitment that was demonstrated as *dynamic involvement* since it is expanding and constantly open to new challenges.

CONCLUDING REFLECTIONS: TO TAME OR NOT TO TAME SOCIETAL VENTURING

Three concepts are induced from the study of Macken – social bricolaging, amplified immediacy and dynamic involvement – signalling genuine characteristics of societal entrepreneurship. On one hand they are about keeping the focus on individual needs, on what is here and now, on the other hand they reflect further social ambitions to nurture and a readiness to intervene whenever new social emergencies appear. Dressed differently, as reflections of the bright and dark sides of societal entrepreneurship, the second part of the book rather talks about the contradictions that societal entrepreneurship accommodates. For example, in Chapter 6 Birgitta Schwartz demonstrates that contrasting national contexts produce a constant need to renegotiate the focus and kind of involvement. However, already the story about Astrid Lindgren's World in Chapter 4 describes how the three societal sectors are mobilized in varying temporal and resourcing patterns.

Further reflections are needed before the lessons from Macken in its unique social setting can be translated, or rather expanded by way of association (Johannisson 2011) or bisociation (Koestler 1964) into new settings. Macken obviously was studied in a specific temporal setting, both with respect to its own chronology (its formative years) and the favourable spirit of the time (global times with a great concern for social and ecological issues) as well as a specific local context (Växjö as a municipality with explicitly 'green' ambitions). Staying with Macken's own situation, forces for as well as against a maintained (social) vitality can be identified. It is a challenge both for Macken itself and those learning from its story to cope with such pressures.

Obviously the characteristics that we ascribe to the practices of societal entrepreneurship put high pressure upon those who are deeply involved, considering that their private lives are influenced to a high degree. As Fredrik Bergman puts it: 'There were times when I wasn't allowed to mention Macken at home.' Of course measures were taken to reduce such strain. In Fredrik's case, as told above, this meant that in the spring of 2011 he was relieved from his CEO position to take charge of 'only the business centre and new venture development'. However, in January 2012 it still happened that he stepped in to support immigrant entrepreneurs on practical matters, people who he had helped to start a business years ago. Obviously, formal (re)arrangements do not make the personal responsibility of a social entrepreneur obsolete, even though they may reduce the overall workload in existing operations. Figure 3.3 illustrates Fredrik's constant urge to launch new social ventures. In addition, when people become more visible they are approached with both problems and solutions. Then dense local networks with a high absorptive capacity for external input become a strength. An indicator of the strengths of that networking is that many contributors to Macken are involved in not just one but in several of Macken's 'quasi'-internal networks – staff, volunteers, board and 'Macken's Friends'. We will return to this in the last chapter when we introduce the notion of 'organizing context'.

Figure 3.4 summarizes the present (March 2012) leadership-in-practice in Macken as reflected in how key actors relate to instrumental and expressive accountabilities. The former reflects Macken as a unit of (social) production, while the latter considers Macken as an arena for civic engagement; see Knutsen and Brower (2010) and Chapter 4 where this dichotomy is elaborated upon. The three women Plemka, Nina and Bisse have, ever since they became involved in Macken, had the responsibility and capabilities to balance instrumental and expressive accountabilities. Fredrik remains extremely focused on protecting the basic values, Macken's social mission, which guides its operations, while Lena, the board chairperson, has a strong social call but is more pragmatic. When the two business angels once entered the scene they were expected to coordinate Macken's instrumental accountabilities. Over time they have, however, become

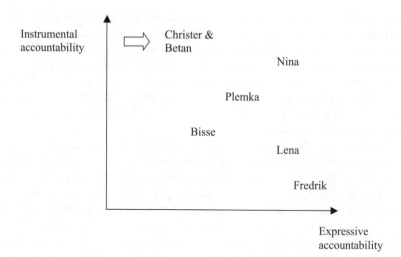

Figure 3.4   Balancing instrumental and expressive accountabilities in Macken – positioning the key leaders (April 2012)

more and more convinced about the need for not just creating economic but social value as well.

I have tried to demonstrate that societal entrepreneurship has to and is able to provide much more variety as regards the potential for self-organized further venture creation than commercial entrepreneurship. There 'sticking to the knitting' is a well-established norm. Besides, traditional entrepreneurship is basically restricted to the imagination and ambition of the founder/the founding team, and possibly to constructive dialogues with customers. In the social enterprise pressures for new ventures have different sources, internal as well as external, and are triggered both according to plan and casually. Macken's broad goals and (still) 'soft' organization create a readiness to absorb different kinds of ideas and resources that in turn make many more ventures enactable. On one hand this gives the social enterprise the discretion to select the most favourable options out of a broad stream of venture offerings. On the other hand the strong social orientation pushes it to accept more challenges than can be properly organized and made financially sustainable. This suggests that new inter-sectoral ventures that are created by the social enterprise run the risk of becoming appropriated by intra-sectoral interests not hesitating to be more efficient in taking advantage of the economic potential of social ventures. It may be argued, though, as I did in a diary conversation with Fredrik, that social enterprises that experience this 'robbery' could be considered as especially valuable in a societal perspective. The business angel Christer and I (BJ) had a brief conversation on this matter (interview 16 May 2011):

> BJ: Applying my business logic – I have no experience as a business angel – I would argue that if Macken doesn't charge at all for their services it means that they sponsor the receiving (social) venture by, say 2000 euros, which makes it able to take off and in turn create social value.

> CN: Then I have another thesis. What is for free is worth nothing. If I get something for free I have to decline because then there is something fishy about it or I cannot complain. If something is for free I cannot come back and say that this was . . . trash but if I pay 2000 euros I can, because then I have the right to expect quality.

> BJ: Then the [delivering] organization becomes infused with a kind of vitality?

> CN: Yes.

The conclusive lesson from the Macken story seems to be that the shared dwelling in the everyday practices of societal entrepreneuring has initiated constructive dialogues between representatives for the different sectors. These dialogues have not only initiated mutual attention to and learning from each other. The ongoing exchange has also created an alertness to the complexities that by necessity characterize societal entrepreneuring as a confluence of different mindsets and logics. Rather than becoming paralyzed by the contrasts, even conflicts, that these opposing rationales produce, they are perceived as challenges that have to be dealt with. Successively a shared understanding of and responsibility for basic human needs have emerged, embedding the contrasting logics of the different sectors that Table 1.1 in the introductory chapter summarizes. This obviously does not mean that, for example, the business angels redefine themselves as 'social angels' or that Fredrik is transformed into an equally efficient manager. It rather implies that they all become more capable of taking advantage of each other's differences in a way that is in the interest of the social enterprise.

REFERENCES

Aldrich, H.E. (1999), *Organizations Evolving*, London: Sage.
Alvesson, M. and K. Sköldberg (2000), *Reflexive Methodology. New Vistas for Qualitative Research*, London: Sage.
Baker, T. and R. Nelson (2005), 'Creating something from nothing: resource construction through entrepreneurial bricolage', *Administrative Science Quarterly*, **50**(3), 329–366.

Barrett, F.J. (1998), 'Creativity and improvisation in jazz and organizations: implications for organizational learning', *Organization Science*, **9**(5), 605–622.

Berglund, K. and A.W. Johansson (2007), 'Entrepreneurship, discourses and conscientization in processes of regional development,' *Entrepreneurship & Regional Development*, **19**(6), 499–525.

Bourdieu, P. (1977), *Outline of a Theory of Practice*, Cambridge: Cambridge University Press.

Bouwen, R. and C. Steyaert (1990), 'Construing organizational texture in young entrepreneurial firms', *Journal of Management Studies*, **26**(6), 637–649.

Chia, R. and R. Holt (2006), 'Strategy as practical coping: a Heideggerian perspective', *Organization Studies*, 27, 635–655.

Chia, R. and B. MacKay (2007), 'Post-processual challenges for the emerging strategy-as-practice perspective: discovering strategy in the logic of practices', *Human Relations*, **60**(1), 217–242.

Dalton, B. (2004), 'Creativity, habit, and the social products of creative action: revising Joas, incorporating Bourdieu', *Sociological Theory*, **22**(4), 603–622.

Davidsson, P. and B. Honig (2003), 'The role of social and human capital among nascent entrepreneurs', *Journal of Business Venturing*, 18, 301–331.

De Clercq, D. and M. Voronov (2009), 'Toward a practice perspective of entrepreneurship. Entrepreneurial legitimacy as habitus', *International Small Business Journal*, **27**(4), 395–419.

Dey, P. and C. Steyaert (2010), 'The politics of narrating social entrepreneurship', *Journal of Enterprising Communities: People and Places in the Global Economy*, **4**(1), 85–108.

Didomenico, L. Di, H. Haugh and P. Tracey (2010), 'Social bricolage: theorizing social value creation in social enterprises', *Entrepreneurship Theory and Practice*, (July): 681–703.

Gartner, W.B. (1985), 'A conceptual framework for describing the phenomenon of new venture creation', *Academy of Management Review*, **10**(4), 696–706.

Grabher, G. (2001), 'Ecologies of creativity: the village, the group, and the heterarchic organisation of the British advertising industry', *Environment and Planning A.*, 33, 351–374.

Hill, L.A., M. Travaglini, G. Brandeau and E. Stecker (2010), 'Unlocking the slices of genius in your organization', in N. Nohria and R. Khurana (eds), *Handbook of Leadership Theory and Practice*, Boston, MA: Harvard University Press, pp. 611–652.

Hirschman, A.O. (1974), *Exit, Voice and Loyalty. Responses to Decline in Firms, Organizations and States*, Cambridge, MA: Harvard University Press.

Hirschman, A.O. (1982), *Shifting Involvements*, Oxford: Martin Robertson.

Hjorth, D., B. Johannisson and C. Steyaert (2003), 'Entrepreneurship as discourse and life style', in B. Czarniawska and G. Sevón (eds), *Northern Light – Organization Theory in Scandinavia*, Malmö: Liber, pp. 91–110.

Jarzabkowski, P. and Wilson, D.C. (2006), 'Actionable strategy knowledge. A practice perspective', *European Management Journal*, **24**(5), 348–367.

Johannisson, B. (1990), 'Community entrepreneurship – cases and conceptualization', *Entrepreneurship and Regional Development*, **2**(1), 71–88.

Johannisson, B. (2000), 'Networking and entrepreneurial growth', in D. Sexton and H. Landström (eds), *Handbook of Entrepreneurship*, London: Blackwell, pp. 368–386.

Johannisson, B. (2005), *Entreprenörskapets väsen*, Lund: Studentlitteeratur.

Johannisson, B. (2011), 'Towards a practice theory of entrepreneuring', *Small Business Economics*, **36**(2), 135–150.

Johannisson, B. and A. Nilsson (1989), 'Community entrepreneurship – networking for local development', *Journal of Entrepreneurship & Regional Development*, **1**(1), 1–19.

Johannisson, B. and L. Olaison (2007), 'The moment of truth – reconstructing entrepreneurship and social capital in the eye of the storm', *Review of Social Economy*, **LVX**(1), 55–78.

Johannisson, B. and C. Wigren (2006), 'The dynamics of community identity making – the Spirit of Gnosjö revisited', in C. Steyaert and D. Hjorth (eds), *Entrepreneurship as Social Change*, Cheltenham, UK and Northampton, MA, USA: Edward Elgar Publishing, pp. 188–209.

Johansson, A.W. (2010), 'Innovation, creativity and imitation', in F. Bill, B. Bjerke and A.W. Johansson (eds), *(De)mobilizing the Entrepreneurship Discourse. Exploring Entrepreneurial Thinking and Action*, Cheltenham, UK and Northampton, MA, USA: Edward Elgar Publishing, pp. 123–139.

Johnson, G., A. Langley, L. Melin and R. Whittington (2007), *Strategy as Practice. Research Directions and Resources*, Cambridge: Cambridge University Press.

Kanter, R.M. (1972), *Commitment and Community*, Cambridge, MA: Cambridge University Press.

Knutsen, W.L. and R.S. Brower (2010), 'Managing expressive and instrumental accountabilities in nonprofit and voluntary organizations: A qualitative investigation', *Nonprofit and Voluntary Sector Quarterly*, 39, 588–610.

Koestler, A. (1964), *The Act of Creation*, London: Hutchinson.

Lévi-Strauss, C. (1962/1966), *The Savage Mind*, Chicago, IL: University of Chicago.

March, J.G. and J.P. Olsen (1976), *Ambiguity and Choice in Organizations*, Oslo: Universitetsforlaget.

Mintzberg, H. (1973), *The Nature of Managerial Work*, New York, NY: Harper & Row.

Nicholls, A. (2010), 'The legitimacy of social entrepreneurship: Reflexive isomorphism in a pre-paradigmatic field', *Entrepreneurship Theory and Practice*, **30**(July), 611–633.

Normann, R. (1977), *Management for Growth*, Chichester: Wiley.

Sarasvathy, S.D. (2001), 'Causation and effectuation: toward a theoretical shift from economic inevitability to entrepreneurial contingency', *Academy of Management Review*, **26**(2), 243–263.

Schatzki, T.R. (2001), 'Introduction: practice theory', in T.R. Schatzki, K. Knorr Cetina and E. von Savigny (eds), *The Practice Turn in Contemporary Theory*, London: Routledge, pp. 1–14.

Schatzki, T.R. (2005), 'Peripheral vision: the sites of organizations', *Organization Studies*, **26**(3): 465–484.

Schön, D. (1983), *The Reflective Practitioner. How Professionals Think in Action*, New York, NY: Basic Books.

Segnestam Larsson, O. (2011), *Standardizing Civil Society*, Stockholm: Santérus.

Stacey, R.D. (1996), *Complexity and Creativity in Organizations*, San Francisco, CA: Berret-Koehler.

Steyaert, C. (2004), 'The prosaics of entrepreneurship', in D. Hjorth and C. Steyaert (eds) *Narrative and Discursive Approaches in Entrepreneurship*,

Cheltenham, UK and Northampton, MA, USA: Edward Elgar Publishing, pp. 8–21.

Steyaert, C. (2007), 'Entrepreneuring as a conceptual attractor? A review of process theories in 20 years of entrepreneurship studies', *Entrepreneurship and Regional Development*, **19**(6), 453–477.

Stryjan, Y. (1987), *Impossible Organizations. On Self-management and Organizational Reproduction,* Department of Sociology, Uppsala: Uppsala University.

Weick, K.E. (1969/1979), The *Social Psychology of Organizing*, Reading, MA: Addison-Wesley.

Weick, K.E. (1995), *Sensemaking in Organizations*, Thousand Oaks, CA: Sage Publications.

Wenger, E. (1998), *Communities of Practice. Learning, Meaning and Identity*, Cambridge: Cambridge University Press.

Winborg, J. (2000), *Financing Small Businesses – Developing our Understanding of Financial Bootstrapping Behavior*, Lund/Halmstad, School of Management and Economics/SIRE.

Winnicott, D.W. (1971), *Playing and Reality*, Harmondsworth: Penguin Books.

4. Narrating Astrid Lindgren's World as societal entrepreneurship

Bengt Johannisson and Elisabeth Sundin

PROLOGUE

In one of Astrid Lindgren's books, *The Brothers Lionheart*, the two brothers have a serious conversation before Jonathan embarks on a dangerous mission (Lindgren 1973, pp. 60–61):

> I thought about the saga of Tengil, I began to think that it was certainly the cruellest of all sagas. I asked Jonathan why he had to undertake something so dangerous, he could easily sit at home by the fire at the Knights Farm and be happy. But then Jonathan said it was something he must do, even if it was dangerous.
> 'Why?' I wondered.
> 'Otherwise you're not a human being but just a piece of dirt.' said Jonathan.
> He told me what he was going to do. He was going to try to rescue Orvar from the Katla Cavern.

THE STORY WE WANT TO TELL

Astrid Lindgren's World (ALW) in Vimmerby in southern Sweden is the country's foremost attraction outside the metropolitan areas, with about half a million visitors every year. Vimmerby is the small town and municipality where Astrid Lindgren, the world-famous author of children's books, was born. Different enactments of entrepreneurship, like commercial, cultural and community entrepreneurship, have over the years jointly produced the societal entrepreneurship that the continuously emerging ALW represents. Our ambition is to demonstrate that this emergence of ALW is anchored in all three sectors. Our story has two main messages, the first being that the institutionalization of sustainable societal entrepreneurship is a long-term process where actors associated with the different sectors in society take turns at energizing the process. Our second point is that societal entrepreneurship as an organizing process in the case of ALW is an outcome of double social embedding: on one hand in the norms and values carried by Astrid Lindgren personally and communicated through her children's books, on the other the norms and everyday practices of the small town. In this process tensions, sometimes destructive, sometimes constructive, between the theme park and the traditional, petty bourgeois Vimmerby have played a main part.

As the vignette communicates, Astrid Lindgren's books carry messages that we can easily associate with entrepreneurship – risk-taking, responsibility and courage. Her first and still most famous character, Pippi Longstocking, entered the Swedish scene as early as 1945. It addressed children aged eight to twelve (Pippi herself was nine), that is the lateral age where human beings reveal themselves as naturally born entrepreneurs (Johannisson 2010). As elaborated on by Berglund in Chapter 8, children spontaneously adopt an entrepreneurial attitude.

The message of Astrid Lindgren is penetrating and well known and she early established herself as an icon and institution not just in Sweden but globally. In the next section we therefore provide a fairly detailed portrait of the author as an appropriate background to the formation of the theme park, which in turn mirrors the childhood world of the author as dramatized in her literary work. After a brief comment on the methodology used in this inquiry we discuss how cultural and symbolic capital, organizing and institutionalization have been instrumental in the making of ALW into an event that we address as societal entrepreneurship. Then we turn to quite a detailed report on how representatives of the market, the public sector as well as of the NPVO sector over the park's 30 years of existence have alternately led and energized the process, sometimes collaborating, sometimes counteracting each other. After reflecting upon this cross-sectorial societal venturing we comment in the last section on the viability of ALW as societal entrepreneurship if compared with a similar but also different Swedish experience in the field.

ASTRID LINDGREN – A SWEDISH ICON, CANONIZED WORLD WIDE[1]

One of the classic works in entrepreneurship research is David McClelland's *The Achieving Society* (1961/67). The author looked into what values, such as the need for achievement, were reflected in children's readers and related those values to indicators of (national) economic growth. The basic message of that research was that if parents raise their children properly the society they belong to will benefit materially. As elaborated upon in Chapter 7 we argue instead that it is our obligation as grownups to listen to and learn from children rather than (only) socializing them into our norms of behaviour (see also Johannisson 2010). Children's approach to life, with play as a major part, is the safest road to progress, economic as well as social. A remarkable spokesperson for children as role models in the making of a socially better world is Astrid Lindgren (1907–2002). As indicated, *Pippi Longstocking* was published in the very years (1950 in the USA) when McClelland conducted his research.

Astrid Lindgren very clearly and consistently put the children in the centre throughout her publishing career. 'Always on the child's side' is the telling title of a contribution to Astrid Lindgren's work (Lundqvist 2007). Her children's books and characters are well known all over the world and have been translated into 90 languages and printed in approximately 145 million copies. The books have inspired productions in many other media and fields such as cartoons, plays, musicals, films and television productions (see also Kümmerling-Meibauer and Surmatz 2011). Edström (1993, p. 2) concludes that Lindgren is an author on a genuinely universal scale.

Astrid Lindgren was born in Vimmerby, where her parents leased a farm that was owned by the Swedish church.[2] The farm was then located on the outskirts of Vimmerby, but today the town has incorporated the farmland. Astrid Lindgren and her two sisters and a brother were very close. Both in her books and in interviews Astrid Lindgren describes her childhood as very happy. 'I think that what made it so happy was that we were given freedom as well as security and care by loving parents', she states (Strömstedt 1999, p. X). The children played all the time; 'we played and played and played. It's a wonder we didn't play ourselves to death', she comments. Literary scholars also emphasize that dimension. 'PLAY', writes Edström (1993, pp. 14–15) in capital letters, 'is the strongest affirmation of life in Astrid Lindgren's world. It is the breath of life itself . . . Play is identical with creative consciousness. What else is there? Only the songs of emptiness and of the birds of sorrow.' Astrid Lindgren wanted all children to experience freedom, security and love and they remained the most important people to her throughout her authorship and private life. 'I want to write for readers who can create miracles and that is what children do when they read. Grownups do not have that gift' (Strömstedt 1999, p. 200). She herself created magic with her words: 'when we listen to Astrid Lindgren we feel how the child inside us wakes up. That is what we have been waiting for – we half dead grown-ups: to come to life again, to feel how the powerful and creating child is reborn and moves, starting to put the questions we in our adulthood have not had the courage to answer for a long time', Strömstedt (1999, p. 317) states in her very affectionate book on Lindgren.

Edström (1993, p. 12) illustrates Lindgren's position through a conversation between the author and a journalist on the Swedish radio. 'Isn't *Mio, my Son* actually a pretty nasty book', the journalist asks and Lindgren answers: 'Of course. That's why children love it!' Loving parents is what she wanted, but she was well aware that children are punished and badly treated, and in her books they are also victims of the power of grownups. Back in 1979 she was one of those who convinced the Swedish parliament to enact a law that forbade the physical punishment of children. Then she very explicitly appeared as an institutional entrepreneur with a strong social and human concern.

Animals and nature were also close to Astrid Lindgren's heart. Their situation in the world, not just in Sweden, made her sad. As she was a well-established author she used her talent and influence to protest. In the spring of 1985 she spoke out publicly about the abuse of domesticated animals. She published a tale about a lovesick cow, protesting against the mistreatment of farm animals, in the form of an open letter in a major national newspaper. With it she started a campaign that lasted for three years. In June 1988 a Swedish Animal Protection Act referred to as 'Lex Lindgren' was introduced (Metcalf 2002, p. 24). The act was given to Astrid Lindgren by the Swedish Prime Minister on the author's 80th birthday.

Beating children and animals is left to villains in Lindgren's writing. Her deeply held belief in non-violence extends to children and animals; indeed, it begins there. 'Never Violence' was the title of Lindgren's speech when receiving the German Booksellers' Peace Prize in 1978 (Metcalf 2002, p. 27). She had then already written about the black race issue in the US after a visit there. In 1976 she published a narrative about 'Pomperipossa in Munismanien' on the extreme Swedish taxation policy entering into polemic with the Swedish Minister of Finance. It is said that her narrative made the Social Democrats lose the general elections that year – after 40 years in power! She also took an active part in the campaigns before the referendum on nuclear power. Astrid Lindgren was an 'unbeatable multiplier', a Swedish website on her concludes. That statement is supported by the top list of the most popular persons in Sweden. Every year she was the most admired woman, even the most admired person, in Sweden, both among women and men. The Queen came second in 2001 and the late Minister of Foreign Affairs (Anna Lindh) took the third place. Astrid Lindgren's death in 2002 was a national concern. Her coffin was carried in a cortege through Stockholm. Police and soldiers on horseback flanked the cortege. Just behind the hearse a white horse without a saddle was led by a girl. The Prime Minister, the Minister of Culture, the Speaker of the Parliament, members of parliament and the royal family, the King, the

Queen and the Crown Princess took part in the funeral. The procedure was broadcast live on national television. Songs written by Astrid Lindgren (now part of the Swedish culture heritage) were sung. The Prime Minister (Göran Persson) in his speech specially mentioned Astrid Lindgren's relation to children. 'She gave us hope and comfort', he said. After the funeral the coffin was transported through southern Sweden to Vimmerby, where she now lies side by side with her parents.

Astrid Lindgren's writings and position in Swedish society reveal that she was very demanding. As the prologue signals, she expected every human being to assume personal responsibility. In many respects Astrid Lindgren was very radical and ahead of her time. Pippi Longstocking obviously forestalled the gender debate that materialized a quarter of a century later. The book about her was so provocative that it was turned down by the first publisher the author approached, and the one who finally published it forced her to make a number of changes in the original manuscript.

Although Astrid Lindgren lived in Stockholm from 1926 onwards she stayed close to provincial Vimmerby, which seems to have crafted her personal and social identity for ever. Many of her most famous books are also set in rural Sweden and thus dramatize traditional Swedish culture, its values, norms and everyday practices. These were seriously threatened by urbanization forces as early as 1945 when she made her debut as an author. Many people wanted to capitalize on her position in society, but her moral positioning constituted not just an enormous source of symbolic capital but also a restriction vis-à-vis the commercial exploitation of her writings. Nevertheless, she contributed to the making of a new industry. The most extrovert and spectacular exponent of her contribution to the rural Swedish creative industry/experience economy was her support of Astrid Lindgren's World (ALW), a theme park on the outskirts of Vimmerby, the story of which we focus on below. But first a few words about our methodology.

SOURCES OF INQUIRY AND THEIR USE

The empirical basis of this chapter mainly consists of different kinds of secondary material. Part of it was compiled when in 2007 we were asked to contribute to projecting an anthology on the different worlds that Astrid Lindgren constructed in Vimmerby (Johannisson and Sundin 2010). The anthology aimed at illustrating the interplay between cultural heritage and local development; see Jonsson 2010. We then adopted a general entrepreneurial perspective to make intelligible the activities and importance of Astrid Lindgren in the making of ALW. Considering the need for 'dwelling' in the context of the phenomenon being researched (see Chia and MacKay 2007), we took part in several meetings arranged in Vimmerby both with politicians and civil servants and with local activists and decision-makers. We have also drawn upon material produced by the municipality as well as material published in the local newspaper and the anthology that we just mentioned. In order to especially highlight entrepreneurial dimensions we made two supplementary interviews – the first with one of the founders of ALW and the second with a leading local politician who has been deeply involved for decades in different (other) roles in local business and the social life that embeds ALW. We also went on reading the local newspaper and kept in touch with local informants while writing this report.

Both the interviews and the other types of material show that there are many stories to be told about the enactment of ALW (not about Astrid Lindgren herself, though – she has remained above any criticism) and about all the different actors involved. The families building the first houses are thus reported both as local heroes and as naïve and bitter losers of ownership control and the municipality is described both as a responsible (even the only responsible) actor and as a hopelessly passive agent, always contributing too late and now, at last, fooled by the children and grandchildren of Astrid Lindgren. The author's family is sometimes portrayed as exploiters of the legacy of a beloved grandmother and sometimes as savers and true carriers of a valuable heritage. Compare the discussion in Chapter 7 on the polarized images of entrepreneurship as either dark or bright. As our story unfolds we try to avoid these extreme standpoints when we present ALW as an entrepreneurial venture. Instead we leave to the next section of this book to contrast the bright and dark sides of entrepreneurship.

Finally, we want to state that, for good or bad, like almost all Swedish persons born in the 1940s, we listened to and read the stories of Astrid Lindgren as children. Later together with our own children we saw the movies based on her books and with our grandchildren we have visited ALW. As native Swedes we have thus become acculturated into the worlds of Astrid Lindgren. We therefore had a contextual understanding of 'what it was all about' already when we accepted the invitation to contribute to the Swedish anthology on Astrid Lindgren (Jonsson 2010). This, as well as our presentation here, has provided an opportunity to refine, focus and make explicit our embodied understanding of what ALW wants to communicate. That experience and further reflections on ALW as an example of enacted societal entrepreneurship we want to share with the readers of this anthology.

THE MAKING OF ALW – CROSS-SECTIONAL VENTURING OVER THREE DECADES[3]

With Astrid Lindgren's status as an icon and institution and with herself and her work canonized, it follows that ALW is richly funded with cultural and symbolic capital, a crucial ingredient in any entrepreneurial venture (De Clercq and Voronov 2009). The values and behavioural norms that she herself once carried and her work epitomizes today (finally) appear as the core of the branding of the small town of Vimmerby (Syssner 2010) as well as for the company Saltkråkan Ltd, through which Astrid Lindgren's heirs now own ALW. On the company's homepage they state: 'The main purpose of the company is to manage the author's works in the same spirit that she herself would have done'. This means that Astrid Lindgren's norms and values provide 'the rules of the game' (see North 1990), which regulate what and how entrepreneurship can be practised in and through ALW. In that respect ALW has itself become an institution; compare for example Selznick 1953 and Czarniawska 2009.

Institution and ideology are closely related concepts, the former of which frame and justify action, while the latter energizes action (see Brunsson 1985; Johannisson 2002; Segnestam Larsson 2011). Ideology provides a foundation for organizing that is both strong and fragile; see for example Kanter (1972). Here we want to narrate how Astrid Lindgren's position in Sweden in general and in Vimmerby in particular has influenced how the interaction between different sectoral interests has produced ALW as a unique and sustainable entrepreneurial venture. Astrid Lindgren's commitment to ALW produced an image of authenticity that has remained essential to ALW – if that image should disappear, ALW would become just another theme park (Persson 2009). Therefore it is important to tell the ALW story in great detail, the way it evolved, as we see it, in quite distinct phases. Since, as indicated, Astrid Lindgren's presence cannot be overestimated, we will begin every subsection with a statement made by or about the author herself.

In Chapter 1 we state that context is important when studying societal entrepreneurship, and elsewhere we have elaborated on this issue; see for example Johannisson 2011, Sundin 2010 and 2011. Here we want to elaborate on the impact of contextualization by adding to the sector-logic framework presented in Chapter 1 and expanding the accountability discourse as applied to the NPVO sector into the broader field of societal entrepreneurship. Accountabilities may be either instrumental or expressive (Knutsen and Brower 2010; see also Segnestam Larsson 2011). Instrumental accountability is based on reciprocity, such as the responsibility to provide a pay-back to resource providers. Expressive accountability is absolute in the sense that some basic values have to be strictly adhered to. While operations in the NPVO have to balance the two accountabilities, instrumental accountability dominates the private and public sectors. Representatives of the three sectors which construct societal entrepreneurship can employ various tools to hold each other accountable. Knutsen and Browser (2010) underline that it is impossible to handle all accountabilities at the same time. Thus they have to be sequentially attended to. This 'managing' of the accountability portfolio especially concerns its instrumental contents, since expressive accountabilities are less negotiable. As regards the enactment of ALW we argue that the moral demands of Astrid Lindgren herself appear as an absolute and dominant restriction. The author, once in person, now her spirit, provides – and conditions! – the unique characteristics of the organization and legitimizes the entrepreneurship in her name; compare De Clercq and Voronov (2009). Yet, ALW's entrepreneurial characteristics can be modified through dialogue and interpreted in different ways even though the tight coupling to societal entrepreneurship remains.

Here we thus argue that the managing of different instrumental accountabilities and the dealing with expressive accountabilities can be considered as one out of two generic features of societal entrepreneurship as associated with place. The second generic feature is the broader local organizing of social life. This is associated here with a range of activities and organizations, from everyday life, which is usually dealt with in cultural studies, via for example the features of the local business community, to the way in which the municipality as a political and administrative body carries out its functions. Keeping these brief conceptual reflections in mind we now want to tell a story about the emergence of ALW.

Phase One: Three Entrepreneurial Families Guided by a Social Vision (1979–1989)

> Dear Rein Soowik! How nice that you will make your dream about a Bullerby come true. It is nice because I really trust you when you tell me that this is not going to be a commercial gimmick to draw money from the innocent small ones. They must be able to walk around for free and have a look at the small, nice village.

Astrid Lindgren in a letter to one of the founders of ALW (published by Althén 2010).

In this pioneering phase of the development of the theme park three actors were important:

- the three families, one of which including Rein Soowik who received the letter that we quote above
- the Vimmerby municipality, and
- Astrid Lindgren herself.

The roots of the Astrid Lindgren theme park go back to the time when three families built small houses retelling Astrid Lindgren's stories for their own children to play in and around. The small houses were built close to the families' own grounds in the vicinity of where Astrid Lindgren herself had played as a child. As Astrid Lindgren owned the right to all her characters, the families needed her allowance and support. Formalities were not a big issue, since the author's moral support was built on personal relations and trust. The three families met her every summer both for doing her different services and for socializing.

Every year the families added a new miniature milieu originating in Astrid Lindgren's stories. Other children living in the neighbourhood joined in and soon enough the families were running an operation that was very much like a business with an expanding demand for facilities like toilets and parking places as well as for coffee and ice cream. Accordingly, the families in due course registered a commercial company and borrowed 30,000 Swedish crowns (about 3000 euro) to make the necessary investments. They used their social network, including the close personal relation to Astrid Lindgren, for bootstrapping, for example for getting white goods from the local stores at a discount and the many other things they needed at favourable prices. They also urged the municipality to make investments required for the infrastructure such as roads and parking lots for visitors. The municipality subsequently did so – but too late and in a too restricted manner, according to the families.

During this period the families were anxious to follow the instructions given explicitly or implicitly by Astrid Lindgren. Her need for tight control went beyond the forerunner of ALW. She was equally strict as regards for example the illustrations of her books. In ALW she wanted her name to be associated only with activities which would benefit *all* children. For example, no one should be excluded because she or he could not afford visiting 'The Village of Fairy Tales', as the theme park was originally named. Whatever was offered there should be free of charge for the children.

The three families – all their members being involved as in any family business – running 'The Village of Fairy Tales' were entrepreneurial in more than one respect. They had an idea which they persistently enacted. They invested some of their own financial capital but used their social capital, their local connections, to identify donors and persuade them to contribute. They were close enough to Astrid Lindgren to stay under her umbrella and use her unique cultural and symbolic capital. This informal resourcing was very important, because at this stage the municipality provided very limited (financial) support and in other respects adopted a wait-and-see policy towards the emerging venture.

In spite of their good flair for business the three families mainly had social ambitions. Their intentions was too make something nice for the children – at the beginning for their own children, then also for children living in the neighbourhood, and later still for the many children visiting Vimmerby from Sweden and from even further away, especially from Germany and the Netherlands. They felt expressively accountable, mainly to Astrid Lindgren but also to each other and their own children as well as to children in general.

The success of the initiative created a demand for systematic management, even incorporation of the operations. The first registered company that was established by the three founding families appeared as a social enterprise with the main purpose of securing the development of the milieu as a playing ground for children. To handle the successful start-up financially the initiating families needed external support. First they had the municipality in mind but for a number of reasons this remained pending at the time. One reason was that the theme park drew visitors' attention from the city centre. Being a traditional rural centre, municipal norms in Vimmerby were dominated by the manufacturing industry and commercial trade. There was no absorptive capacity for the emerging experience industry. The municipality therefore did not want to get involved in the social activities that ALW offered, especially not since its owners expected financial support. A convenient excuse was that Swedish municipalities were, and are, not allowed to support individual enterprises – the activities they get financially involved in must be appropriate for the whole or a substantial faction of the business community.

Phase Two: The Market Invades the Village, Turning it into a Theme Park (1989–1992)

> How she was convinced? I really do not know. Maybe by songs from the churches she visited when she was a child. But it was a hard decision. It felt risky. But mother was such a nice person. She wanted to make people happy. So she agreed – but she was anxious to keep it non-commercial so she established a Programme Board to secure the quality of the park in the future.

Astrid Lindgren's daughter when interviewed by journalist Kajsa Althén (Althén 2010).

The initiative by the 'Fairy-Tales brothers' in Vimmerby was soon enough communicated all over Sweden and also to the many other countries whose children and parents were well acquainted with Astrid Lindgren's authorship. In 1988 the target of 100,000 visitors was reached. The huge number of children and accompanying families who went to Vimmerby obviously called for further investments in public facilities far beyond what the three founding families could finance. By then commercial interests had, however, realized the great potential of ALW, and a conglomerate led by a (then) successful regional entrepreneur entered the scene and became the majority owner. To the founders exit seemed to be the only way to make it possible to develop the theme park, make use of its commercial potential and get pay-back for themselves. The entrepreneurial families, however, all kept a very small share, as they were still emotionally attached to ALW and Astrid Lindgren herself. It was more difficult to convince Astrid Lindgren that the new owners were trustworthy. However, as the quote above indicates, her consent was necessary, according to all stakeholders. Without that the founding entrepreneurs did not want to sell and nor did the municipality want to be involved as an owner.

With the new financially strong owners the 'village' was turned into a professionally run theme park. More and more small houses and appropriate surroundings materialized Astrid Lindgren's storied milieux were built, enforcing the core of a theme park. Further huge investment plans were presented both to Astrid Lindgren herself and to the municipality. Again we want to point out that Astrid Lindgren was paid respect to as the dominant holder of the symbolic capital that made ALW unique; neither she nor her family had at the time any financial ownership in the theme park. The municipality supported the new owners in a pliable way – mainly with infrastructural investments at their request.

The leading actors during this period were private-sector representatives, that is, the new owners, whose main business was the production of pre-fabricated detached houses. The municipality through its politicians and civil servants was quite involved as well, but then as facilitators and intermediaries only (compare Chapter 5). As a commercial company the corporation was instrumentally accountable only to its shareholders, but as regards its ownership in ALW it was also expressively accountable to Astrid Lindgren personally. Every change in the park that was proposed had to be accepted by her. This called for time-consuming face-to-face negotiations and hands-on quality control. Items in the park's store that were too commercially oriented in her view were literally taken away by the author herself. Astrid Lindgren did not want to sign a formal contract but preferred to build trust in the old-fashioned way and confirm an agreement with a handshake. She eagerly maintained her opinion that

ALW should be run with social intentions, which created problems for a company working in a market.

The municipality, too, considered Astrid Lindgren's opinions to be the adequate subject of accountability. The leading politicians and civil servants mediated and supported changes and demands, not the least in order to avoid a situation that would confront Astrid Lindgren's own interest. Before the take-over by the corporation, leading local politicians had asked for her opinion, and encouraged by them and together with some of the local people who she really trusted she met the new owners and 'blessed' them. The new commercial owners were, however, not as submissive as the author wanted. Nevertheless, the main discussions between the leading actors at this point concerned strategic issues including what should be offered to the children and their parents and how the park should develop and be managed.

Even if the creative industries represented an expanding market, the competition for public attention was becoming sharper in Sweden. The large corporation was hard to handle for the five women constituting the Programme Board. Astrid Lindgren's law stated: no advertisements, no plastic toys and no junk food in 'her' theme park. Maybe the tensions between the Programme Board and the management of the park would in the long run have torn the unholy alliance between strong social concerns and eager profit-seeking apart. But before that potential crisis occurred an (inter)national financial crisis changed the situation for the main owner.

Phase Three: Representatives of the Private and the NPVO Sectors Enter as Rescuers of the Park (1992–1994)

> I do not want my name to be associated with bankruptcy!

A statement by Astrid Lindgren published in the local paper *Vimmerby Tidning* (in Althén 2010: 84) repeated in the interviews made by the authors of this article.

The recession at the beginning of the 1990s played into Astrid Lindgren's hands and helped her to preserve the social profile of the theme park. The private-sector majority owners had to exit. This was not because of any financial problems in the operations of ALW itself but because the main business units in the conglomerate ran into problems. In 1992 the theme park was thus hit by an acute financial crisis. Astrid Lindgren herself was very upset and demanded that the municipality should do something to prevent such a scandal: 'Now it is time for you to act. Do not just use me!' If the municipality did not take what she considered as its responsibility, she threatened to leave Vimmerby and ALW for ever and take all the rights associated with her work with her.

A leading local politician, who was personally close to Astrid Lindgren, was chosen to assure the stubborn author that whoever the new owners would be they would have to run the park according to her rules. The politician came to the conclusion that the municipality itself had to be one of the owners. Then two more new owners entered the scene. One was a national insurance company that had guaranteed the loans taken by the failing corporation. Obviously it wanted to save the money it had invested. The third new owner was a voluntary organization, a branch of the Swedish temperance movement and thus a member of the Swedish NPVO sector. The latter organization was persuaded to get involved because one of Astrid Lindgren's main characters Emil (*Emil in Lonneberga*) as a young boy joined the movement. The new owners were all triggered by the ambition to prevent the economic, social, cultural and symbolic values embodied in the theme park from eroding and they also wanted to contribute to its further development.

The insurance company was instrumentally accountable to its shareholders and the temperance movement expressively to its members. The municipality as a democratic and economic organization had incentives and responsibilities of both kinds. In addition, the demands from Astrid Lindgren were recognized as a strong obligation as she explicitly addressed the municipality as the one organization in charge of what could now be considered a major part of her legacy. After all, one of the local politicians had persuaded Astrid Lindgren to accept the regional company as an owner. All three new owners also had close personal relations to Astrid Lindgren, which enforced their strong financial and social commitment.

Phase Four: The Public Sector takes on Further Responsibilities 1994–2010

'If you do I will haunt you at night – and who wants an old hag at the bed?'
'Don't! – you know what I feel about animals in cages?'

Arguments presented by Astrid Lindgren when presented with potential owners of ALW told by persons handling the negotiations. These statements are well-known and published in Althén 2010: 88.

The voluntary organization and the insurance company never had any intention to stay on as majority owners. When the acute financial crisis had been dealt with and their economic investments had been saved they wanted to exit. Thus new owners were needed. Several other actors were also interested in acquiring the theme park, but Astrid Lindgren loudly opposed some of them. A leading corporation in the national theme-park sector with an outspoken commercial orientation was banned by her, according to the first quote above. Another proposal, delivered by a constellation of theme parks including a zoological park, was refused as well. Astrid Lindgren, as the second quote above states, was opposed to keeping animals of any kind in cages. As the local business community remained uninterested in getting involved in ALW, the municipality in 1999 decided to use its pre-emptive option and acquired the majority of the shares – with the founding families staying as minority owners. Reconstructed and with a professional management ALW then became a profitable operation and the municipality's decision to take over was not locally opposed. However, a successful local entrepreneur, later to become mayor, who was associated with the highly influential local newspaper, launched the idea of turning ALW into a 'community enterprise' by inviting local people to share ownership. This idea was occasionally on the local agenda but was never realized.

Astrid Lindgren and the values she represented developed into an accountability norm for the municipality. While the leaving owners' major objective was return on investment, the municipality now rather looked upon the theme park as a social community enterprise. The municipality had finally learnt to fully appreciate the cultural and symbolic capital carried by Astrid Lindgren as a person and as an icon. The leading actors in the municipality realized that the time for both enthusiastic amateurs and market-oriented capitalists was gone. ALW needed professional management that was able to unconditionally accept and build further on the unique values associated with the theme park. Only then would it be possible to keep it sustainable, both financially and as a manifestation of the legacy of Astrid Lindgren.

Astrid Lindgren died in 2002. Her daughter and grandchildren's inheritance included the rights to her characters, and the intellectual capital that they represented was collected in a joint stock company, Saltkråkan Ltd. Since trust in social relations is difficult to transfer, the family found the informal relations that Astrid Lindgren had used to control the operations at ALW inadequate. Besides, times had changed since Astrid Lindgren was a child and when a word and a handshake was all that was needed to make both life and businesses work. With a (grand)mother who left Vimmerby at the age of 19 Astrid Lindgren's descendants were not personally connected to Vimmerby, neither to the place and nor to its people.

Phase Five: 2010 – Control and Ownership Finally Integrated

Our goal is to preserve the intentions expressed in Astrid Lindgren's books.

Source: www.Saltkrakan.se

Now, in 2012, Astrid Lindgren's family, her daughter and grandchildren, are the owners of ALW through Saltkråkan Ltd. The municipality keeps a minority of 16 per cent. This solution was reached after a verbal fight between many of the actors we have presented above – mainly the original social entrepreneurs building the first houses, the municipality, different commercial interests, the inhabitants of Vimmerby and Astrid Lindgren's family.

Who is the proper interpreter of the visions of Astrid Lindgren? The answer to that question is crucial. The family and their incorporated interests see themselves as the 'natural' owners and the only legitimate guardians of Astrid Lindgren's legacy. Their case also has a material twist since they own the right to use the characters that populate her books. There was an obvious risk that they would claim their legal rights to royalty or even abandon their involvement in ALW and Vimmerby altogether. Realizing this threat and being caught by having used some of the surplus of the theme park operations to strengthen the municipal budget rather than reinvesting it in the park, the municipality decided to transfer their ownership to the Lindgren family. Even the three pioneering families were then forced to sell their remaining shares, a decision they consider to be outrageous. According to the local newspaper this forced exit has also been heavily criticized by 'everyone'.

Thus, at the end of this (final?) act in the ALW drama the entrepreneurial families, crafting the original idea and building the first houses, have no influence left. They have certainly been financially compensated, both when they sold their majority ownership to the regional entrepreneur and by being employed at the park for several years. They are, however, dissatisfied because their original entrepreneurial initiative, which was driven by social and cultural concern rather than pure greed, has in their view never been fully recognized. For example, they were never acknowledged and awarded for their contribution to Vimmerby's cultural life. The municipality has lost its ownership control but is convinced that with the Lindgren family as the owner of ALW the park, and the community, will develop further. The legacy of Astrid Lindgren will be preserved in Vimmerby, even though all family members live in Stockholm. Considering that Astrid Lindgren's son-in-law now (2012) is the CEO of Saltkråkan Ltd, the theme park is nowadays (again) run as a family business.

INSTITUTIONALIZING SOCIETAL ENTREPRENEURSHIP

In the traditions of TWA [Total Work of Art], ALW strives to transform the illusion, the literary fiction, into reality of a kind in which the visitors become active actors that complete the artificial world and transform the humanistic ideas into reality. Thus, ALW equals the conception of the unity, integrity, or wholeness of the work of art.

Source: Führer 2011, p. 254.

The making of the park into a remarkable living tribute to a great author and her imagination is the outcome of multiple agencies where representatives of the three sectors have taken turns as leaders of the process. The development of the Astrid Lindgren theme park has obviously been a very complex and dramatic venture that has over three decades repeatedly crossed the boundaries between the private, public and NPVO sectors. Different enactments of entrepreneurship have entered the stage, sometimes fighting, sometimes enforcing each other, but always submitting to the insurmountable wall of expressive accountability that Astrid Lindgren and her core values represent.

In our report the Vimmerby municipality has appeared as both a (potential) resource provider and as beneficiary of Astrid Lindgren's and ALW's concerns. For many years there was almost an antagonistic relationship between the park and its financial and symbolic ownership on one hand, and a reluctant Vimmerby municipality on the other. Finally, both its politicians and its inhabitants have realized the potential of the park as an important contributor to the emerging Swedish creative industries. Today it has managed to match this commercial and cultural potential with the municipality's own capabilities and agenda. The municipality has even managed to institutionalize the generic message of Astrid Lindgren in her stories – responsibility, courage and imagination – by presenting them as the basic values on which its general development plan rests. The municipality pays this tribute to its most recognized citizen even though it has lost the formal influence over the theme park that its ownership once provided. The municipality has demonstrated its responsibility towards its citizens and guaranteed the sustainability of the theme park. This leadership has meant bridging between different entrepreneurial initiatives and ownerships, as they turned out to be incapable of running ALV in a way that made it able to pass the Charybdis of 'raw' capitalism and the Scylla of strong-willed Astrid Lindgren.

In contrast to all the other owners and stakeholders passing by, the municipality has been and will remain stuck to, and even be regarded as synonymous with the locality of Vimmerby. This may in a purely economic perspective be considered as a drawback but appears, when it comes to the societal dimension of entrepreneurship, as a strength. Even if the local attachment means limited access to financial capital it mobilizes the emotional capital, including pride, which a shared history and everyday life may produce (see also Berglund in Chapter 7). The relations between Astrid Lindgren and the municipality are emphasized in the branding of Vimmerby as a protection against other organizers of activities and establishments referring to Astrid Lindgren or her characters (Syssner 2010). Today ALW contributes to the making of an integrating collective self-identity, based on the insight that the Vimmerby community makes a difference, a local insight that harmonizes with the image of the municipality that outsiders have.

In order to make intelligible the eventing of Astrid Lindgren's life and work into what emerged into the ALW of today you have to realize that the status of the author was and still is after her death that of an institution. As elaborated upon in the introductory chapter, institutions direct, that is, facilitate and restrict, the making of entrepreneurial events. Different bonds – the concern for children and their worldview, the reconstructed and materialized stories, the taming of commercial forces – actually turned the author and her writings into a structure that framed all initiatives, whether mainly voluntary, as those of the founding families and the temperance movement, commercial as the private conglomerate, or public as those initiatives taken by the municipality.

Considering her ardent concern for children and their playful approach to life as well as her alert defence of humanistic values, Astrid Lindgren the writer can be considered to be a social entrepreneur. However, she also appeared as an unintentional institutional entrepreneur. With her huge cultural and symbolic capital she controlled by a comfortable margin the resources needed to enact her own institution (see DiMaggio 1988). All those taking advantage of her in the making of ALW can be considered to enforce her iconic status by playing around in and with her reconstructed fairy tales milieux. The children who visit ALW further enforce the institutionalization and thus the sustainability of the theme park by coming and experiencing, by participating in the events and by telling stories about the visit to ALW once back home. This is what Führer (2011 – see the vignette) also relates to, albeit from a quite different perspective, that of a seeing ALW as a 'total work of art'. In the language of that approach Führer states that 'ALW creates a utopian world of simplicity and innocence to evoke the feeling of being in childhood's "lost paradise" in harmony with nature and with the proper balance between freedom and security.' (Führer 2011, p. 246). Elsewhere (Johannisson 2010) we also see the world of children as a world of entrepreneuring, a view that is further elaborated on in Chapter 8 by Berglund. Besides, however intriguing Führer's reasoning may be, it neglects the paradox that ALW as a paradise for children is the outcome of the intense battles between ideas and sectoral logics that we have narrated here.

The tensions and conflicts that on one hand threatened the survival of ALW and on the other hand kept it vital and crafted its sustainability appeared on the individual as well as on the organizational and the community levels. The vocabulary that is outlined in the introductory chapter can be used to analyse ALW's different stakeholders, why and how they professed themselves to the private, public or NPVO sectors and their specific logics, see Table 1.1. Multiple memberships in different constituencies only made it natural for individuals and organizations to move between different sectors and their different social and mental spaces. However, they all, individuals and organizations, had to submit to the same standard: the moral sentiments that Astrid Lindgren mainly expressed in her books but also practised in her explicit involvement in the making of ALW. She also made 'strategic' statements when radical changes were about to happen. As illustrated above in the vignette to phase four, she for example vetoed the proposed acquisition of ALW by a zoological garden. When the theme park was on the edge of bankruptcy she threatened to withdraw all the property rights that ALW had for free if the threatening financial catastrophe should materialize. Only then did the municipality finally engage financially in ALW – the local business community, however, remained indifferent.

In perspective of our concern for societal entrepreneurship it is interesting that ALW in the early 1990s, due to the national financial crisis in Sweden and its implications for the corporate owner of ALW, was reconstructed as a (formal) partnership between the private sector – represented by the insurance company and the three founding families who kept a minority share of the equity, the public sector (Vimmerby municipality) and the NPVO (an organization associated with the temperance movement which was attracted by the core values communicated by ALW). This reformed ownership was paralleled by a formalization of both the influence of Astrid Lindgren's control and the management of the theme park. ALW's new board and executive management included financial and (tourism) industry expertise. This partnering and formalization guaranteed that the norms and values of Astrid Lindgren were respected. With the theme park becoming increasingly profitable further dramatic events could be avoided. This also meant that the municipality in 1999 acquired the shares controlled by the other major partners. By then the professional management of the theme park had realized that only careful attention to Astrid Lindgren's legacy could guarantee ALWs sustainability. In this perspective Astrid Lindgren's surviving relatives in 2010 had a strong case for taking over.

CONCLUSIONS: ALW AND THE MAKING OF AN ENLIGHTENED COMMUNITY

As stated in Chapter 1, institutional forces were originally associated with the internal environment of an organization. In the 1970s and 1980s the focus in research was instead on institutions as an inter-organizational phenomenon, a 'field' (see for example Powell and DiMaggio 1991 and Chapter 6 by Birgitta Schwartz). That view does not leave much space for entrepreneurs – neither intellectually nor in practice – since it states that there is a pressure towards conformity in order to gain legitimacy. The 'old' institutionalism, however, pointed out the uniqueness of organizing and institutionalization processes, including infusing means with a value beyond what is needed to complete different tasks. We here propose a return to this 'old' institutionalism in order make intelligible how ALW emerged into what it represents today, thanks to the legacy of Astrid Lindgren.

In their systematic comparison of the old and new institutionalism Powell and DiMaggio (1991: 13, Table 1:1), for example, argue that the old institutionalism was characterized by underlining the ongoing conflict between different stakeholders representing different interests. These tensions were in the ALW case energized by and channelled through the local newspaper both as part of its editorial policy and due to the intense debates that it invited the public to. This debate was energized by the fact that ALW as a representative of the new emergent experience economy challenged Vimmerby and its traditions in the manufacturing industry and commerce. In addition, while Vimmerby ambitiously presented itself as a town, many of the stories that appeared as local milieux in ALW idealized rural life. Some, however, realized the potentials of materializing Astrid Lindgren's story-telling, besides the pioneering entrepreneurs who originally were also all independent businesspersons, as well as some further members of the business community. Our point is that the combination of Astrid Lindgren's own and non-negotiable social concerns and the small-town location with its traditional values and norms triggered institutionalization processes that made it possible to understand the enactment of ALW as a viable project because of, and not in spite of, tensions between different local outlooks (compare Berglund and Johansson 2007). Viable small town/business communities turn out to preserve Gemeinschaft values, yet see conflicts and tensions between different factions as creative.

See reports from the Swedish context by, for example, Wigren (2003) and Johannisson (2000a). At least it is better than the individualism and indifference that Gesellschaft-orientated (rural) settings provide.

A major organizing vehicle, according to the old institutionalism, is personal networking. In Vimmerby and ALW two forces contributed to making informal relations important. First, the only way to get access to the author's stories was to create a personal and trustful relationship to her. No formal relations would do. As the vignette to the second phase in the development of ALW hints at, even the established business entrepreneur who bought the pioneering entrepreneurs out had to mobilize all his charm to convince Astrid Lindgren that he was the right person to turn the then minor operations into a new great 'world' for children. It is thought that the negotiations ended with him and the author jointly singing traditional Swedish gospels (the entrepreneur having a background in the Baptist church). A second reason for intense personal networking as the way of making things work was the context of a local town where social networks are dense and where physical proximity makes people meet casually in different settings only to nurture multiple loyalties. That in turn created the feeling of being unique and different with neither the need nor the possibility to compare with other similar towns. This produced a kind of conceit that both facilitated and opposed the appropriation of ALW by the different local stakeholders. The small town is a setting that invites local political processes that are easily mobilized. But they have to fit into the local interpretations of what is valuable and good and, not the least, what is local. Locality is highly valued, and what is foreign, often expressed as related to 'Stockholmare' (that is, people from Stockholm), is looked upon with suspicion. In Vimmerby the local newspaper with its different initiatives in creating a local opinion on different issues in addition to reporting everyday local life operated as an interpreter and amplifier of what was considered to be local and proper.

Personal networking means intertwining different roles and interests, social and professional (Johannisson 2000). It then goes without saying that intertwining between different sectors happens on the individual level; see Malin Tillmar's comparative study in Chapter 2. The two persons who were interviewed by us epitomize such intertwining. One of the pioneering entrepreneurs combined already in the formative years of ALW (then known as the The Village of Fairy Tales) his voluntary work with running a (naprapathy) business (including Astrid Lindgren herself as one of the clients) and used his commercial experience to find ways to finance ALW when it grew to become something more than just amusement for the founding families' own children. He was also involved in local politics where in different ways he tried to make the municipality realize the potential of The Village of Fairy Tales. He and his entrepreneurial partners constantly looked for financing that did not confront the rules stated by Astrid Lindgren. Her diktat said that they could not charge the children with an entrance fee, but they could make the parents pay for parking the car. Further ideas for financing, not realized however, included putting advertising signs on the fences that surrounded the different milieux in the theme park.

Surprised at the commercial potential of ALW this entrepreneur and his family now operate a hotel business in the summer season where visitors to ALW are accommodated. He and his friends never planned or wished this tremendous expansion to happen. But now that it is a fact they want 'their share' as well. The other person is well established and for several years successfully ran a local medium-sized business in the media industry. He recently sold it only to activate his involvement in local politics and was, due to his personal qualities, voted to the highest political office in Vimmerby. He also operates a hotel business that trades on the attractiveness of the ALW theme park. In addition, he was the person who ten years earlier in collaboration with the local newspaper, where he had worked as a journalist, launched the idea of inviting the local (business) community to buy shares in the theme park, compare above. Whatever his intentions may have been, the initiative itself may be considered as an attempt to recreate a sense of community.

Our own research into community entrepreneurship in Sweden as a mode of societal entrepreneurship goes back to 1979, the same year that ALW came into existence. (Johannisson and Nilsson 1989; Johannisson 1990). I have kept in touch ever since, see for example Johannisson (2007). The original mobilization was triggered by a strong expressive accountability to the community, a small peripheral locality (Målerås) in southern Sweden dominated by a glassworks that was threatened with closure. Led by a local glass artist a rescue operation was organized, sedimented out of dense local social tissue but also attracting external subjects from the private sector (such as craftsmen and would-be entrepreneurs) as well as the public sector (such as researchers and, subsequently, state financing). The operations were successful and the local glassworks, acquired by a community cooperative including the workers, a considerable share of the local population and several researchers, in a few years' time became the most successful company in the industry, and a decline in the local population that had been going on for three decades was turned into a slight increase thanks to jobs created in the glassworks and further emergent companies. However, soon enough larger companies in the industry realized the potential of the glassworks and made it the target for a hostile take-over bid. Threatened by external ownership the designer and social

entrepreneur mobilized the financial resources needed to acquire ownership majority. Today the glassworks is run as his family business employing several more family members. The company has also paid back to
the community by, for example, running the grocery store, investing in a
sports hall and supporting other local firms with services like design and
financing.

There are a great many similarities between Målerås/the glassworks and
Vimmerby/ALW: a community with a strong sense of place, a 30-year
record, a dominant, strong-willed individual directing innovative change,
a major local enterprise with global markets and auxiliary local operations
and with a family business as the formal outcome of the societal venturing
being enacted. However, there are also considerable differences: Målerås
is a village of 250 people, while Vimmerby is a municipality with about
10,000 inhabitants; in Målerås the industrial traditions were reinforced as
the glassworks was revitalized, in Vimmerby traditions were challenged;
in Målerås the social entrepreneur was personally involved in the concrete
enactment of societal entrepreneurship, in Vimmerby Astrid Lindgren
and her legacy provided an institutionalized value setting and mainly left
to others to use it. What, however, seems to be the most important difference is that in Målerås life-giving societal entrepreneuring has made itself
dependent on a mortal person while in Vimmerby it is based on institutionalized values and norms that were founded almost 40 years before the
creation of ALW and seem to be made immortal by Astrid Lindgren's
authorship. Genuine involvement appears as a generic driver of societal
entrepreneurship, however in different shapes and with varying stamina.

NOTES

1. Throughout the chapter Swedish quotes have been translated into English by the
    authors.
2. The presentation of Astrid Lindgren is mainly inspired by *Astrid Lindgren. En levnadstec-
    kning* by Margareta Strömstedt (1999) but also Vivi Edström (1997).
3. For a contrasting perspective of Astrid Lindgren's World in Vimmerby, see Führer 2011.

REFERENCES

Althén, K. (2010), 'Att våga tänka annorlunda', in L. Jonsson (ed.), *Astrid
    Lindgrens världar i Vimmerby*, Lund: Nordic Academic Press, pp. 64–104.
Baumol, W.J. (1990), 'Entrepreneurship: productive, unproductive, and
    destructive, *Journal of Political Economy*, **98** (5), 893–921.
Berglund, K. and Johansson, A.W. (2007), 'Entrepreneurship, discourses and

conscientization in processes of regional development', *Entrepreneurship & Regional Development*, **19** (60), 499–525.

Brunsson, N. (1985), *The Irrational Organization*, London: Wiley.

Chia, R. and MacKay, B. (2007), 'Post-processual challenges for the emerging strategy-as-practice perspective: discovering strategy in the logic of practices', *Human Relations*, **60** (1), 217–242.

Czarniawska, B. (2009), 'Emerging institutions', *Organization Studies*, **30** (4), 423–441.

Dagens Nyheter (newspaper) (2002), 'Astrids sista farväl' (The last goodbye from Astrid), 8 March.

De Clercq, D. and Voronov, M. (2009), 'Toward a practice perspective of entrepreneurship. Entrepreneurial legitimacy as habitus', *International Small Business Journal*, **27** (4), 395–419.

DiMaggio, P. (1988), 'Interest and agency in institutional theory', in L. Zucker (ed.) *Institutional Patterns and Culture*, Cambridge, MA: Ballinger Publishing Company, pp. 3–21.

Edström,V. (1993), *Astrid Lindgren*, Stockholm: The Swedish Institute.

Edström, V. (1997), *Astrid Lindgren och sagans makt*, Falun: Rabén & Sjögren.

Führer, H. (2011), 'Astrid Lindgren's World in Vimmerby – a "Total Work of Art"?', in B. Kümmerling-Meibauer and A. Surmatz (eds), *Beyond Pippi Longstocking. Intermedial and International Aspects of Astrid Lindgren's Works*, London, UK and New York, NY: Routledge, pp. 239–257.

Johannisson, B. (1990), 'Community entrepreneurship – cases and conceptualization', *Entrepreneurship & Regional Development*, **2** (1), 71–88.

Johannisson, B. (2000), 'Networking and entrepreneurial growth', in D. Sexton and H. Landström (eds), *Handbook of Entrepreneurship*, London: Blackwell, pp. 368–386.

Johannisson, B. (2000a), 'Modernising the industrial district: Rejuvenation or managerial colonisation?', in E. Vatne and M. Taylor (eds), *The Networked Firm in a Global World: Small Firms in New Environments*, Ashgate: Aldershot, pp. 283–308.

Johannisson, B. (2002), 'Energising entrepreneurship. Ideological tensions in the medium-sized family business', in D. Fletcher (ed.), *Understanding the Small Family Business*, London: Routledge, pp. 46–57.

Johannisson, B. (2007), 'Enacting local economic development – theoretical and methodological challenges', *Journal of Enterprising Communities: People and Places in the Global Economy*, **1** (1), 7–26.

Johannisson, B. (2010), 'In the beginning was entrepreneuring', in F. Bill, B. Bjerke and A.W. Johansson (eds), *[De]mobilizing the Entrepreneurship Discourse. Exploring Entrepreneurial Thinking and Action*, Cheltenham, UK and Northampton, MA, USA: Edward Elgar Publishing, pp. 201–221.

Johannisson, B. (2011), 'Towards a practice theory of entrepreneuring', *Small Business Economics*, **36** (2), 135–150.

Johannisson, B. and Nilsson, A. (1989), 'Community entrepreneurship – networking for local development', *Journal of Entrepreneurship & Regional Development*, **1** (1), 1–19.

Johannisson, B. and Sundin, E. (2010), 'Astrid Lindgrens Värld. Ett mångbottnat entreprenörskap',in L. Jonsson (ed.) (2010), *Astrid Lindgrens världar i Vimmerby. En studie av kulturav och samhällsutveckling*, Lund: Nordic Academic Press, pp. 150–168.

Jonsson, L. (ed.) (2010), *Astrid Lindgrens världar i Vimmerby. En studie av kulturav och samhällsutveckling*, Lund: Nordic Academic Press.

Kanter, R.M. (1972), *Commitment and Community*, Cambridge, MA: Cambridge University Press.

Knutsen, W.L. and Brower, R.S. (2010), 'Managing expressive and instrumental accountabilities in nonprofit and voluntary organizations: A qualitative investigation', *Nonprofit and Voluntary Sector Quarterly*, **39**, 588–610.

Kümmerling-Meibauer, B. and Surmatz, A. (eds) (2011), *Beyond Pippi Longstocking. Intermedial and International Aspects of Astrid Lindgren's Works*, London, UK and New York, NY: Routledge.

Lindgren, A (2004), *The Brothers Lionheart*, Cynthiana, KY: Purple House Press. (In Swedish in 1973.)

Lundqvist, U. (2007), 'Always on the child's side', in *Barnboken*, Stockholm: Svenska Barnboksinstitutet.

McClelland, D.C. (1961/1967), *The Achieving Society*, New York, NY: The Free Press.

Metcalf, E.M. (2002), *Astrid Lindgren*, Stockholm: The Swedish Institute.

North, D.C. (1990), *Institutions, Institutional Change and Economic Performance*, Cambridge, MA, Cambridge University Press.

Persson, J. (2009), *Kulturarv som en turistisk resurs. En studie av Astrid Lindgrens Värld*, C-uppsats. Turismprogrammet. Linköpings universitet.

Powell, W.W. and DiMaggio, P.J. (1991), 'Introduction', in W.W. Powell and P.J. DiMaggio (eds), *New Institutionalism in Organizational Analysis*, Chicago, IL: The University of Chicago Press, pp. 1–41.

Segnestam Larsson, O. (2011), *Standardizing Civil Society*, Stockholm: Santérus.

Selznick, P. (1953), *TVA and the Grassroots. A Study in the Sociology of Formal Organization*, Los Angeles, CA: University of California Press.

Strömstedt, M. (1999), *Astrid Lindgren. En levnadsteckning*, Stockholm: Rabén & Sjögren.

Sundin, E. (2010), 'Vem är egentligen företagare?', in N. Brunsson (ed.), *Företagsekonomins frågor*, Stockholm: SNS Förlag, pp. 30–47.

Sundin, E. (2011), 'Entrepreneurship and the reorganization of the public sector: A gendered story', *Economic and Industrial Democracy*, **32** (4), 631–654.

'Sveriges populäraste personer', available at http://www.learning4sharing.nu, (accessed 10 January 2012).

Syssner, J. (2010), 'Visioner, miljöer, människor', in L. Jonsson (ed.), *Astrid Lindgrens världar i Vimmerby*, Lund: Nordic Academic Press, pp.133–149.

Wigren, C. (2003), *The Spirit of Gnosjö. The Grand Narrative and Beyond*, Doctoral dissertation. Jönköping: Jönköping International Business School.

PART II

Penetrating societal entrepreneurship: dark and bright sides

Part II penetrates societal entrepreneurship from a critical perspective, with three chapters focusing on, discussing and problematizing the outcomes of societal entrepreneurship processes. In the chapters we discuss societal entrepreneurship from individual, organizational and societal perspectives. In doing so we are able to see more than one side of these processes compared to the entrepreneurship discourse of success stories with individual entrepreneurs as heroes of implementing and driving change processes. In this part of the book, our aim is to penetrate societal entrepreneurship from more than the success perspective, which could be seen as the bright side, and also discuss the other darker side of the processes. Twisting the analysis from different angles will bring up the complexity in the processes we have studied demonstrating that societal entrepreneurship is not done from a prescribed recipe. To act with a view to changing society is a challenge both for individuals and for organizations, which is related to contextual issues as well as to different institutional logics in the private, public and NPVO sectors, as discussed in Chapter 1. In all chapters we have been able to see that societal entrepreneurs cross these sectors with different institutional logics, which will result in both dark and bright sides, depending on which rules of the game they have to relate to.

The three chapters discuss different examples of societal entrepreneurship, showing diversity rather than a common empirical base and therefore also bringing to light different dark and bright sides of the field. Two of the chapters (Chapters 5 and 6) also relate to different geographical contexts and discuss how societal entrepreneurship processes are developed in different cultural settings. What is possible in one geographical context is not always possible in another. The role of the researcher is also crucial for the analysis in the three chapters presented. The research methods differ between the chapters and in some chapters several methods are applied, from literature studies (Chapters 5 and 7) and interviews (Chapters 5 and 6) to ethnography and interactive research (Chapters 5, 6 and 7) with great involvement of the researcher in the societal entrepreneurship processes of the actors studied. The analyses of the dark and bright sides are concluded by the researchers but are based on the respondents' expressions in interviews and during participatory observations. The analysis from the literature studies, in Chapters 5 and 7 is also an interpretation from secondary sources but highlights another dimension of possible readings of these texts.

In Chapter 5 – *Small business promotion and intermediating as societal entrepreneurship* – Lena Andersson and Anders W. Johansson discuss the role of the government with the help of intermediaries as societal entrepreneurs with the mission to promote entrepreneurship and small businesses and increase employment in the local community. The authors discuss how activities in the public sector for promoting and supporting small businesses in the private sector are organized, and they compare cases from different geographical contexts like Germany and Sweden. The analysis of these initiatives recognizes both bright and dark outcomes. The chapter discusses the intermediaries' role as a bridge between sectors. In the German case of Borken the public actors focus on small business support starting from the need of individual businesses, while in the Swedish case of Norrköping the initiatives for solutions come from the public actors. This different focus could be an explanation of the different outcomes as for example the increase of employment in the Borken case, while in the Norrköping case the unemployment figures increased during the period. The Swedish case illustrates the absence of a market mechanism to judge whether the support from the public sector provides economic or social value to the companies receiving it. This opens up for cuckoos in the nest, that is, if an initiative costs more than it generates in terms of increased revenue in supported businesses. However, unexpected outcomes were noticed in intermediaries not only focusing on companies but also connecting important actors from other sectors and acting in between the societal structures to make new arrangements possible in order to develop society.

How actors act in and between several sectors as well as geographical contexts is also penetrated in Chapter 6 – *Societal entrepreneurship contextualized: the dark and bright sides of Fair Trade* – where Birgitta Schwartz discusses the diffusion and translation of the Fair Trade idea by actors in and between the NPVO and private sectors and between Sweden and India. The bright and dark sides are penetrated from an organizational and an individual perspective. One dark side discussed concerns postcolonial tendencies in the many controls made by European and Swedish actors in India when checking how the Fair Trade and other CSR standards are met by the Indian Fair Trade suppliers. The darker side is also connected to entrepreneuring, the everyday life of the societal entrepreneurs, which highlights the challenges the Swedish Fair Trade societal entrepreneur recognizes when she combines her social mission with her business. These challenges are discussed as a Fair Trade paradox, where the Swedish Fair Trade societal entrepreneurs must act regarding to the for-profit logic in the Indian private sector while striving for changes in Indian society with the help of Fair Trade, which is related to the NPVO sector's non-profit logic.

In Chapter 7 by Karin Berglund and Anders W. Johansson – *Dark and bright effects of a polarized entrepreneurship discourse and the prospects of transformation* – the individual perspective is in focus. With two quite different cases, IKEA and the Moon House, represented by two charismatic entrepreneurs, Ingvar Kamprad and Mikael Genberg, the authors elaborate on the bright and dark sides of the entrepreneurship discourse. They claim that this is a polarizing discourse, creating a gap between the view of the mythicized entrepreneur as a saviour and the dark side of the villain. However, the polarization is also discernible in the disconnection between mundane and everyday life in contrast to spectacular entrepreneurial events. From this reasoning about the tendency of the entrepreneurship discourse to create polarized views of the entrepreneur on the one hand and entrepreneuring on the other the authors argue that two entrepreneurs and their surrounding contexts respond differently. In the Moon House case the entrepreneur seems to be reconstructed as a hero, down-playing the dark side, whereas the entrepreneur in IKEA invites integration of the bright and dark side of him as an entrepreneur. Furthermore, the polarization disconnects the entrepreneur in the Moon House case from the collective efforts of entrepreneuring, while in the IKEA case the mundane and the spectacular effects of a polarized discourse are integrated. Eventually the authors point towards the potential of societal entrepreneurship to bring about a discourse that transforms contemporary entrepreneurship discourse. Still, it remains an open question whether societal entrepreneurship, too, tends to be polarized. The authors therefore argue for societal entrepreneurship acknowledging both the bright and the dark sides of entrepreneuring.

5. Small business promotion and intermediating as societal entrepreneurship

Lena Andersson and Anders W. Johansson

PROLOGUE

> Closer-to-Companies is both a new venture and a stand-alone working method for starting a dialogue between the municipality, small businesses, the Swedish Public Employment Service, and others. The idea is to facilitate growth and more jobs. We create personal contacts by visiting entrepreneurs in Norrköping and discuss the business situation and growth prospects. Your task will be to conduct a dialogue about opportunities and obstacles. You will simultaneously capture and analyze various support needs that you then pass on to the 'providers' that will be of assistance to the business. This also means keeping in touch with the 'providers' and reconciling the fulfilment of support. In doing this you will be cooperating with the Swedish Public Employment Service. Together we will develop the Closer-to-Companies working model.

The text above is an excerpt from the advertisement made by the Swedish municipality Norrköping (130,000 inhabitants) to recruit staff who could function as an intermediary between the municipality, the Swedish Public Employment Service and the small business community within the municipality.

INTRODUCTION

Governments taking on the mission to promote entrepreneurship and small businesses have emerged over a long period of time. In 1953, with US president Eisenhower signing the Small Business Act, the Small Business Administration was established to aid, counsel, assist and protect the interests of small business concerns. Even before that support initiatives had been taken in the US and in other Western countries. Today most countries have made the promotion of small business a prioritized political agenda. Increased entrepreneurship and growth through small business support has also been a prime focus of the European Union since the implementation of the Lisbon strategy in 2000 (Lambrecht and Pirnay, 2005; Selegård, 2011). Birch (1979), with his seminal work on job generation, found small businesses to be extremely important as drivers of economic growth. As subsequent studies have underscored Birch's findings, though not to the extent Birch's methods suggested (Neumark et al., 2011), the argument for public intervention in small businesses has been accentuated.

Governmental small business promotion is not least concerned with the creation and maintenance of a suitable macroeconomic framework (Storey, 1994). This is done by issuing laws and introducing tax systems implying formalized interaction between governmental authorities and small businesses. Governments have also formed institutions aimed at guiding individuals in the formation of successful and growing businesses. This has been done by providing advisory services, sometimes connected to financial support. These services are often delivered directly from a governmental institution (in Sweden the public agency 'Almi Business Partner' is such an organization), and sometimes the government provides means for services to be delivered by a third party, such as a private business consultant (see for example the Marketing Initiative reported by Wren and Storey, 2002). This means that governments intervene in the market for consultancy services. The main legitimating reason governments have based this intervention on is the existence of market failure in information markets (Hjalmarsson and Johansson, 2003).

When governments and other public authorities intervene in the market for consultancy services they cross the borders between the public and the private sector and thus act as a societal entrepreneur in the way the concept is positioned in Chapter 1 by Berglund and Johannisson. However, not all these entrepreneurial acts create additional value. While the ways in which the governmental mission to promote small businesses has been carried out have varied over time and from country to country, the efforts to evaluate the effects in terms of wealth creation and the generation of new jobs have been limited. Sophisticated evaluation studies (Greene, 2009; Norrman and Bager-Sjögren, 2010) present quite a disappointing picture. Generally speaking, evaluations that have been carried out in the European context indicate a low return on the money spent (Johansson, 2011). Public support for small businesses seems to have become a cuckoo in the nest, swallowing more and more resources from those that were supposed to receive it – that is, the entrepreneurs (compare Bill et al., 2009). Such lack of value creation is, we argue, a dark side of societal entrepreneurship. As has been pointed out in Chapter 1 by Berglund and Johannisson, each sector has its own logic, and it is reasonable to assume that if the public sector logic, in the form of policy implications, is imposed on the private sector, the outcome cannot be expected to be altogether positive.

The eagerness of governments to issue policies for the support of small businesses seems to correspond to a disinterest in finding out whether or not these policies, when implemented, really add value. This is to say that governments apparently are not really interested in finding out whether or not the initiatives are needed. While actors in the private sector are judged by the market, governments are judged by democratic processes. But if all political parties proclaim the relevance of publicly supporting small businesses, the voters have no influence, since the support will continue more or less unchanged regardless of which political party is in power. From a societal point of view our argument is that if governments and other actors in the public sector keep crossing borders in ways that are entrepreneurial but do not create value, be it economic or social, we encounter a dark side of societal entrepreneurship. From a societal perspective it is a tragedy if public money is spent on something that instead of adding value takes value away. In contrast, if these initiatives can be found to add value by increased employment and economic growth, we argue that they demonstrate bright sides of societal entrepreneurship.

In this chapter we present a review of evaluation studies of public support for small businesses. The general conclusion from the rather few sophisticated evaluation studies that have been published is that they provide a disappointing picture of the capacity of public advisory services to create economic value, even if there are some exceptions. Our review points out that there may be reason to further address the way in which the support function is organized in order to find out how small business support can be generative and successful. The existence of intermediary functions might help to explain instances of positive outcomes of small business support. The case of the German County (Kreis) of Borken (Hull and Hjern, 1987), in particular, illustrates how intermediaries play an important role in an extraordinary community development by linking small businesses with relevant support providers. The concept of intermediation therefore deserves attention, as few studies have addressed this function in the public support of small businesses.

The aim of this chapter is to critically analyse the intermediary function in the business support context and to relate intermediation to societal entrepreneurship. The examination of the function is based on two cases. The Borken case (Hull and Hjern, 1987) demonstrates how existing agents can play an important role as providers of intermediation services requested by small businesses. The Norrköping case demonstrates the initiation and enactment of a proactive intermediary function that was launched to improve small business support and generate local community development. Unlike in Borken, where societal development really took off, the businesses visited by the intermediary function in Norrköping were reluctant to grow and expand. Thus, there seem to be limits to its effects in terms of how it comes into existence. The two cases are based on quite dissimilar empirical sources and differ in many respects. What they have in common, though, is the intermediary function enacted to link other actors and create societal development. In doing that, both are cases of entrepreneurship in terms of brokerage (compare Kirzner, 1973). The analysis of the two cases furthers the discussion of the dark and bright sides of business support initiatives and of how intermediation can be seen as an act of societal entrepreneurship.

Next, we will present the review of previous literature scrutinizing the effects of public support for small businesses, followed by presentations of the two cases: the Borken case and the Norrköping case. As the Borken case is based completely on secondary sources, we do not have access to the same kind of detailed information on micro level processes of intermediation as in the Norrköping case. The former case is therefore presented on a more general level than the latter. The chapter ends with a discussion of in what ways intermediaries can enact societal entrepreneurship aimed at supporting small businesses and generating societal development.

METHODS AND EMPIRICAL SOURCES

In this chapter we employ several methods and make use of quite different sources, from a review of previous research to organizational ethnography, to fulfil our purpose.

The literature review of evaluations reported in published research was conducted by one of the authors (Johansson, 2011). It is based on a selection of articles concerned with entrepreneurship and public policy (Smallbone, 2010). This two-volume publication brings together both classic and recent articles on the impact of public policy published in mainly high-ranked journals. Some articles not included in Smallbone (2010) and some published later, such as the evaluation of the Sweden Innovation Centre (SIC) program (Norrman and Bager-Sjögren, 2010), were also included. Here only a few of the reviewed articles are explicitly referred to.

The Borken case is based on the published works of Hull and Hjern (1987). This study aimed at evaluating local business support structures and was designed as a comparison between four localities in Germany. The localities were selected to reflect the highest possible variation in contexts; Borken to represent a rural area in the periphery, Paderborn a small county seat, Oberhausen an old industrial district marked by big firms, and Hamburg was selected to represent an urban metropolis. Manufacturing firms with 10–200 employees in each of the localities were approached by a postal survey, asking about their major concerns for development and growth in their businesses. In a second phase, 20 per cent of the respondents were selected for personal interviews in order to increase the understanding of what kind of problems the firms experienced. The firms were then asked about what external actors they used to handle the identified problems. After that the actors mentioned by the firms were interviewed.

In this chapter we refer only to Hull and Hjern's discussion of the results of the study of Borken, as that explicitly amplifies how intermediaries can play important roles in relation to business support. This is further explained in the case description section of the chapter.

The Norrköping case is based on field research conducted by one of the authors (Andersson, 2010). The study was designed as an in-depth, longitudinal real-time study focusing on the organizing of the Closer-to-Companies initiative. Inspired by organizational ethnography (compare Rosen, 1991), observations of more than 70 meetings in different groups partaking in the organizing effort were conducted between 2004 and 2007. Some 26 interviews with key actors were conducted and organizational documents were collected and read.

REVIEW OF EVALUATIONS OF SMALL BUSINESS SUPPORT EFFORTS

In 2008 Robert Bennett published his article 'SME policy support in Britain since the 1990s: What have we learnt? '. The overall conclusion is that the occurrence of market failure, which has been the main theoretical reason for public intervention in advisory services for small businesses, is more or less non-existent. If failures occur, they are not significant. According to Bennett (2008), it is also possible to compare advisory services based on unitary national programs with different decentralized setups, as a wave of decentralization has swept across the system in Great Britain during this longitudinal range of surveys. Bennett's study shows that through decentralization advisory services have expanded the outreach. However, this has also caused substantially increased costs, which are by no means motivated from a national economic point of view.

While Bennett's study encompasses a broad evaluation of advisory support to businesses in Great Britain, the study by Norrman and Bager-Sjögren (2010) is built on a thorough evaluation of a specific Swedish program, SIC, and was conducted during the years 1994–2003. The study shows that there is no measurable difference between businesses that have once received support compared to businesses that were denied support; the two groups of firms perform alike. For businesses that received support two or more times the results indicate that they perform worse than those denied support and those who received support only once. The overall conclusion of the study is clearly disappointing with respect to the effect of a support program allocating almost 100 million euros over a ten-year period.

Some evaluation studies of public support for small businesses report more positive findings than Bennett's and Norrman and Bager-Sjögren's articles do. On the basis of a large national survey Chrisman and McMullan (2004) found that advisory services from the Small Business Development Centres (SBDC) in the US had generated considerable effects on turnover and employment among firms which had received advisory services. They calculated that for every dollar spent to run the SBDC, $2.61 was generated in increased tax revenues – for one year only. They further found that 80 per cent of the new and established firms perceived the services rendered as valuable.

Most evaluations are not, however, evaluations in the sense that they reliably measure the outcome of a policy initiative against specified objectives of the policy concerned, as argued by Storey (2002). Storey presents a six-step model for evaluation, beginning with the simplest and ending up with the most sophisticated step. The first three steps are all labelled monitoring. The simplest form (Step 1) is nothing more than a report of expenditures and receivers, a 'take up of schemes'. Step 2 involves the recipients' opinions of the program, which in Step 3 includes the recipients' opinions of the difference the provided support made. To make it a real evaluation, the support provided must be evaluated in terms of how the support has affected the performance of the firms that received the support. This requires a control group to compare with. Steps 4–6 in Storey's model account for how such evaluations can be designed with different degrees of sophistication. Step 4 means a rather simple comparison with typical firms, while in Step 5 measures are taken to compare with firms which 'match' the firms that received support and, finally, in Step 6 selection bias is taken into account.

Greene (2009) compared five evaluations of the Prince's Trust program in Great Britain. He categorized these five evaluations as to which step they belonged to according to Storey's (2002) model. He found that evaluations placed on the lower steps in the model reported a more positive outcome than those on the higher. The most sophisticated evaluations (on the highest step) showed no effect of the program.

US studies from before the year 2000 can be criticized for not being real evaluations when related to Storey's model, but rather monitoring the support. Chrisman and McMullan (2004), however, actively take on the problem of self-selection addressed by Storey (2002). This problem means that firms which consume advice are in a much better position to become successful compared to firms that do not consume advisory services. By means of regression analysis Chrisman and McMullan show that the advisory services have had a positive value as the rate of survival increased the more such services were consumed and, as expected, with diminishing return on the time spent with the consultant.

Wren and Storey (2002) evaluate 'The Marketing Initiative', which was part of the UK Enterprise Initiative executed in the late 1980s. The program subsidized the cost for using external private consultants by 50 per cent. The firms participating could either contact the consultants themselves or use a mediator. Firms had to apply for the program and could choose to turn down the offer if they did not find it attractive enough. The evaluation by Wren and Storey demonstrates that the effects of the program, with respect to turnover and the number of employees, are positive independently of the size of the firm. Wren and Storey found that by 1996, on average, the turnover had increased by £138,700 and by 4.8 employees at the corresponding subsidy of £4600. For the whole program this should mean that the initiative led to an increased turnover of £2,100 million and created 72,500 new jobs. Another way of calculating the effect of the program is to say that the turnover increased by 10 per cent for the firms which participated in the program and that subsidies of £1000 generated an increased turnover of £30,000 and created one new job. This strongly positive effect of the program made the authors question their research design. They found, however, that their results resonated reasonably with the Department of Trade and Industry's (DTI) own evaluation. On the other hand, the authors assume that the program might have had substantial displacement effects (which means that the positive effect for the firms receiving the support corresponds to an analogous negative effect for those which did not receive support), something that the study did not include. It is also noticeable that the evaluation by DTI states that 'most firms already had a clear idea of the project they wished to carry out prior to the assisted consultancy'. Wren and Storey conclude that this positive effect of the program was probably a one-time effect. It brought about an awareness of the value of outside assistance, but the same positive effect could not be expected to be repeated.

There seems to be a different way of organizing business support efforts in cases where the outcomes are more positive. The British case referred to by Bennett (2008) in his study has one main 'actor', the Business Link Program, which gradually developed an organization with regional public offices. These offices had consultants who were supposed to establish a broad competence in order to match the need of different types of businesses. This was apparently not so successful. Similarly, the SIC program (Norrman and Bager-Sjögren, 2010) was run by a public organization, also on the basis of the idea that advisors could match different kinds of customers. In cases where support outcomes have been more positive, such as Borken, the public organization seems to have collaborated with private consultants and other actors who have been able to act independently towards that organization, thus acting as intermediaries. In this way the interplay between sectors gives more room for the coexistence of logics; the private sector logic is allowed to operate in the private sector and is not suppressed by the public sector logic. The intermediary role lies in the balancing of an initiative from the public sector with the private sector logic. Instead of advising the small businesses themselves, the intermediaries linked the small businesses to others that matched each business well, depending on the specific competence asked for. We therefore turn now to a discussion of the concept and the function of intermediation.

INTERMEDIATION CONCEPTUALIZED

The intermediary concept has been used in a variety of ways and across many disciplines (Moss et al., 2009). A review of the use of this concept referred to by Moss et al. (2009) reveals that it is used to denote many different types of actors, such as systemic intermediaries (van Lente et al., 2003) and commercial intermediaries (Brousseau, 2002). Benner (2003) and Bäckström (2006) use the concept of intermediaries to discuss labour market organizations working in between employers and employees, supporting employees during job transition, and employers when downsizing. In regional development studies intermediaries are discussed in terms of organizations having different roles depending on their aim and function in the system (Mittilä, 2008). At the local level intermediaries can act as linkages, bridging institutions and gatekeepers.

The intermediary function in relation to business support has been described as that of acting out several roles. Stevenson and Lundström (2001), for instance, describe the Dutch organization 'Dreamstart' as a platform that provides information, stimulates entrepreneurship and brings together all parties that are potentially relevant for increasing efficiency in start-ups. Some business intermediaries specialize in particular niches, such as ethnic minority business support (Ram et al., 2010).

Other concepts are used to describe intermediary types of organizations and functions, such as boundary organizations (Guston, 2001) or brokers

(Ram et al., 2006). Burt (2005) discusses brokerage and closure in relation to social networks. People are brought together by events, such as employment. A firm then represents a cluster of people who are more or less closely connected as a network. A closed network involves plenty of interaction between the members of the network, but people in a network also have ties to other networks. A social structure is thus made up of clusters of more or less closed networks and ties between these. There are empty spaces between the clusters – structural holes – in Burt's terminology. The value of structural holes, according to Burt (2005), is that they prevent the circulation of redundant information. People in a firm who know each other well can communicate more effectively. On the other hand, weaker ties, as Granovetter (1983) argues, include the strength to provide links to other networks. When entrepreneurs bridge structural holes, they shape these important weaker ties. Kirzner (1973) uses the term brokerage to denote this entrepreneurial key feature. This, we argue, is another way to articulate the shaping of weak ties. There is thus always a balance between closure and brokerage in networks, as these two need to be combined (Burt, 2005).

Public support for small businesses, where intermediary actors work in between public and private sectors, can be conceptualized as ways to provide important weak ties from the outside so that small businesses will connect to appropriate outside networks for the effective functioning of the firm. The public support provides add-on brokerage capacity to the small business by way of intermediaries. This presupposes that small businesses by themselves do not include entrepreneurs that are alert to enacting the brokerage or intermediation function.

In this chapter we use the concept of intermediary to denote an actor spanning the realm between public and private sectors and acting as a mediator between different interests and sector logics (see Chapter 1 by Berglund and Johannisson). Forester (1999) provides narratives of mediating in the context of city planners, illustrating how some city planners enact an intermediary function, linking and negotiating public and private sector interests. In city planning different interests often stand in opposition to one another and block the progress of planning activities. City planners sometimes function as resolvers of interest disputes by acting as mediators.

Forester-like narratives are still missing in the small business support context, illustrating how intermediaries work in order to link small businesses with external resources that are needed, such as expert advisors, financial capital, and so on. Arguably, such narratives could increase the knowledge of local support structures. There is also a need for narratives and analyses of how local contexts block effective support structures. The disputes Forester's narratives illustrate could, in the context of small business support, consist of walls between support actors, personal conflicts between advisors, or conflicts between support institutions. Resource providers, and even intermediaries, could thus be available but still not function together. With this chapter, and the Norrköping case in particular, we aim to provide narratives of public business support enacted by intermediaries.

INTERMEDIATION IN SMALL BUSINESS SUPPORT

Two cases will now be presented, first the case of Borken and then that of Norrköping.

The Borken Case

The case of Borken (Hull and Hjern, 1987) stands out for pointing out intermediaries as particularly important for linking public support to private businesses. Borken is described by Hull and Hjern as a German County that went from economic decline to a profound and positive increase of employment compared to other localities included in the same study (Hull and Hjern, 1987). The way the support to small businesses was organized in Borken differed markedly from that of other localities. In Borken three actors were identified as being very intensely utilized by the small businesses.

Between 1974 and 1980 there was an increase in employment by 35 per cent in the area of Borken, compared for instance to a one per cent increase in the Hamburg area. This remarkable increase in Borken was mainly a result of increasing employment in small firms. Hull and Hjern (1987) conducted a multivariate analysis to help explain the cause–effects and found that the pattern of small business support providers differed between Borken and other localities. In Borken three actors were frequently contacted by small businesses in need of support: the Borken County Economic Development Agency (private sector), the County Savings Bank (public sector), and the Coesfeld-based Labour Office (public sector). What these actors had in common was that they functioned as intermediaries taking an active part in problem definition, problem solving and resource mobilization. To a high extent small businesses were guided to other actors and programs, meaning that these three actors did not do all the support work themselves, but rather mediated contacts between the public and the private sectors which were beneficial for the small businesses.

According to Hull and Hjern (1987), historical and cultural circumstances along with the mediation efforts help to explain how the remarkable development in Borken during these years could take place. The three mediating actors, that is, the intermediaries, all helped to raise levels of employment, but they did so in somewhat different ways and to differing degrees. The Agency stands out as the most important actor in that it contributed the most to problem definition and resource identification. The Agency was the actor providing the most comprehensive support, reaching more firms than the others, covering more types of problems, and using a wide range of public programs as well as drawing mostly upon other actors in order to supply assistance. The Labour Office helped firms to handle staff problems and granted resources in accordance with AFG (the Employment Promotion Act). The Bank helped by identifying and mobilizing resources available in public programs that were administered via the banking system. Hull and Hjern argue that the Borken case demonstrates that resource identification and problem definition form an important but neglected business support function.

In sum, the Borken case illustrates an intermediary function where the key element seems to be to assist small businesses in finding the most adequate expertise and other resources elsewhere and thus promoting these businesses by facilitating a best possible solution with the help of external resources.

Bearing the results of Borken in mind, as shown by Hull and Hjern (1987), the results of other evaluations of support efforts could be reread to display that the intermediary function is also present in other studies illustrating positive effects. In the study by Wren and Storey (2002), for instance, the role of the public organization was also a mediating one. Organizations operating between private and public sectors as intermediaries have also proved successful in national economic development as in the case of Ireland. Frankelius and Ogeborg (2009) demonstrate how the Industrial Development Authority (IDA), a semi-governmental authority, managed to promote export and achieve an increase in the establishment of 994 companies in Ireland during the 1980s and 1990s. Some of the keys to IDA's success was, arguably, the combination of competencies, including people recruited both from the state and from the trade and industry sector, as well as the ability to take action, and acts of border-crossing and role-expanding leadership (Frankelius and Ogeborg, 2009).

The Case of Norrköping

For some 400 years, the city of Norrköping was a centre of industry, shipping and commerce. The textile industry was the main hub of the community, around which most things revolved. By the turn of the twenty-first century, however, the industry structure had changed dramatically from a few large manufacturing firms employing the majority of the workforce to a much more diversified trade and industry sector. Today some 9000 businesses are established in Norrköping, and the trade and industry is quite differentiated, although stronger in sectors such as retail and communication, pulp and packaging. At the beginning of the twenty-first century, some 2000 people more than in comparable Swedish cities were unemployed in Norrköping. The restructuring of the industry has left parts of the workforce unqualified for the new jobs that emerged.

The municipality and the County Administrative Board blamed each other for not doing enough to reduce the unemployment. In 2004 the municipality initiated a collaboration effort (Closer-to-Companies) to take steps to turn the situation around. The initiative took the notion seriously that small firms are highly important as creators of jobs as well as the normative demand for local governments to support small businesses.

Closer-to-Companies was regarded as a long-term investment in a new way of working with business relations and promotion on behalf of the municipality. There had been an increase in the municipality's interest in economic development issues, the manager of the municipal Trade and Industry Office explained in early 2005, meaning that Norrköping was moving 'from an authority perspective to a customer perspective'. In this way the municipality aimed at integrating private sector logic within the public sector logic. With the launch of the Closer-to-Companies initiative, the municipality recognized that it only had strong relations to the largest employers in the city. This new way of working aimed to turn that around, creating a wider net of relations with small businesses as well.

The political motive for financing the Closer-to-Companies initiative was that growth in small businesses would entail the creation of new jobs. There was, however, some debate as to how the job creation process was to take place. The Closer-to-Companies venture was financed as part of a municipal growth agenda, launched under the heading '2006 more in jobs by 2006', envisioning that the unemployment rate of the city would be reduced to the same level as in comparable cities (almost equivalent to 2006 jobs) by the time of the Swedish general elections in September 2006. The main purpose of the agenda was to reduce the unemployment, argued the top responsible politician, that is, the municipal Executive Committee chairman.

The basic idea behind the agenda was that more could be done to get the manpower reserve into jobs. Previously, some public actors (that is, the local office of the Swedish Public Employment Service, the municipal Labour Market Office, and others) devoted their work completely to the manpower reserve, while others (the municipal Trade and Industry Office, Jobs n' Society, the Science Park, and others) primarily targeted companies. Previous to Closer-to-Companies no constellations for collaboration were in place. With this new way of working collaboratively it was argued that an increase in efficiency in initiatives would be made possible. The collaboration idea was materialized mainly in the Closer-to-Companies project and with the bringing together of a team of representatives of the municipality and the local office of the state-governed Swedish Public Employment Service. The team's mission was to visit all small and medium-sized businesses in the Norrköping area.

Intermediary activities in Closer-to-Companies

In forming the team of people to execute Closer-to-Companies, it was argued that they needed to be able to speak with the managers in managers' own language. Thus, the municipality recruited four business developers on the basis of their background in the private sector and their experience of working as consultants, entrepreneurs or business managers (compare the chapter's introductory preamble). The representatives of the Swedish Public Employment Service, hereafter called employment officers, were all well experienced in working with business contacts.

The team targeted all companies with five to 200 employees in the Norrköping area, initiating contacts and requesting a meeting with the senior manager. During the visits, the Closer-to-Companies representatives endeavoured to listen for what the managers thought to be the aims and aspirations of the business and whether there were any hindrances for the business to achieve its goals that they could help to eliminate. The attractiveness of the Closer-to-Companies initiative was said to be the simultaneous and proactive offer of concrete support and a meeting with representatives of two important public organizations who, taken together and with help of others, could provide suitable support for the individual business. The offers included assistance in creating networks, help at finding new localities, aid in finding risk capital, assistance in change of generations as well as in-service training, and a great deal more.

Out of 9000 businesses registered in the Norrköping region, some 1100 fitted the profile of an established business having between five and 200 employees. All 1100 identified businesses were targeted in order to generate information about the business sector, information that was previously unavailable to the municipality. The information gathered was registered in a 'customer database', providing information of requests made and development issues discussed and thus enabling future follow-ups.

The proactive approach, by which the Closer-to-Companies team initiated contacts with businesses, was argued to be an important aspect of the working model. This way the business managers would realize that the public support providers were interested in actively supporting them. On the basis of experiences of visits made, the team realized that many of the managers experienced a conflict with or dislike of the municipality. The issues often concerned the municipality's role as a local authority providing and issuing permits and the like. The dislike was based on previous contacts or errands, but also on rumours. The Closer-to-Companies team took it as their mission to engage in turning the managers' view of the municipality around, trying to create a more positive image. This effort received much support from municipal managers and politicians, who had high hopes of a regenerated image aided by the Closer-to-Companies initiative.

Closer-to-Companies made an active effort at creating a system of contacts and contact channels, as well as gathering knowledge of what these different actors could offer small businesses. The support providers identified included different municipal offices, the Swedish Public Employment Service, the university, business financing channels, support channels, consultants, and others. This way, Closer-to-Companies could to work as a knowledge bank and a broker for mediating contacts. Intermediation in Closer-to-Companies thus had to do with establishing relationships, identifying needs for support among the companies, and providing businesses with contacts to relevant support providers.

Swedish municipalities' abilities to provide support for individual companies are restricted by the 1991 Local Government Act, which stipulates that municipalities may provide general support to promote trade and industry, whereas support to targeted individual businesses may only be given in extraordinary circumstances. Thus, Closer-to-Companies had no financial means to offer the companies they visited. What they could offer, in terms of financing, was contact information to financial support actors such as the Almi Business Partner.

Mediation was the obvious and concrete way in which the business developers and employment officers could help businesses during the visits. One of the business developers demonstrates this activity by using an example where the surplus of personnel in one visited company came to good use in a company in need of employing personnel:

> During a visit with an IT company here in the city the manager said: 'I could surely use some ten to twelve new IT developers, where could I get hold of them?' At the time we had become aware of another company in a city nearby that had given notice to people with precisely the skills requested by this manager. Thus, our employment officers contacted the Swedish Public Employment Service in the nearby city and asked if they could accomplish a match of competences to see if they fit. We are not yet sure of how this will work

out but I think it is a great example of what we actually can contribute with. (Business developer during an official meeting, 5 March 2005.)

The role of the business developers was not given beforehand, and in order to be able to mediate between managers, support providers and authorities and still remain legitimate in the eyes of the others they used their experiences and roles differently depending on who they were in contact with. In some instances they stressed their background as consultants or entrepreneurs, when meeting with managers. In other situations they emphasized their role as municipality representatives, thus adapting to different sector logics.

In addition to the four business developers one municipal team member had a special mission to act as an intermediary between the education sector and the trade and industry sector. His 42 years in the education sector, many of which he worked as a school principal, had provided him with relevant contacts to use in the mediation activities between the municipality and the businesses.

In sum, the intermediary function of Closer-to-Companies was motivated by the idea that the current business support system was not enough, that there was a need for a middleman to initiate contacts between service providers and service receivers in order to facilitate a more prosperous business climate that would benefit the community as a whole. The intermediary was supposed to have good capacity to recognize external resources needed by the service receivers, as well as a very good network among service providers in order to match the small businesses with the best available resources, with a thorough understanding of the different logics between the public and private sectors.

Results of the intermediation effort
All in all, Closer-to-Companies got in touch with 1049 small and medium-sized businesses out of the 1100 regarded as relevant to contact. 40 per cent of the visits resulted in errands for Closer-to-Companies to deal with, mainly concerning networks and contacts, recruitment and staffing, as well as land and premises.

It is difficult, if not impossible, to measure what effects Closer-to-Companies may have had both in terms of small business development and in terms of generating jobs. Assessments conducted under the project indicate that the majority of the managers visited supported the idea of Closer-to-Companies, particularly regarding the possibilities of making use of established contacts and networks.

During the period of the Closer-to-Companies project, unemployment in Norrköping continued to increase and by the turn of 2007 it was higher than it had been when the Closer-to-Companies initiative was launched in 2004.

The business developers reflected disappointedly on the number of businesses that were uninterested in growing:

> Having completed almost 1000 company visits, we have made the unsatisfactory observation that relatively few companies express a desire to grow. Several of them argue that they are 'satisfied as things are', that 'growing only means more trouble and hassle', and that 'keeping the operations at its present level is convenient and good enough'. This is an obvious indication of how important continued small business support is, i.e. encouraging more companies to strive for growth and to be able to grow. (The Final Report of the Closer-to-Companies Project, 2007.)

When the project period of the Closer-to-Companies initiative ended, the municipal Trade and Industry Office was provided with the generated information and took over the intermediary function. Today, the municipal Trade and Industry Office in Norrköping actively markets its support to established businesses, and all the support providers now use the business developer title. The role of the Trade and Industry Office as an intermediary between societal support providers and enterprises is incorporated in the mainstream way of working, although on a smaller scale than was made possible with the funding provided to carry out the Closer-to-Companies initiative.

Unintended consequences of intermediation
The Closer-to-Companies initiative did not by itself generate new jobs. That was not the intention of those engaged in the enactment of the initiative either. The aim was rather to generate societal development by improving the local business climate. With the initiation of communication across the public–private sector borders, as well as across organizational borders, Closer-to-Companies wanted to enact a better common future for all involved.

For those hoping that Closer-to-Companies would provide new jobs the results were of course somewhat disappointing. However, with a little perspective, additional and unintended consequences were brought to the fore. For instance, the initiative generated further ideas as to how Norrköping could improve its efforts at societal development through increased dialogue with businesses. One of the representatives of the political reference group initiated company visits where local politicians together with business developers and employment officers met with business managers. At first the Closer-to-Companies team expressed reluctance to the idea, fearing that the business managers would disagree with having politicians discussing their businesses. The results showed quite the opposite. Company visits where Closer-to-Companies were accompanied by local politicians were often fruitful and resulted in positive responses from the business managers. As a result of the positive reactions, the initiator launched regular visits with companies including all representatives of the municipal council. According to the initiator, the result was a council that was better informed regarding the situation of small businesses in the Norrköping area.

There were also unintended consequences related to the intermediary function and the organization of Closer-to-Companies. The ambition of the venture was to construct a function that would span the borders and connect the public and the private sectors. However, for those engaged as links between the municipality and businesses, the intermediary role was a mixed blessing. 'Among the benefits is the potential of belonging to several places at once', the project leader stated towards the termination of the project when the issue of Closer-to-Companies enacting an intermediary function was explicitly discussed during a workshop. 'The downside is that you do not belong anywhere, really', he continued. 'Business managers will probably never regard Closer-to-Companies as a part of the enterprising community', he pondered. 'And will the municipality accept Closer-to-Companies as a legitimate part of the municipality? Perhaps', the project leader contemplated, 'or perhaps not, depending on how much autonomy is instilled in the intermediary organization'. The intention was to be a double insider but it turned out in such a way that the project leader felt himself more as a double outsider.

Dark and Bright Sides of Intermediation

The company visits conducted by Closer-to-Companies meant that they engaged in a proactive way of working with small business support on behalf of the municipality of Norrköping, unlike in Borken, where the intermediaries became mediators by request from local businesses. Thus, the initiative of the intermediation differs between the two cases. In the Norrköping case, the municipality is actively engaged in societal entrepreneurship as its agents strive to contribute to societal development. In the Borken case the three intermediaries contribute to societal development by doing what the local businesses requires them to do, that is, their job. They seemed to be adapting well to the private sector logic in this way. Paradoxically, the Borken case demonstrates a much more profound societal development, while it is in the Norrköping case that the act is truly entrepreneurial in the sense that the initiative is proactive. This could, hypothetically, be explained by a difference in growth orientation among the companies in Borken during 1974–1980 and in Norrköping during 2005–2007. The companies in Norrköping did not actively request the intermediary function, but it was rather the public actors that identified an information gap and engaged in filling it. It is impossible to say, of course, what this new way of working will mean for the trade and industry climate of Norrköping in the long run. What is well established, though, is that such a climate is a complex system of many factors (Storey, 1994), of which only a few are available for the municipality and other local actors to actively influence.

Proactive societal entrepreneurship enacted by intermediaries engaged by public actors is very much in line with the discourse on public support of small businesses and can be legitimated as such. But it seems that the prospects of adding economic value in the Norrköping case were quite limited, as many small businesses were not interested in growing and hiring more people. If they had been, the initiative might have been prolonged. The difficulty of adding value is a major problem of legitimacy on behalf of the municipality. On the other hand, it is little expected that such a complex problem as unemployment could be solved by one single project. In order to remain legitimate difficulties in reducing the unemployment was down-played and the positive effects of Closer-to-Companies were highlighted. These positive effects were argued to be the relations established between the public and private sector, as well as a better informed municipality when it comes to trade and industry matters.

Public institutions face a dilemma in offering public support to small businesses, as policies are decided via top-down logic, where politicians make decisions to be carried out by the public officials. Besides, there is no market mechanism to judge whether this support provides economic or social value to those receiving it, if it is provided for free. This absence of a market mechanism for public interventions is a dark side of societal entrepreneurship as it opens up for cuckoos in the nest.

Further, the public officer's freedom to form his or her role is usually limited. It seems that in order to be effective, the intermediary function should be organized as a bottom-up approach, as represented by the Borken case. This resonates fairly well with how societal entrepreneurship is conceptualized as cross-sectoral in Chapter 1 by Berglund and Johannisson, and as sectoral intertwinement in Chapter 2 by Tillmar. It also resonates well with the suggestion by Hjalmarsson and Johansson (2003) that public advisory services should be provided on an experimental basis. The bottom-up perspective was used by Hull and Hjern (1987) and it is further discussed by Selegård (2011). The latter advocates a low bottom-up perspective, which means that initiatives should originate from a close dialogue between actors in the public and private sectors. The

Borken case is based on a bottom-up perspective, as intermediaries were responding to a direct demand from the small firms in the locality. The Norrköping case can be viewed as an experiment based on a bottom-up perspective. Both the experiment and the ending of the initiative can be argued to be instances of bright cases of societal entrepreneurship, as the ending might be followed by new initiatives, based on better informed knowledge about what would be recognized as value adding to the small businesses of Norrköping.

The story of the Closer-to-Companies initiative provides a narrative of the enactment of an intermediary, demonstrating benefits and drawbacks of working between organizations and sectors in striving for societal development. The issue of how societal entrepreneurship is social and not limited to the actions of single agents, as discussed in Chapter 7 by Berglund and Johansson, is again relevant to note. The municipality alone cannot contribute to societal development in terms of decreased unemployment. For societal development to take off companies need to share and enact the same vision. Here, the logics of different sectors clash. The municipality has to handle complex and often unsolvable problems like unemployment, even when they do not control the ways of handling them. Thus, in order for the municipality to remain legitimate, the work done is sometimes more of image work than of activities that can really solve the problem (compare Brunsson, 2002).

Societal entrepreneurship is about a desire for community development, not small business development, write Frankelius and Ogeborg (2009). However, small business development initiatives can be an act of societal entrepreneurship when aimed at community development. In this respect the case of Norrköping demonstrates an ambition at creating a better city to live in for its inhabitants, including the entrepreneurs. The aims and desires of the intermediaries of Borken are more concealed and it is possible that the aims vary between actors and over time.

CONCLUDING DISCUSSION

Public sector initiatives to support small businesses are acts of societal entrepreneurship because they cross the boundaries between the public and the private sectors. On the basis of current knowledge about the value which is really added by such initiatives there is reason to question this kind of societal entrepreneurship. It seems in many cases to represent a dark side of societal entrepreneurship, a cuckoo in the nest, which swallows more resources than it generates.

Although we need to remain sceptical of causation in the case of

Borken, as well as of the effects on employment in the Norrköping case, we suggest an opening to a solution for the continued efforts at supporting small businesses by showing that intermediaries might be a way forward. The success of the intermediary function seems to be linked to the role of working as a catalyst rather than generating local development by itself. Several conditions could be noticed as important for whether or not an intermediary will be successful, such as a desire among firms to develop and grow, trust between societal intermediaries and small businesses, as well as an awareness of services available – be it provided by the intermediary itself or by someone else.

It could be that intermediaries benefit from acting from a position at the very cross-roads between the public and private sectors, thus being as much as possible an independent actor in relation to both sectors: supported by both and still independent. And yet, as the project leader of Closer-to-Companies pondered, the position might also be a mixed blessing as in-between can also imply not belonging anywhere.

REFERENCES

Andersson, L. (2010), *När strävan efter samsyn blir en kamp: meningsskapande och meningsgivande i mångtydiga sammanhang (Clashing meanings – sensemaking and sensegiving in equivocal contexts)*, Department of Management and Engineering, Linköping: Linköping University, PhD dissertation.

Benner, C. (2003), 'Labour flexibility and regional development: the role of labour market intermediaries', *Regional Studies*, 37 (6&7), 621–633.

Bennett, R.J. (2008), 'SME policy support in Britain since the 1990s: what have we learnt?', *Environment and Planning C: Government and Policy*, 26 (2), 375–397.

Bill, F., B. Johannisson and L. Olaison (2009), 'The incubus paradox: attempts at foundational rethinking of the "SME support genre"', *European Planning Studies*, 17 (8), 1135–1152.

Birch, D.G.W. (1979), *The Job Generation Process*, Cambridge, MA: MIT Program on Neighborhood and Regional Change.

Brousseau, E. (2002), 'The governance of transactions by commercial intermediaries: an analysis of the re-engineering of intermediation by electronic commerce', *International Journal of the Economics of Business*, 9 (3), 353–374.

Brunsson, N. (2002), *The Organization of Hypocrisy: Talk, decisions, and actions in organizations*, Oslo: Abstrakt Liber.

Burt, R.S. (2005), *Brokerage and Closure: An introduction to social capital*, Oxford: Oxford University Press.

Bäckström, H. (2006), 'Arbetsmarknadsintermediärer: omställningar och institutionella förändringar på arbetsmarknaden', in E. Ekstedt and E. Sundin (eds) (2006), *Den nya arbetsdelningen – arbets – och näringslivets organisatoriska omvandling i tid, rum och tal*, Stockholm: Arbetslivsinstitutet, pp. 105–124.

Chrisman, J.J. and W.E. McMullan (2004), 'Outsider assistance as a knowledge resource for new venture survival', *Journal of Small Business Management*, **42** (3), 229–244.

Forester, J. (1999), *The Deliberative Practitioner: Encouraging Participatory Planning Processes*, Cambridge, MA: The MIT Press.

Frankelius, P. and J. Ogeborg (2009), 'När samhällsentreprenörskap lyfter en hel nation – fallet Irland', in M. Gawell, B. Johannisson and M. Lundqvist (eds), *Samhällets entreprenörer: En forskarantologi om samhällsentreprenörskap*, Stockholm: Stiftelsen för kunskaps- och kompetensuteckling (KK-stiftelsen).

Granovetter, M. (1983), 'The strength of weak ties: A network theory revisited', *Sociological Theory*, **1** (1), 201–233.

Greene, F.J. (2009), 'Assessing the impact of policy interventions: the influence of evaluation methodology', *Environment and Planning C: Government & Policy*, **27** (2), 216–229.

Guston, D.H. (2001), 'Boundary organizations in environmental policy and science: an introduction', *Science, Technology and Human Values*, **26** (4), 399–408.

Hjalmarsson, D. and A.W. Johansson (2003), 'Public advisory services – theory and practice', *Entrepreneurship & Regional Development*, **15** (1), 83–98.

Hull, C.J. and B. Hjern (1987), *Helping Small Firms Grow: An Implementation Approach*, London: Croom Helm.

Johansson, A.W. (2011), *Effekter av företagsrådgivning – En forskningsöversikt*, Stockholm: Tillväxtanalys, WP/PM 2011:30.

Kirzner, I.M. (1973), *Competition and Entrepreneurship*, Chicago, IL: University of Chicago Press.

Lambrecht, J. and F. Pirnay (2005), 'An evaluation of public support measures for private external consultancies to SMEs in the Walloon Region of Belgium', *Entrepreneurship & Regional Development*, **17** (2), 89–108.

Mittilä, T. (2008), *Intermediary Organisation in a Regional Development Network*, Conference on Regional Development and Innovation Processes, Borgå, Finland.

Moss, T., W. Medd, S. Guy, et al. (2009), 'Organising water: the hidden role of intermediary work', *Water Alternatives*, **2** (1), 16–33.

Neumark, D., B. Wall and J. Zhang (2011), 'Do small businesses create more jobs? New evidence for the United States from the National Establishment Time Series', *The Review of Economics and Statistics*, **93** (1), 16–29.

Norrman, C. and L. Bager-Sjögren (2010), 'Entrepreneurship policy to support new innovative ventures: Is it effective?', *International Small Business Journal*, **28** (6), 602–619.

Ram, M., T. Jones, P. Edwards, et al. (2010), *Engaging with Super-Diversity: New Migrant Businesses and the Research-Policy Nexus*, Institute for Small Business and Entrepreneurship's (ISBE) 2010 conference, London.

Ram, M., T. Jones and D. Patton (2006), 'Ethnic managerialism and its discontents: Policy implementation and "ethnic businesses"', *Policy Studies*, **27** (4), 295–309.

Rosen, M. (1991), 'Coming to terms with the field: understanding and doing organizational ethnography', *Journal of Management Studies*, **28** (1), 1–24.

Selegård, P. (2011), *Tillväxtbilder, regionala intentioner samt entreprenörers orsaksförklaringar av tillväxt – En penroseisk syn på regional tillväxt*, School of Innovation, Design and Engineering, Västerås: Mälardalen University, PhD dissertation.

Smallbone, D. (ed.) (2010), *Entrepreneurship and Public Policy*, Cheltenham, UK and Northampton, MA, USA: Edward Elgar Publishing.

Stevenson, L. and A. Lundström (2001), *Patterns and Trends in Entrepreneurship/ SME Policy and Practice in Ten Economies*, Örebro: Forum för småföretagsforskning.

Storey, D.J. (1994), *Understanding the Small Business Sector*, London: Routledge.

Storey, D.J. (2002), 'Methods of evaluating the impact of public policies to support small businesses: the six steps to heaven', *International Journal of Entrepreneurship Education*, **1** (2), 181–202.

van Lente, H., M. Hekkert, R. Smits, et al. (2003), 'Roles of systemic intermediaries in transition processes', *International Journal of Innovation Management*, 7 (3), 1–33.

Wren, C. and D.J. Storey (2002), 'Evaluating the effect of soft business support upon small firm performance', *Oxford Economic Papers*, **54** (2), 334–365.

6. Societal entrepreneurship contextualized: the dark and bright sides of Fair Trade

Birgitta Schwartz

PROLOGUE

I am in India with Sandhya Randberg, the owner of the Swedish Fair Trade company Oria, where we meet with her suppliers and visit their factories. Today she is going to have a meeting with the supplier who is now producing Oria's T-shirts and we will later see the stitching and packaging procedures of these T-shirts. The visit is introduced with a meeting with the CEO and three more managers in the conference room, and Sandhya starts to present her company and her products. 'My products are used for showing my Swedish customers' belief in Fair Trade, so I sell cotton bags to large food retailers and different interest organizations'. She explains: 'It is not only important for me that the cotton is Fair Trade; also to see how your factory deals with social issues such as the working conditions for your employees and how you work with committees are very important for me'. She continues: 'The name of my company, Oria, reflects that it is a person from Orissa [in India], and I have adopted my daughter from Orissa and I am adopted from Mother Theresa's orphanage in India to Sweden. So, my company is very much myself and my story is important for the company's image.'

INTRODUCTION

With a growing debate on sustainable development in Western society environmental and social issues are put into focus. These issues, raising demands on Western companies not to exploit the workforce in low income countries, have created the Fair Trade market. However, as markets are not only constructed by profitability, efficiency and resource allocation, they could also be seen as organizations embedded in organizational fields

(DiMaggio and Powell, 1983). These organizational fields consist of politicians, public authorities, NGOs, labour unions, trade associations, journalists and consumers, together with different kinds of companies such as producers, suppliers, retailers, investors, and so on. They are all important stakeholders determining how institutions, norms and values regarding specific issues such as Sustainable Development and Fair Trade develop when organizations interplay. This interplay is in this chapter viewed as processes of societal entrepreneurship, as the actors or entrepreneurs act in and between the private sector and the non-profit voluntary sector (NPVO) in order to make changes with the help of the Fair Trade idea. Fair Trade is mostly looked upon as a tool for consumers and NGOs to help farmers and employees in low-income countries to reach a better life. However, we seldom discuss this Fair Trade idea from a critical perspective, at least not from that of a low-income country, and what happens when this idea is diffused and translated into that context. As we will see in this chapter, this critical perspective of viewing Fair Trade from different angles will show both the dark and the bright sides of societal entrepreneurship.

As the prologue reveals, this chapter is based on a study of Sandhya Randberg and her company Oria, a Swedish Fair Trade textile company, producing Fair Trade and organic certified cotton clothes and bags in India, which are sold to Swedish customers. The way Oria interplays with other organizations such as business customers, Fair Trade suppliers in India and NGOs in its organizational field is discussed in the chapter. The aim is to understand how these different organizations and companies acting in contrasting contexts like Sweden and India interpret the idea of Fair Trade and translate it into practical actions in order to change the business community.

In Figure 6.1, which shows the organizational field demarcated from the perspective of Oria, the actors and how they relate to Oria and other actors in the field are presented. Some actors promote Fair Trade ideas in the organizational field and are marked '1' in the figure. These actors, such as the International and Swedish Fairtrade organizations, FLO-Cert, SwedWatch, Fair Trade Center, Swedish World Shop's Association and Fair Trade network, are NGOs acting in the NPVO sector. Mass media could also be seen as promoting Fair Trade ideas, since they publish and discuss NGO reports and activities regarding human rights issues. It is, however, difficult to place mass media in one of the three sectors, since this actor involves itself in all three sectors when discussing these issues. Actors marked '2' in the figure are market players connected to Oria as suppliers, customers or competitors. Most of them act in the private sector, but some, like the Church of Sweden, are in the NPVO sector. Actors marked '3' promote other sustainable development ideas which are related to Fair

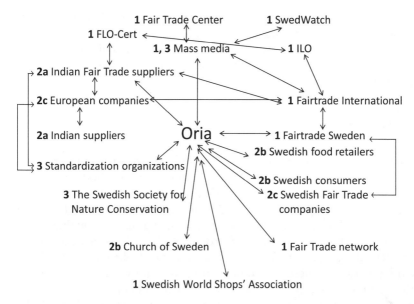

1 Fair Trade Center   **1** SwedWatch

1 FLO-Cert

1, 3 Mass media   **1** ILO

2a Indian Fair Trade suppliers

2c European companies   **1** Fairtrade International

2a Indian suppliers   Oria   **1** Fairtrade Sweden

2b Swedish food retailers

3 Standardization organizations

2b Swedish consumers

3 The Swedish Society for
Nature Conservation   **2c** Swedish Fair Trade
companies

2b Church of Sweden   **1** Fair Trade network

1 Swedish World Shops' Association

Notes:
1. Actors promoting Fair Trade ideas in the organizational field.
2. Actors as market players, 2a. Suppliers, 2b. Customers, 2c. Competitors.
3. Actors promoting sustainable development ideas connected to Fair Trade.

Figure 6.1   *The organizational field of Oria with interplaying actors*
institutionalizing Fair Trade ideas

Trade and Oria's products. They are NGOs fighting for environmental issues acting in the NPVO sector, standardization organizations handling environmental standards, and health and safety standards acting in the private sector. This classification marking is also relevant for mass media, since this actor also discusses these sustainability issues in the public debate. Oria could be classified as belonging to all types, since it promotes Fair Trade ideas, it is a market player and it also promotes other sustainability ideas. Several of these actors and how they relate to each other in the organizational field will be presented later in the chapter. How they act, some of them as societal entrepreneurs, to change the situation in India as regards social and environmental issues is discussed in relation to context and sector logics such as the for-profit logic in the private sector and the non-profit logic in the NPVO sector, showing both the dark and bright sides of societal entrepreneurship.

The chapter goes on to present the methodological approach of the study and its theoretical framework. The empirical findings are then discussed in the framework of theories presented. The chapter concludes with the argument that the national and local relevance of context in different geographical settings as well as organizational logics in the private and NPVO sectors are of crucial importance for discussing how and why different actors act as they do.

METHOD

Since the concept of Fair Trade is seen as socially constructed and defined by the actors in the organizational field, a qualitative method is well suited for collecting different actors' experiences and views of the concept. The methods used are qualitative, including in-depth interviewing, observation through shadowing, mentoring, and an ongoing dialogue with Sandhya Randberg. This is in line with the strong belief that knowledge in the field of societal entrepreneurship as a complex social phenomenon calls for close-up studies where the contextual setting can be further considered through those concerned (see Chapter 1). This kind of field work is also a way to understand entrepreneurial behaviour since it is possible to follow what the entrepreneur does in everyday life (Gartner, 1988).

The data were collected through 16 personal interviews and 14 observations from September 2009 to June 2011 in Sweden. Interviews were also made in India in January 2012 with persons from five Fair Trade suppliers with whom Oria has or had business, and one consultancy company; in total 12 interviews and five visits to Fair Trade suppliers' factories. Some of the interviews made in India are in this chapter referred to when discussing general conclusions in the specific case of the Fair Trade supplier. The personal interviews in Sweden were made with persons from different organizations and companies besides Sandhya Randberg, namely the CEO of an Indian Fair Trade textile supplier (also interviewed a second time in India), Oria's customers such as a purchaser at a Swedish food retailer and the purchaser at the Church of Sweden, an investigator at the Swedish Fair Trade Center NGO and the Secretary General of the Swedish Fairtrade organization. In Sweden shorter interviews were also made with other Swedish companies producing and selling organic and Fair Trade textile products at business and Fair Trade fairs.

In India interviews were made with two CEOs, four factory managers, one export manager, one marketing and communication manager and one employee of an Indian Fair Trade textile supplier, as well as three consultants at an Indian consultant agency working with the implementation of quality, social and organic standards. The companies and organizations were chosen because of their interactions with Oria and because they were defined as important actors by Sandhya. As regards the companies that are Oria's customers it was also important to choose persons who were working practically with Sandhya, such as the purchasers. They are the persons who make the final decisions on whether to cooperate with Oria and buy the company's Fair Trade and organic products or not. It was important for me to understand how they interpreted and evaluated the Fair Trade idea in their decision-making process. The interviews with Sandhya were conducted repeatedly over time and could be described as ethnographic interviews, being open and extensive and aimed at achieving an account of the events that took place between the interviews (Czarniawska, 2007). Each interview was approximately 1–2 hours long and was recorded and afterwards transcribed.

In addition, participating observations and shadowing (Czarniawska, 2007) took place while I accompanied Sandhya to six fairs in Sweden, six business meetings in Sweden and three in India. Three of the fairs were related to Fair Trade issues where Sandhya also sold the company's products and participated in Fair Trade network meetings. Another was a business fair specializing in children's products, where only a few of the other companies were selling Fair Trade products to retailers. Most companies were not selling Fair Trade or organic products but were acting in accordance with business for-profit logic, in comparison with the actors at the Fair Trade fairs where the actors largely followed the non-profit logic. These different fairs positioned Sandhya and the Oria company in different roles, which resulted in varying challenges. I also attended four seminars/conferences in Sweden on my own, where CSR and Fair Trade issues were discussed in relation to different kinds of industries.

During the business meetings I attended I took notes when listening to Sandhya and the other person. I did not involve myself actively in the business conversations or discussions, but my presence may have influenced the two even though they did not explicitly comment on that during their discussions. However, I could never be 'a fly on the wall' (Barinaga, 2002; Czarniawska, 2007). As the shadowing technique does not separate the actor and the observer, they engage in a dialogical relationship (Czarniawska, 2007), and before and after their business discussions I talked and discussed with them as well. The interaction between me and Sandhya has also influenced Sandhya's role as seeing herself as an entrepreneur running a business and not only working for social change. She realized that as a researcher I gave her and her company legitimacy when she interacted with other actors at conferences or business meetings. This phenomenon is especially present in interactive research where the involvement of the practitioner also has implications for the research process and thus contributes to knowledge creation (Johannisson, 2011). This is also shown in other studies in this book; Johannisson in Chapter 3, Berglund and Johansson in Chapter 7 and Johansson and Rosell in Chapter 10.

In this chapter the interviews and the observations form the basis of the empirical material analysed and discussed. The dark and bright sides which are shown in the actors' translation of Fair Trade are interpreted and expressed both by the actors themselves during the interviews and in confidential conversations, but also by me as a researcher in the analysis of the empirical data. For example, the dark side of Fair Trade, explained as just another kind of postcolonialism, was not explicitly articulated by the Indian Fair Trade supplier but recognized by me as a researcher. The supplier rather expressed the European customers' management standards and additional controls as customer demands which he needs to follow in order to do profitable business. Other dark sides are expressed by Sandhya in the different challenges she meets in her everyday life and by other Swedish Fair Trade companies. So, dark and bright sides are interpreted differently depending on which actor, including me as a researcher, analyses the outcome of the Fair Trade idea and from which context and culture the actors relate their interpretations. This shows the range of cultural differences and how people with diverse perspectives interact (Spradley, 1979).

THEORETICAL INSPIRATIONS

In institutional theory organizations are constructed analytically as acting and interacting in organizational fields where ideas and practices are diffused by coercive pressure, normative forces or imitation (DiMaggio and Powell, 1983). In this study the organizational field includes the studied companies and organizations which act and interplay in relation to the Fair Trade idea. They are all important actors determining how institutions, which can be explained as norms and values regarding specific issues such as Corporate Social Responsibility (CSR) and Fair Trade, develop when organizations interplay. For example, in the creation of Fair Trade markets not only companies are involved, but these markets are also created by NGOs with the aim of improving human rights and living conditions for people in low-income countries. In the diffusion of ideas by imitation between organizations, there is a tendency in organizations to implement the latest ideas (Sahlin-Andersson, 1996; Sevón, 1996). Ideas like those of Fair Trade travel with actors such as standardization organizations, consultants, media, and academics are translated into organizations by a transformation of the original idea (Sevón, 1996; Czarniawska and Joerges, 1996). The Fair Trade idea could also be seen in relation to

Sustainable Development (SD), where SD as a master idea for environmental and social responsibility is translated into a Fair Trade label and other CSR standards.

The continuous interaction between actors and the context in which they are embedded is also of importance, according to Mair and Martí (2006). Individual actions are decided by the organizing context which establishes rules for their behaviours (Hjorth and Johannisson, 1998; see also the concluding Chapter 11). However, it is also important to see the connection between the global and the local contexts (in this chapter consisting of both Sweden and India) as a glocal logic seen from a Western perspective as well as from that of the low-income country (Gawell et al., 2009). An adverse context may often lead social entrepreneurs to seek to change the context itself, since the social problem is often deeply embedded in contextual factors (Austin et al., 2006). This wish to change contextual factors could be recognized by the NGOs but also among companies focusing on Fair Trade and environmental issues.

However, this wish for change as well as the methods for change are often based on and developed from a Western context, so that consequences in another context, like that of a low-income country, are not highlighted and are often of no interest to actors in the West (Khan et al., 2007). This is exemplified in the article (ibid.) when the authors discuss institutional entrepreneurship in relation to power and postcolonialism. The diffusion of norms and values from the West and the de-institutionalization of child labour in the production of hand-stitched soccer balls in Pakistan gave unintended consequences. A large part of the employed women could not continue to work when production was moved from home to stitching centres with the ambition to control that child labour was not used.

As the French colonial rhetoric of civilizing mission was based on the conception of Western society as superior regarding morals, culture, society structure, political and economic development, science, and technology (Conklin, 1997) also the British colonizers saw it as their responsibility or duty to 'civilize' or 'enlighten' people in foreign countries by their own norms (Mann, 2004). Neocolonialism could be seen as a continuation of direct Western colonialism with elements of political, economic and cultural control (Banerjee and Prasad, 2008). However, the West is discussed by Gregersen (2010) as a historical and cultural construction rather than related to a specific geographic territory, and the idea of the West is based on a society which is secular, industrialized, capitalistic and modern. As we will see in this chapter, Western society and its ideas are represented by several actors both in Sweden and in India.

THE FAIR TRADE IDEA

The Fair Trade idea and market could be seen as an answer to demands from NGOs and customers in Europe and the US for a fairer trade with low-income countries. On this market several organizations and companies work for and present an alternative to a profit-maximizing logic where products made in low-income countries and sold in Europe and the US should be produced by workers with higher wages and better working conditions. A Fair Trade label developed on the basis of the International Labour Organization's criteria for indigenous people regarding human and labour rights,[1] which states that farmers will be paid a minimum price and a premium for their products (for example cotton, cacao or coffee). The farmers decide how to invest the premium and often act collectively as community entrepreneurs (Johannisson, 1990; Johannisson and Nilsson, 1989) when they invest the premium in schools, water wells, health care institutions, and so on in their local societies. The aim of the Fair Trade label idea is to help poor farmers in low-income countries to develop their societies while simultaneously being able to make a reasonable income.

The Fair Trade standard setting or certification organization Fairtrade International is responsible for the Fair Trade label and sister organizations in 20 countries worldwide. The organization develops its criteria[2] for different products, controls farmers and producers with its organization FLO-Cert and promotes the Fair Trade label by campaigning (Fairtrade Sweden's conference, March 2010; www.fairtrade.se). The certification is also linked to production in the whole supply chain, where producers can be licensed as Fair Trade producers if they follow the criteria of the Fairtrade International organization (www. fairtrade.se). Since NGOs like the Fair Trade Center consider the criteria of minimum wages as not enough for workers, they promote living wages instead, which are higher and better enable people to obtain life's basic necessities (interview, Fair Trade Center, 24 November 2009).

ORIA: TO DO BUSINESS FROM SOCIAL AND ENVIRONMENTAL ENGAGEMENT

Oria sells organic and Fair Trade-produced cotton bags to large Swedish retail companies, cotton clothes for children and clothes such as T-shirts and shirts to adults, cotton bedclothes for children and cotton towels. The combination of both organic and Fair Trade certified textile products is not common in Sweden. Sandhya Randberg, the owner of Oria, also runs a small shop in the Swedish town of Västerås where she sells her own products as well as other Fair Trade and organic products. Her own products are made of organic GOTS[3] and Fair Trade certified cotton and are manufactured by Indian companies registered as Fair Trade producers at their certification organization. This means that it is not only cotton, the raw material, which is certified according to these criteria, but the production with its different stages like ginning, spinning, colouring, knitting and stitching also follows the organic and Fair Trade principles based on ILO's conventions.

Sandhya was born in India and lived until she was 5 years old in one of Mother Theresa's orphanages. She was adopted by a Swedish family and has lived in Sweden since then. She has also adopted a girl from India. One of her reasons for manufacturing Oria's products in India is related to her own background and her wish to help poor children and workers in India. Sandhya has a personal engagement in environmental and human rights issues and is also a member of Amnesty International and other NGOs related to human rights issues. Since 1995 she has worked with Fair Trade issues. At first, when she was a teacher, she worked for the teachers' union in their international engagement. Later on she voluntarily started a World Shop[4] in Västerås in order to push Fair Trade issues, but she felt that there was not enough force in the World Shop concept. One of the problems was that all the staff worked voluntarily, which made it difficult to rely on whether the shop staff would show up to their scheduled work or not. Besides, when she took care of the shop, she had a heavy workload including campaigning, coordination of the financing organizations, the purchase and sales of Fair Trade products and so on while working full time as a school teacher. She decided to start her own business relating to Fair Trade issues instead of putting in so much energy for other organizations, as she says:

> Now I do this for myself so I can get something out of it. (Interview, 6 October 2009; my translation.)

She felt restrained as voluntarily employed and started her own business in order to also take a share of the revenues and receive an income from her work. Her social ideas about human rights and environmental responsibility were realized through a business initiative (Sundin, 2009). So, Oria was established in 2006 and since 2009 Sandhya has received help now and then from temporary employees and from 2011 she has one person employed in her shop.

The choice to start a Fair Trade company for her social mission seemed to have given a successful start to her business career. When Sandhya launched Oria her goal was to be the first licensee in the Swedish Fairtrade organization. She reached this goal in 2006 and that was the reason why a large Swedish retailer found Oria through a contact with the Swedish Fairtrade organization. The retailer placed a large order of cotton bags with Oria. These bags were sold in food stores as an alternative to plastic bags. Oria still gets new customers due to being a Fair Trade licensee, and Sandhya is now working to become the first person getting licensed for the Swedish organic label 'Bra Miljöval' (Good Environmental Choice), which is hosted by Naturskyddsföreningen (The Swedish Society for Nature Conservation), an NGO organization.

The Fair Trade Paradox

To be a social entrepreneur involves the dual aim of making profits and surviving in a market context, and having a social mission (Smith et al., 2010). This dual aim, which in Sandhya's case also illustrates her activities in both the private and the NPVO sector, makes everyday life as a societal entrepreneur complex and sometimes challenging (also discussed in Berglund and Schwartz, 2012), as she could also be seen as the translator of the Fair Trade idea between the Swedish and Indian contexts. These challenges illustrate a paradox; the societal entrepreneur strives for social change but must sometimes act in accordance with the for-profit principles she fights against. This complexity is shown when Sandhya reflects on her business and her work for human rights.

Sandhya thinks that the requirements and demands on the Indian Fair Trade producers could be stronger, for instance the criterion for minimum wages, which are too low. Nevertheless, she looks upon the situation for the workers at the Fair Trade suppliers as much better than the average in India.

Still, a Fair Trade company in Sweden has an ethical challenge, according to Sandhya. There is a moral limit to how large a profit you can make on Fair Trade products, since the workers in India will still have low wages, and the gap between the company's profit on each product and the workers' wages should not be too large.

> Can I make a profit? I must make a profit but there is a limit to how large it could be in comparison with how much the workers get if I earn more, if the argument is Fair Trade. If the argument is not Fair Trade and instead quality, then I can take any margin I want. But, I can't take too much if it is Fair Trade, because the workers who should benefit get such a small proportion anyway and I so much more. (Telephone interview, 15 March 2010; my translation.)

This ethical reflection shows the challenge of being a societal entrepreneur, as Sandhya wants to help the workers in India and identify herself and her company as a caring company, but still has to make a profit. So, where is the bottom line for being a fair company?

She also finds it troublesome to make a profit in Sweden from selling, for example, T-shirts and cotton bags, since the Swedish customers will not pay for her higher production costs for Fair Trade and organic products. Sometimes she needs to sell at a lower price and her profit will then be too low.

Researcher: So sometimes you need to sell at a lower price even if you shouldn't?

Sandhya: Yes, sometimes I need to do that. Cotton bags, which I sell, are actually a loss. To sell 100 bags, it is almost the same work to make a cotton bag as making a T-shirt. And people will buy a cotton bag for 5–10 SEK [0.5–1 euro] and you don't make a profit on that. It is not possible to get so much profit. (Interview, 6 October 2009; my translation.)

So, it is not only in the Indian context that the Fair Trade idea is challenged. For Swedish customers there is a limit to how much social responsibility they want to have for workers in India. However, even if Sandhya sometimes makes an economic loss she still contributes to the workers in India with her Fair Trade business.

According to Sandhya, the Swedish Fair Trade companies which act with social engagement and commitment to help the workers in India sometimes have problems with the Indian Fair Trade producers, who are skilled businessmen. They take advantage of the Fair Trade companies' lack of business experience. They want high prices, they do not keep delivery times, their products are faulty, they do not want to write agreements with small customers, so if there are faults the customer needs to place a new order and pay again. Sandhya's opinion is that the Fair Trade producers in India are quite few and take advantage of that position. They are convinced that their customers will wait for their products, since the Swedish Fair Trade importers will do everything they can to be able to supply their customers in Sweden. These problems are also, in her view, expressed in Fair Trade seminars by Fair Trade importers in Sweden dealing with products other than textiles.

So, a dark side of societal entrepreneurship emerges when the Swedish Fair Trade companies in the Indian context are forced to do business according to the profit-maximizing logic, a logic that they, in their capacity as agents for Fair Trade, try to change. This Fair Trade paradox shows that the concept is framed in the economic discourse despite what its companies in Sweden want. The economic discourse has its roots in the Western ideology of industrialization but is well adapted by companies in the Indian context. Since the Indian Fair Trade producers are embedded in the Indian context they are, as Holm (1995) states, conditioned by the very institutions that are the framework for their actions, and they do not consider changing existing rules.

Nor is, according to Sandhya, the consequence of the Fair Trade business for its companies in Sweden taken up by NGOs like the Fairtrade Sweden organization. They focus on producers in low-income countries and do not support the Swedish Fair Trade companies in business matters. According to Sandhya, Fairtrade Sweden wants its Swedish licensees to make agreements with their non-Swedish suppliers but gives no support to the licensees by putting pressure on Indian suppliers that do not want to sign agreements. The reason is that the organization does not want to get involved in business matters. Besides, the fee for the Fair Trade license is high, in that 2 per cent of the sales price is paid by the company to Fairtrade Sweden. This is high compared with the fee for organic certifications, which is 0.5 per cent of the sales price. Sandhya argues that 'this is not fair' to the Fair Trade companies in Sweden but is something of a paradox, since Fairtrade Sweden stresses that the trade should be fair in all parts of the trade chain, although this seems to be only directed to farmers and producers in low-income countries. It is obvious that the organization acts according to the non-profit logic in the NPVO sector and distances itself from the Swedish Fair Trade companies. Sometimes, too, people in the NPVO sector with whom she still works in a Fair Trade network irritate her when they can make use of their paid working time for their social mission, while she must pay with her working time, which she also needs for selling her products and running the company.

In the next section we will meet some of the actors in the organizational field and their interplay. They could all be seen as societal entrepreneurs although in different degrees, and the experiences of their interplay with other actors will show both dark and bright sides.

THE INTERPRETATION AND TRANSLATION OF FAIR TRADE

Standardization as Coercive Demands

One of Oria's Indian Fair Trade suppliers, who has been interviewed both in Sweden and India, produces cotton bags, clothes/uniforms to restaurants, T-shirts and so on to customers in France, Germany, England and Sweden. Sandhya is very satisfied with their business relation and the way he runs his company in India and treats his employees. He runs the company together with his British partner, who mainly focuses on sales and marketing activities aimed at the European market. The Indian Fair Trade supplier also holds a master's degree from a British university. Before he started his company he was a sourcing agent for European companies, helping them to find Indian producers. He purchases the cotton raw material from certified Fair Trade and Organic farmers (90 per cent) in India, but also purchases conventional produced cotton (10 per cent). At the beginning of the supplier's business he did not know what the Fair Trade label was, but the company followed Indian law (where several requirements correspond with the Fair Trade criteria, such as minimum wages) and paid even better wages than the law stated, but this was not formalized with labels and certifications. He said:

> We had the procedure but if you asked me to prove some documentation it may not be there but I was following the law of the land. But, I could not prove it to you; I could not say for sure that this is absolutely perfect. And that is what the certification and the standards taught us. (Interview, CEO Indian Fair Trade supplier, 9 November 2009.)

It seems that the standards are not the reason for the company to take social responsibility, but rather that the standards fulfil the need for proving social responsibility to the European customers according to the Fair Trade idea developed in Western society.

The supplier's business card shows all the standards and labels that the company uses: Fair Trade, Global Organic Textile Standard (GOTS), SA 8000,[5] OHSAS 18001,[6] ISO 9001,[7] ISO 14001[8] and UKAS Quality Management.[9] The supplier sees the opportunity of adapting to the standardized management approach and also focuses on European customers only. According to the CEO, the standards have helped the company to make the customers realize that the company is serious and wishes to build up customers' confidence.

With regard to this, the need for a Fair Trade standard and certificate is also emphasized by some of Oria's major customers in Sweden, a large food retailer and the Church of Sweden, which stresses that this is an important control instrument for purchasing Fair Trade products from Asia. How could they otherwise be sure that the products have been produced fairly, they say. The standard will reduce their uncertainty. However, it seems as though the uncertainty among the European customers remains, as we will see below.

The standards seem to be very important for formalizing the Fair Trade and other sustainability issues in the Indian supplier's company and also for legitimizing the social responsibility for its employees and environmental awareness to the European customers. The standards are viewed as a way of seeking legitimacy from the surrounding world (Jacobsson, 2000).

It seems necessary for the Indian supplier who chooses to focus on European customers to embrace the management model with its logic of standards developed by companies and organizations in the European context. Fair Trade and other sustainability ideas such as health and environmental improvements are in that sense diffused and translated as certifications and management standards. The customers' demands are coercive (DiMaggio and Powell, 1983), forcing the Indian supplier to implement the Fair Trade standard and other CSR standards, since the economic logic that the Customer is King is strong in India, as he explains how a French customer asked him to get licensed for Fair Trade:

> The customer is the king, the customer tells you, you gonna do it, you have to do it. (Interview, CEO Indian Fair Trade supplier, 9 November 2009.)

Therefore the Indian supplier neither questions the implementation of the different standards nor the customers' additional demands on workers' rights and the customers' own controls and audits (discussed below). In this interaction the European customers control the Indian supplier, which influences the institutional framework of the organizational field of Fair Trade (Czarniawska and Joerges, 1996; Schwartz, 2009), and hence management standards and controls are institutionalized as a common practice.

Sandhya's experience of making business with Indian Fair Trade producers is that as a customer she can exert an influence on labour rights, since Indian producers regard all customers as important and are desirous to take all orders. For example, when she placed her first order she effectively asked for information about labour rights, because the supplier needed to be able to show this. She emphasized:

> Only ask for contact information if there is a labour union. We want to know if there have been any meetings about the union, how it is possible to know your rights, have there been any meeting about this . . . only that you raise these questions. (Interview, 6 October 2009; my translation.)

However, her experience is that there are only a few people employed at the Indian Fair Trade producers that know what Fair Trade is and could push it to the customers. It is usually only the managers who are familiar with the Fair Trade concept. Indian companies have a hierarchical organization, Sandhya reminds us, and as an employee you should know your position and not make any claims for anything more. The interview with an Indian employee at one of the suppliers reveals that at least this person knows that Fair Trade means that the farmers get a higher price for the cotton, but he does not recognize that Fair Trade improves his own working conditions at the textile factory.

The conclusion drawn by Sandhya is that many Indian Fair Trade suppliers see their Fair Trade license as PR, which primarily could give them the legitimacy to sell their products to foreign customers. Sandhya also realizes the importance of the Fair Trade label for her Oria business and has managed to reach new customers who specifically demand Fair Trade products, since European customers will also be granted greater legitimacy and self-satisfaction by adopting a social standard (Schwartz and Tilling, 2009) like Fair Trade.

Mistrust and Control as Postcolonial Power

Another consequence related to Western countries' postcolonial power in framing, interpreting and addressing social issues in low-income countries (Khan et al., 2007) is revealed by the relation between the European customers and the Indian Fair trade suppliers. European companies mistrust Fair Trade and other CSR certifications and audits and also put large resources into building up their own parallel control systems. The purchaser at the Swedish retailer explains:

> We do both, because it is possible to copy a paper [certificate] or to buy it. (Interview, purchaser, 14 January 2010; my translation.)

Earlier scandals make European companies afraid of future ones and they consider all suppliers in India as potential risks. Even if the Indian supplier makes all the necessary audits with a third party, some customers still make their own audits on site. He says:

> We have independent audits like some customers, we tell them that we got certified, but they still send their auditors to audit . . . and because of that . . . our factory is open 24 hours for customers to come to check and see. They want to do it themselves, so they have the satisfaction of seeing it with their own eyes. But, there is nothing new that they do or nothing extraordinary. (Interview, CEO Indian Fair Trade supplier, 9 November 2009.)

He also told me in the interview conducted on14 January 2012 that each year the company does two internal audits for all standards and 15 customers do third party audits of the standards, and on top of that there are also 3–5 audits of customers' own control of their codes of conduct. Two or three managers need to use two to three days of their time for each audit. Altogether between 100 and 200 days will be spent during working hours by the company on customers controlling that they follow the standards. Customers' own controls of suppliers are also confirmed by the other Indian Fair Trade suppliers interviewed. So, there are a great many controls of the supplier's compliance to the standards. In this respect producers with different definitions of sustainable development could view European companies as infusing their values in the Asian context (Egels-Zandén, 2007). The customers' demands for making their own controls could also be explained as a wish to exert control over the supplier by power and dominance (Mir et al., 2008) and the customers seem to be suspicious about the supplier's ability to follow the standards. Would they treat certified suppliers in Europe in a similar way, one might question. Why don't they trust the suppliers and auditors in India? According to Oria's customers, the reason is that mass media regularly reveal scandals when investigations by NGOs show that producers in Asia that sell products to large Western companies use child labour or have poor working conditions for employees. This happens even if the national law prohibits this, and the Western companies use codes of conduct in order to prevent such mistreatment. The Swedish companies are afraid of losing legitimacy and customers on account of these scandals.

Another big problem in his country, according to the Indian Fair Trade supplier, is that the law states minimum wages for workers, but the Indian companies which are not Fair Trade companies usually do not follow this law; they use child labour and have poor working conditions with low wages. Nor does the government have any interest in controlling these companies. Besides, the penalties are very low since they are based on the Workers' Act from 1948, which was constituted by the British colonizers before they left India. So, the driving force for better working conditions only includes European and US companies and not the government, he says. Referring to an interview with an Indian standardization consultant, he is experiencing that more and more European companies now move to suppliers in other developing countries such as Bangladesh and Vietnam in order to get lower prices. However, the suppliers in these countries have not institutionalized the ethical standards, so the European companies must start the process of standardization all over again. Now that many suppliers in the export industry in India have invested in these social and environmental standards and the wages have increased, the European companies seem to abandon the Indian suppliers, he says. So what will happen in the future; will the process of ethical and environmental efforts survive in India?

Regarding the European customers' own controls of the Indian Fair Trade supplier, the customers are largely looking at the ethical part of his business, he explains. That is, whether the company pays the workers properly, looks after them, gives them their own freedom of bargaining, and whether it has a union, or workers' committee, what issues are raised by the workers and how the company solves them. Many of these issues are not included in the standards but are additional demands from the customers, which they also control in meetings with the workers. This indicates that the standards implemented by the Indian Fair Trade supplier are not enough to handle the issues of workers' rights according to the values and norms in the Swedish or European context. The explanation might be that standards diffuse very rapidly compared with norms, which develop by socialization processes over a long period and require particular social conditions to emerge at all (Brunsson and Jacobsson, 2000). Or, as Welford (2010) argues, the problem with codes of conduct or other CSR models when copied from the West and used in developing countries is that they are unlikely to work well. The challenge is to move CSR from a Western to a truly global agenda, which involves working on the capacity building of companies, NGOs and consumers (Welford, 2010). This was recognized at conferences when NGOs stressed the importance of labour unions, which could empower the workforce to change their own situation and improve their working conditions (Fair Christmas gifts, 3 December 2009; MakeITfare conference, 26 October, 2009). This indicates that employees together with labour unions would act as activist entrepreneurs (Gawell, 2006) in order to promote necessary changes.

Fair Trade as Mainly Meeting European Customer Demands

Even if the Fair Trade demands appear to be exclusive to customer demands from European companies, the Indian Fair Trade supplier seems after a while to see the advantages of taking more care of the workers. They remain in the company and the supplier claims that he feels better personally when he sees that the workers are able to improve their standard of living, and the local community develops. Besides following the standards criteria, the Indian Fair Trade supplier gives other benefits to his employees which are related to the Indian context. The employees could apply for interest-free loans to finance weddings, children's higher education, medical emergency issues and housing. Annual medical examinations, free consultation with a lawyer for personal problems in the first step of a juridical process, and free transportation to the factory for 50 employees are other benefits.

However, the Fair Trade certification and the other standards for quality, environmental issues, health and safety and so on, seem mainly to offer business opportunities for the Indian Fair Trade supplier on the European market, because the Indian market is not yet ready for the Fair Trade ideas, and certainly not for this kind of standard. About the low awareness among the Indian public he says:

The common man doesn't have the disposable income to pay a premium to Fair Trade farmers and has no interest when he cannot afford things for himself . . . The premium doesn't go well with the Indian mentality because there are a lot of poor people. (Interview, CEO Indian supplier, 9 November 2009.)

Sapre (2000) discusses this phenomenon, arguing that issues which shape the twenty-first century such as the emphasis on ethics, morality and values in private and public life, human rights, empowerment and so on surfaced first in the industrialized countries and are foreign and therefore irrelevant to India, since large sections of the Indian people cannot identify with them.

ORGANIZING SOCIETAL ENTREPRENEURSHIP IN AND BETWEEN CONTEXTS: DARK AND BRIGHT SIDES

In order to understand the process of organizing societal entrepreneurship in the organizational field and the way the actors interpret the idea of Fair Trade and translate it into practical actions, it is important to discuss it from the perspective of contextualization. The study shows that the societal entrepreneurship processes of Fair Trade in Sweden and India are dependent on actions driven by the actors' contextualized values and norms. The Swedish and European actors focus on Western management models such as standards and certifications, as they regard control and legitimacy as important. The food retailer and the Church of Sweden act in relation to the values and norms in the Swedish context, where management standards and control systems are popular management methods and legitimized company practices. The institutional logic in the Swedish context determines which solution is the focus of management's attention (Thornton, 2002; see also Chapter 1). Another explanation is that the Swedish food retailer seems to be automorphic (Schwartz, 2009), which means that it imitates its earlier behaviour. The retailer repeats the routines of management standards for social issues in the same way as is done for environmental issues when using environmental standardization like ISO 14001. In addition, the importance of being a good citizen and being legitimate in the eyes of Swedish customers determines the food retailers' actions and interest in Fair Trade.

In Table 6.1 the dark and bright sides occurring in the translation of Fair Trade are expressed with regard to the Swedish and Indian contexts in relation to the private sector's for-profit logic and the NPVO sector's non-

Table 6.1   *The dark and bright sides of the contextualized translation*
             process of Fair Trade

Sector and context	Sweden	India
Private sector	*Dark side*: − Oria has difficulties to always make a profit for ethical reasons − Or to be profitable − Sandhya does voluntary work during working hours *Bright side*: − Oria and its customers acquire legitimacy in the market	*Dark side*: − Indian FT suppliers are controlled by additional customer controls − Low interest in FT/Organic products in Indian domestic market − Oria and Swedish FT companies struggle with problematic suppliers and the profit maximizing logic − Only European customers who could easily move to other low-income countries *Bright side*: − Good business for FT suppliers acting in the export industry
NPVO sector	*Dark side*: − FT companies get little support from the Fair Trade organization *Bright side*: − Oria, its customers, other FT companies and NGOs acquire legitimacy in the Swedish society	*Dark side*: − Conventional Indian companies have low interest in better working conditions and environmental issues *Bright side*: − Oria and Indian FT suppliers improve standard of living for Indian workers with the help of Fair Trade criteria, CSR standards and context-related benefits

profit logic. As we can see, there are both dark and bright sides depending
from which actor's perspective we interpret the translation process.

The Indian Fair Trade supplier adapts to the standards and certification
processes and utilizes them for doing business outside India. The dark side
of his adaption of the standards is when the supplier needs to put large
personnel resources into auditing and controls, which could be viewed as
a result of postcolonial coercive forces, while the Swedish and European
customers also add their own control on top of the supplier's compliance

with the CSR and Fair Trade standards when interplaying in another context. The major Swedish and European companies acting in India set their standard of control and use their power as customers for changing institutions in the Indian export industry.

A brighter side from the perspective of the Indian Fair Trade supplier is his ability to understand the European context thanks to his British partner, British education and experience of working with European companies as a sourcing agent. This implies that he can combine the possibilities both in the European context with its Fair Trade demands and in a growing Fair Trade market with the business norms in the Indian context. The additional benefits for his workers are also related to the Indian context. However, as a Fair Trade producer and societal entrepreneur in India contributing to the local community and to employee welfare, the supplier also challenges the values and norms of working conditions and environmental issues in the Indian business society. But, as an export-oriented company only selling to European customers like the other Fair Trade suppliers interviewed, it is doubtful whether any change will occur, since the consumer demand for Fair Trade and/or organic products is still very low in India.

The story of the Fair Trade company Oria and Sandhya's struggle shows that Oria is placed in a Swedish context where the norms and values of human rights and employees' situation are similar to those forming the basis of the development of the Fair Trade label and standard. When these norms are diffused to the Indian context by Oria as a translator of Fair Trade, some dark aspects emerge in Sandhya's struggle with her company which force her to act in the private sector with the for-profit logic while simultaneously striving for a social mission. Interpreting her business failures as successful in a non-profit logic is a way for her to rationalize her actions and go on until a new challenge occurs. This shows some dark sides of societal entrepreneurship when Sandhya, with her values and norms based in the Swedish context, meets suppliers in the Indian context where the actors are very much into the for-profit logic and challenge the social values on which she wants to base her business.

This darker side of societal entrepreneurship is expressed in the Fair Trade paradox, which emerges when Swedish Fair Trade companies in the Indian context are forced to do business according to the profit-maximizing logic, a logic that they try to change as societal entrepreneurs, since they stress that actors should be fair in their business relations. As the Swedish Fair Trade companies act from a Swedish solidarity perspective and want to change the business society in India, it becomes difficult for them to handle the Indian business context. This shows that when translated by the actors, Fair Trade also maintains asymmetrical power relations, as Swedish Fair Trade companies interplaying in another context are in a weak position against Indian Fair Trade suppliers.

The Fair Trade paradox is further highlighted through Sandhya's everyday struggle. The need to combine her vision of changing poor working conditions in India and making a living in her business poses an existential challenge to her and she sees constraints in making too large a profit in her business. The duality between her non-profit ideology, based on her human rights engagement, clashes with the business ideology of profit maximization and ends up in an ethical challenge for her. She does not want to exploit the Indian Fair Trade workers by making too much money at their expense. Still, this view also causes her financial challenges as she cannot make enough profit from selling Fair Trade products to Swedish customers but sometimes needs to sell at a loss. In this perspective she also struggles with the norms and values among Swedish customers, who do not want to pay high prices for products produced in low-income countries, even if they are Fair Trade labelled, since Swedish customers are used to low prices from these countries.

And yet, sometimes she is able to contribute to the Indian workers when she finds that she can influence the Indian Fair Trade suppliers as a customer of Fair Trade and organically produced textile products who asks for human rights issues to be considered. In these situations she could be identified as a change agent (Sharir and Lerner 2006; Khan et al., 2007), or, as we prefer, societal entrepreneur, with the help of the Fair Trade idea.

The study shows that it is a challenge to be a Fair Trade societal entrepreneur, because of the need to handle different norms and values in different contexts and contrasting logics in the private and NPVO sector. Both dark and bright sides emerge, since the actors in Sweden and India and their actions are dependent on which values and norms they are familiar with and guided by. The different degrees of societal entrepreneurship among the actors are recognized in that the actors play different roles in the organizational field. Some, as NGOs, promote the Fair Trade idea more from an ideal picture of what the world should be like, while some actors are more involved as market players, as Indian Fair Trade suppliers, or struggle with both roles like Sandhya in her Oria company when she tries to cope with the everyday life of a societal entrepreneur. To discuss both the dark and the bright sides of these processes in relation to context and logics highlights and reaches beyond the general discussion of good and bad outcomes and instead increases the understanding of different actors' behaviour and their interpretation of the Fair Trade idea.

NOTES

1. The ILO criteria are: elimination of forced labour, abolition of child labour, elimination of discrimination (www.ilo.org).
2. The Fairtrade criteria are: premium for products sold, minimum price for products, minimum wages at the same or higher level than the national law, the right to organize in labour unions, democratic organizational structure, health and security, environmental awareness, no child labour (www.fairtrade.se).
3. Global Organic Textile Standard (GOTS) is a standard for organic products.
4. The Swedish World Shops' Association was mainly supported by the Church of Sweden when it started in 1969. The aim is to sell craft and food products from small-scale producers in developing countries which have been produced according to specific Fair Trade criteria based on WFTO's Fair Trade principles. The association also works with information and campaign activities (www.varldsbutikerna.org).
5. SA 8000 is a voluntary international management standard for social accountability applied to working conditions based on several international human rights conventions (Social Accountability International, 2008).
6. OHSAS 18001 is a health and safety management standard.
7. ISO 9001 is a quality management standard.
8. ISO 14001 is an environmental management standard.
9. UKAS Quality Management is a British accreditation service organization providing certification to ISO 9001.

REFERENCES

Austin, J., H. Stevenson and J. Wei-Skillern (2006), 'Social and commercial entre-preneurship: Same, different, or both?', Entrepreneurship Theory and Practice, **30** (1), 1–22.

Banerjee, S.B. and A. Prasad (2008), 'Introduction to the special issue on "Critical reflections on management and organizations: a postcolonial perspective"', *Critical Perspectives on International Business*, **4** (2/3), 90–98.

Barinaga, E. (2002), *Levelling Vagueness: a Study of Cultural Diversity in an International Project*, Doctoral thesis. Stockholm: EFI.

Berglund, K. and B. Schwartz (submitted 2012), 'Holding on to the anomaly of social entrepreneurship: Solving dilemmas and dealing with disharmonies', *Journal of Social Entrepreneurship*.

Brunsson, N. (2000), 'Organizations, markets and standardization', in N. Brunsson and B. Jacobsson (eds), *A World of Standards*, Oxford/New York: Oxford University Press, pp. 21–39.

Brunsson N. and B. Jacobsson (2000), 'The contemporary expansion of standard-ization' in N. Brunsson and B. Jacobsson (eds), *A World of Standards*, Oxford/New York: Oxford University Press, pp. 1–17.

Conklin, A.L. (1997), *A Mission to Civilize: The Republican Idea of Empire in France and West Africa, 1895–1930*, Stanford: Stanford University Press.

Czarniawska, B. (2007), *Shadowing and Other Techniques for Doing Fieldwork in Modern Societies*, Malmö: Liber.

Czarniawska B. and B. Joerges (1996), 'Travels of ideas', in B. Czarniawska and G. Sevón (eds), *Translating Organizational Change*, Berlin: Walter de Gruyter, pp. 13–48.

DiMaggio P.J. and W.W. Powell (1983), 'The iron cage revisited: Institutional isomorphism and collective rationality in organizational fields', *American Sociological Review*, **48** (2), 147–160.

Egels-Zandén, N. (2007), 'Suppliers' compliance with MNCs' codes of conduct: Behind the scenes at Chinese toy suppliers', *Journal of Business Ethics*, 75, 45–62.

Fairtrade, www.fairtrade.se (accessed 4 October 2010; 27 January 2012).

Gartner, W.B. (1988), '"How is an Entrepreneur?" is the wrong question', *Entrepreneurship Theory and Practice*, **13** (4), 47–68.

Gawell, M. (2006), *Activist Entrepreneurship. Attac'ing Norms and Articulating Disclosive Stories*, Doctoral thesis. Stockholm: Stockholm University.

Gawell, M., B. Johannisson and M. Lundqvist (2009), 'Mot ett mångsidigt entreprenörskap i samhällets intresse', in M. Gawell, B. Johannisson and M. Lundqvist (eds), *Samhällets entreprenörer: en forskarantologi om samhällsentreprenörskap*, Stockholm: KK-stiftelsen.

Gregersen, M. (2010), *Fostrande förpliktelser: representationer av ett missionsuppdrag i Sydindien under 1900-talets första hälft*, Doctoral thesis. Lund University.

Hjorth, D. and B. Johannisson (1998), 'Entreprenörskap som skapelseprocess och ideologi', in B. Czarniawska (ed.), *Organisationsteori på svenska*, Malmö: Liber Ekonomi, pp. 86–104.

Holm, P. (1995), 'The dynamics of institutionalization: Transformation processes in Norwegian fisheries', *Administrative Science Quarterly*, **40** (3), 398–422.

International Labour Organization, www.ilo.org (accessed 4 October 2010).

Jacobsson, B. (2000), 'Standardization and expert knowledge', in N. Brunsson and B. Jacobsson (eds), *A World of Standards*, Oxford/New York: Oxford University Press, pp. 40–49.

Johannisson, B. (1990), 'Community entrepreneurship: Cases and conceptualization', *Journal of Entrepreneurship and Regional Development*, **2** (1), 71–88.

Johannisson, B. (2011), 'Towards a practice theory of entrepreneuring', *Small Business Economics*, **36** (2), 135–150.

Johannisson, B. and A. Nilsson (1989), 'Community entrepreneurship: Networking for local development', *Journal of Entrepreneurship and Regional Development*, **1** (1), 1–19.

Khan, F.R., K.A. Munir and H. Willmott (2007), 'A dark side of institutional entrepreneurship: Soccer balls, child labour and postcolonial impoverishment', *Organization Studies*, 28, 1055–1077.

Mair, J. and I. Martí (2006), 'Social entrepreneurship research: A source of explanation, prediction, and delight', *Journal of World Business, Special Issue: Social Entrepreneurship: New Research Findings*, **41**, 36–44.

Mann, M. (2004), 'Torchbearers upon the path of progress: Britain's ideology of a moral and material progress in India. An introductory essay', in H. Fischer-Tiné and M. Mann (eds), *Colonialism as Civilizing Mission: Cultural Ideology in British India*, London: Anthem Press, pp. 1–26.

Mir, R., S.B. Banerjee and A. Mir (2008), 'Hegemony and its discontents: a critical analysis of organizational knowledge transfer', *Critical Perspectives on International Business*, **4** (2/3), 203–227.

Sahlin-Andersson K. (1996), 'Imitating by editing success: The construction of organizational fields', in B. Czarniawska and G. Sevón (eds), *Translating Organizational Change*, Berlin: Walter de Gruyter, pp. 69–92.

Sapre, P.M. (2000), 'Realizing the potential of management and leadership: Toward a synthesis of Western and indigenous perspectives in the modernization of non-Western societies', *International Journal of Leadership in Education*, **3** (3), 293–305.

Schwartz, B. (2009), 'Environmental strategies as automorphic patterns of behaviour', *Business Strategy and the Environment*, **18** (5), 192–206.

Schwartz, B. and K. Tilling (2009), 'ISO-lating' corporate social responsibility in the organizational context: A dissenting interpretation of ISO 26000', in P. Dobers and M. Halme (eds), *Corporate Social Responsibility and Environmental Management, Special Issue: CSR and Developing Countries Perspectives*, **16** (5), 289–299.

Sevón G. (1996), 'Organizational imitation in identity transformation', in B. Czarniawska and G. Sevón (eds), *Translating Organizational Change*, Berlin: Walter de Gruyter, pp. 49–67.

Sharir, M. and M. Lerner (2006), 'Gauging the success of social ventures initiated by individual social entrepreneurs', *Journal of World Business, Special Issue: Social Entrepreneurship: New Research Findings*, 41, 6–20.

Smith B.R., J. Knapp, T.F. Barr, C.E. Stevens and B.L. Cannatelli (2010), 'Social enterprises and the timing of conception: Organizational identity tension, management, and marketing', *Journal of Nonprofit & Public Sector Marketing*, **22** (2), 108.

Social Accountability International, (2008).

Spradley, J. (1979), *The Ethnographic Interview*, Belmont: Wadsworth, Cengage Learning.

Sundin, E. (2009), 'Det dolda samhällsentreprenörskapet: omsorgsmotiv i småföretag', in M. Gawell, B. Johannisson and M. Lundqvist (eds), *Samhällets entreprenörer: en forskarantologi om samhällsentreprenörskap*, Stockholm: KK-stiftelsen, pp. 96–114.

Thornton, P.H. (2002), 'The rise of the corporation in a craft industry: Conflict and conformity in institutional logics', *Academy of Management* Journal, **45**, 81–101.

Welford, R. (2010), 'Epilogue corporate social responsibility: The next agenda?', in P. Dobers (ed.), *Corporate Social Responsibility: Challenges and Practices*, Stockholm: Santérus Academic Press, pp. 309–322.

Världsbutikerna, www.varldsbutikerna.org (accessed 4 October 2010).

7. Dark and bright effects of a polarized entrepreneurship discourse . . . and the prospects of transformation

Karin Berglund and Anders W. Johansson

PROLOGUE

Early in the morning of Tuesday 26 May 2009 a helicopter took off from the ground close by the largest sports arena in Sweden, the Globe. In a rope underneath the helicopter a ten-square-meter red house with white gables was swinging. When the helicopter made a sudden move, making the house oscillate, the crowd of about 70 people gathered at the ground went completely silent presumably visioning a possible crash at the 'Nynäsvägen' motorway in the Stockholm morning traffic. However, everything went well. The helicopter could successfully place the house on the top of the Globe, where it was anchored in a pre-made frame by the five climbers waiting. At this point I recall one of the people in the crowd reflecting on the idea of decorating this red house with IKEA furniture and wondering if that would not be an outstanding symbol of Sweden.

The above episode is told by one the authors of this chapter, who was witnessing the spectacular event when a prototype of the Moon House was placed on top of the Globe arena in Stockholm. The spontaneous reflection of one of her fellow witnesses to connect the Moon House with IKEA is in this chapter taken as a point of departure for comparing two in many ways very different expressions and cases of societal entrepreneurship. As will be illustrated, these two cases also share some similarities. However, from interpreting the cases from the perspective of a polarizing entrepreneurship discourse – sometimes denoting the bright and at other times the dark shades of entrepreneurship – this chapter winds up with an unexpected proposal. Whilst societal entrepreneurship may clear the way for novel ways of perceiving entrepreneuring as a cross-sectoral phenomenon, it may also be subsumed by contemporary understandings of 'traditional' entrepreneurship. At stake is how to view the entrepreneur, success and activity emanating from processes of societal entrepreneurship.

INTRODUCTION

The Moon House is about a project of putting a red Swedish cottage on the surface of the moon, which has gained a lot of public attention as a contemporary entrepreneurial project. IKEA, the Swedish company, has become a global symbol of Sweden but also of entrepreneurship. While the Moon House is taking place as described in this chapter, IKEA has already proved to be successful, valued and mythicized. Today for more than half a century IKEA has made people relate to design and furniture in new ways, facilitating many people to decorate their homes. Conversely, the Moon House is only emerging as an entrepreneurial endeavour, aiming to provoke people in contemporary society about what is possible to do by, literally as well as metaphorically, trying to open up new spaces by which places and beliefs can be transformed.

Despite the differences of the two cases, both share strong similarities, for instance illustrating cross-sectoral organizing (see Chapter 1). A legitimizing base for the Moon House is an NPVO ('Friends of the Moon House'), while the realization of the project is commercial by way of a private company with a wide range of potential investors. Further, the project has close links to research and the public sector. IKEA crosses sectors in the way the company interacts with its customers in one of the most private areas of customers' lives (their homes). Whereas IKEA was in its early stage a company in the furniture industry, social initiatives and environmental concern have become a conscious part of the company strategy since the 1990s. The company works together with organizations like Save the Children, UNICEF and World Wide Fund for Nature (WWF), and is involved in projects concerned with children's health and schooling in southern Asia, related to climate change, and many other projects. Mirroring this philosophy, the former CEO of IKEA, Anders Dahlvig (2012), states that 'a company's reason for existence should be to contribute to a better society'. The endeavour to contribute to a better society is also stated as a vision and aim in the Moon House case, supported by the NPVO 'Friends of the Moon House', which has partaken in promoting all sorts of activities related to constructing a house that can be sent to the moon in a small package, unfolded by some ingenious (not yet invented) mechanism to the size of a ten-square-meter large and full-height house, symbolizing human beings' enterprising capability. However, from an artistic point of view – and due to the many paintings made – the house also reminds us about its loneliness in outer space, with its cold and dark surroundings, echoing that we need to work together with the challenges we are facing on earth. In the Moon House work public organizations, manufacturing companies, high-tech businesses, the Swedish Space

Corporation, universities and individuals have come together to meet, discuss and take action on account of the different challenges that have been brought up by the project; from efforts involved in inventing new materials and methods in order to make the construction of the house function, promoting young people to take on the engineering path, to the prospect of communicating communal values to the global community. Whilst the Moon House is, concretely, an engineering challenge, it involves public, private and NPVO sectors as well as individuals who are part of it 'just for fun', transgressing the way the idea of entrepreneurship is known in each of the sectors.

Furthermore, both cases are characterized by having a charismatic entrepreneur and an idea that is recognized as outstanding. Even if the two entrepreneurs are sometimes called into question – the IKEA founder Ingvar Kamprad for being part of the Nazi movement in his youth and the artist Mikael Genberg for making space commercials – the projects themselves are seldom contested. These endeavours are rather depicted as successful and bright and even make up some sort of 'role models' of entrepreneurial projects. From following these two cases over a long period of time we have seen that there are also dark sides to the success involved in both cases. Thus, despite all success, the entrepreneurs themselves, as well as those taking part in the two endeavours, face accusations and are subtly positioned in ways that obstruct action and the unfolding of entrepreneuring. In this chapter this is discussed from the notion of a polarized entrepreneurship discourse, idealizing the entrepreneur and disconnecting the everyday, humdrum part of entrepreneuring from spectacular events (such as placing a red house on the Globe arena).

Hence, the view taken in this chapter is that entrepreneurship has become a discourse in the sense that it exercises power over individuals and collectives as to how entrepreneuring (see Steyaert, 2007; Berglund and Johansson, 2007b; Johannisson, 2011) can be enacted. We illustrate that the entrepreneurship discourse seems so strong that the dark sides of entrepreneuring are seldom portrayed or talked about. Instead, the dark side appears to be part of an entrepreneurs' everyday life as a silent, inconvenient, misplaced, and yet inescapable, shadow. Adopting the idea of bright and dark sides, the polarized tendencies of the entrepreneurship discourse is recognized. From discussing entrepreneuring in the Moon House and the IKEA case, some down sides of success and how they affect individuals and collectives in entrepreneuring endeavours, are illustrated. Finally, the effects created by the polarized discourse are elaborated on, on the assumption that 'success' created by an 'autonomous entrepreneur' can be counterproductive.

In the following two sections of the chapter we will outline our understanding of the entrepreneurship discourse and its polarizing effects on the entrepreneur and the context around. This will be followed by a section about the methodology we have been using as well as about some similarities and differences between our two cases. After that we elaborate on the cases in a section about the Moon House, followed by a section about IKEA. In the concluding parts of the chapter we analyse the polarizing effects of the entrepreneur and entrepreneuring in the two cases and at the end return to their societal prospects.

THE ENTREPRENEURSHIP DISCOURSE AND ITS LIMITATIONS

In the initial stages of the entrepreneurship discourse Joseph Schumpeter (1883–1950) saw the entrepreneur, at least in his early writings, as an individual who carries out new combinations (innovations) that throw the market out of equilibrium. Not many within a human population have this quality which is often limited to a certain period of time. The relevant question to ask from a Schumpeterian perspective was: Who is an entrepreneur? Even if Schumpeter (1934, 1939, 1942) pointed towards the function of entrepreneurship, a great deal of research has ever since been devoted to understanding the make-up of the entrepreneur. What were sought after were the inner qualities, the personal characteristics of a person who could be predicted to become a successful entrepreneur. As these efforts were shown to be less fruitful, a dominating stream of research within entrepreneurship turned towards studying new business creation, attaining a slightly more inclusive notion about who can be included in the herd of entrepreneurs. We could say that the initial question, 'Who is an entrepreneur?' was reformulated into a new question: 'What should a person do in order to become a successful entrepreneur?' Many entrepreneurship textbooks today therefore emphasize how to develop successful business ideas, how to recognize opportunities, how to build an entrepreneurial team, how to write a business plan and how to manage a growing entrepreneurial firm (for example Barringer and Ireland, 2006).

What both these questions assume is a strong belief in the agency of actors. Schumpeter had in mind individuals such as Henry Bessemer, the great inventor of, among other things, the technique for making steel out of iron (Henreksson and Stenkula, 2007). There are a few, though not very many, individuals in Western countries, according to early Schumpeter, who have been very influential because they were able to create innovations that could throw the market out of equilibrium and thus drive the whole economy forward. Had he lived now, he might have mentioned Ingvar Kamprad as one such individual. The later Schumpeter however, recognizing the changing character of the capitalist system, also saw other actors as important for innovation processes (Lindgren and Packendorff, 2003). He claimed that the capitalist system grew more and more bureaucratic and that innovation was to an increasing degree based on calculations and aggregated behaviour. So he more or less abandoned the idea of the great hero entrepreneur. Maybe Schumpeter towards the end of his life became quite pessimistic about the agency of the individual?

Despite Schumpeter's doubts concerning the status of the entrepreneur and despite the problems of identifying these men and women in real life, the discourse has lived its own life seemingly unaffected by such doubts. According to this discourse, entrepreneurs have certainly come to stand out as special persons and, as illustrated by way of discourse analysis, there exist a number of superlatives for describing these people (Ahl, 2004). In this respect, the majority of entrepreneurial traits also go in line with how masculinity and ethnocentrism are constructed in Western society (Ogbor, 2000). With a closer look at the discourse, the heroizing tendencies make each and every one of us turn into 'the other' in relation to the entrepreneur (Jones and Spicer, 2005).

Thus, rather than providing us with a vocabulary for talking about entrepreneuring, the discourse of entrepreneurship provides us with superlatives depicting the fully furnished human being in contemporary society. This implies that the entrepreneurship discourse limits our ability to see what is entrepreneurial. The focus on the individual prevents an understanding of entrepreneuring as a social process. The emphasis on entrepreneurship as a vital part of growth rhetoric (and connected to progress) presents entrepreneurship both as something necessary and as something inherently good and bright, neglecting the everyday greyness as well as the dark sides of entrepreneuring. Consequently, the entrepreneurship discourse presents a one-eyed view, providing us with words that depict the 'good' future and the 'ideal' human being. These limitations of entrepreneurship discourse therefore call for a review of how destructive aspects of entrepreneuring have been discussed in the literature.

ENTREPRENEURSHIP: A POLARIZING DISCOURSE

The concept of destruction (creative destruction), familiarized by Schumpeter (1942) as an economic theory of radical innovation and progress, seems to have been lost in the discourse. There are exceptions, however. Baumol (1990), building on Schumpeter, differentiates between productive, unproductive and destructive entrepreneurship, but his analysis is on a macro level like Schumpeter's – it is concerned with the economic effects of the behaviour of (individual) entrepreneurs. Further, we have the notion of extreme entrepreneurs (Johannisson and Wigren, 2004) acting in ways that generally challenge institutions and sometimes being criminal. Rehn and Taalas (2004), on the other hand, elaborate mundane entrepreneurship in a dysfunctional setting (the former Soviet Union), and Abdukadirov (2010) argues for terrorism as a dark side of social entrepreneurship. Kets de Vries (1985, 1996) has explicitly addressed the dark side of entrepreneurship from a psychoanalytical perspective, which has been picked up by Shepard and Haynie (2009). Moreover, Beaver and Jennings (2005) discuss the abuse of entrepreneurial power and its consequences, whilst Khan et al., (2007) emphasize the dark side of institutional entrepreneurship, privileging an actor-centred perspective with a limited awareness of the unintended consequences that entrepreneurial endeavours may bring about. Despite these accounts, the dark sides of entrepreneuring are rarely examined (Lockwood et al., 2006).

Considering that the two-sided concept of creative destruction laid the ground for theorizing on entrepreneurship, one side of the coin – destruction – seems to have been lost in mainstream research. Instead, the entrepreneurship discourse keeps flourishing, creating a prospering myth of a creature that does not exist. The effects of the discourse exercise are somehow that what is put in the limelight is not only the entrepreneur, but also 'growth' and 'success' and features whatever bright side we associate with creation, whereas the dark side is downplayed and put aside. Seemingly, the discourse works in a direction in which it continuously and increasingly hails creation, making the connection between entrepreneuring and destructing more and more obsolete. Our argument is that this may have serious consequences. Entrepreneuring need neither be something utterly good nor does it have to be positioned as totally bad. It is 'merely' part of human conduct. As such, there is always good and bad – creation and destruction – in inescapable harmony. When the discourse represses one side, it has consequences for those involved.

These consequences are emphasized by Bill et al. (2010), taking a point of departure in the case of Stein Bagger, a celebrated entrepreneur who even won Ernst & Young's Entrepreneur of the Year award in Denmark. However, on the day of the award ceremony, Bagger was gone, running away from the 'castle in the air' he had built. His company was nothing but a fake. One day the hero, in his glory, while the next he was put in the corner being revealed as a scam. How could Bagger one day be seen as the best of the best of entrepreneurs, and the next be dismissed as an impostor? Bill et al. (2010) give the following explanation:

If almost anyone learning to play the role of an entrepreneur can be perceived as an entrepreneur, even without any tangible artefacts in the world that we perceive as real; and if done well enough, the imagery of success will appear, even though the enterprise evidently is, in a sense 'incomplete' (p. 160).

Bill et al. trace this to the tendency, in academic and public discourses, to emphasize the spectacular aspects of entrepreneurship at the expense of mundane entrepreneuring. Thus, the scope between the spectacular – our fascination with the imaginary, creative and innovative – and the dull and boring dwelling in the mundane is not insignificant. It detaches entrepreneurs from the doing of it: the building, working, staying, writing, hanging around, waiting, and other daily routines inevitable for viable entrepreneuring to proceed. The entrepreneurship discourse seems in its best scenario to produce optimistic visions. Or, to be a little more pessimistic, optical illusions, which inevitably fail unless a connection is created between the spectacular and the mundane.

A similar split emerges if we take a look at how the subject – the entrepreneur – is constructed by media. In a content analysis of a major British broadsheet newspaper by Nicholson and Anderson (2005) a 'rational undercurrent' was found, which discloses a figure that is not always successful, but more like a natural human being. The image of the entrepreneur changes over a period of ten years from entrepreneurs as male dynamic and successful skyrockets to corrupters, which results in two opposite myths. In 1989 the two were much the same, while in 2000 the gap between them has widened. In 2012 it is expected to have widened even more and that the pattern of entrepreneurial action will swing between the building and contradiction of myths. The consequence is that the media only allow either a very dark or a very bright character in the entrepreneur, while real humans do both good and bad things all the time. The point is thus that the social construction of the entrepreneur and of entrepreneurial action will deviate more and more from the 'real' individual (Berglund and Johansson, 2007a).

Hence we propose that the entrepreneurship discourse should be viewed as a discourse of polarization, which is fuelled by, and fuels, the description of present society as a world of massive contradictions. Media is continuously presenting another 'hit list' versus a 'shit list'. The contents of the two lists constantly shifts, but the headlines leave us with a world depicted as either black or white. Still, we live in a society permeated by the idea of individualism, which fosters detachment from people and institutions that provide reassuring rapprochement (Bauman, 2001/2002). Perhaps we have lost the idea of an integrated Self on this trip, resulting in a struggle for polishing the façade by taking up the right professional positions, being seen in the right contexts, getting the proper degrees and buying ourselves a sense of Self through consumption. The triumph of emptiness, as Alvesson (2006) states, seems to lurk behind every corner in a society that is characterized by polarization. This polarization, turning the world and its heroes into 'good and bad', emphasizing the spectacular and downplaying the mundane, has consequences for those we come to call entrepreneurs, but also all of those who relate to entrepreneurs.

Something that in one moment is seen as a creation can in the next be perceived as a destructive fact. Considering the notion of entrepreneurship as destructive creation, entrepreneurs walk the tightrope between being a person who creates and one who destroys. The content of entrepreneurship, as well as the persons we call entrepreneurs, may shift, but the connection between entrepreneurship and creation as part of the progress of society seems inescapably inviolable and unshaken. Some persons are called entrepreneurs and placed on a pedestal. Separating the wheat from the chaff, the entrepreneurs-to-be are picked out. But after moments of fame they are dangerously close to the abyss. As soon as the wind picks up they risk falling down into a deep hole. What is often forgotten is that the entrepreneurship discourse is collectively reconstructed. We all invest in the discourse, not least in this book, addressing entrepreneurship as important. Whether we conduct entrepreneurship research or are involved in entrepreneurial projects such as the Moon House or IKEA, this 'investment' can be made differently, making the move between heaven and hell more or less apparent.

METHODOLOGICAL CONCERNS

Ethnographic, enactive and biographic methods have been used to provide the two cases (see van Maanen, 1988; Johannisson, 2011). The Moon House has been studied since 2002, when the idea was first made public, until today. The process has sometimes been pursued at a distance with occasional contacts, but for two periods (2002–2004 and 2008–2010) the process was followed more closely, during which the researcher (Karin Berglund) had almost daily contacts with key actors. During the last period (2008–2010) she even took part in initiating activity. In particular, two workshops were staged, one with the purpose of developing ideas on the Moon House construction, and the other with the aim of developing plans for concretizing how an innovative idea could be commercialized. Additionally, several student projects and a number of meetings took place where academic, industry and public sector representatives met. These activities involved not only the entrepreneur of the Moon House, but also many other entrepreneurs and artists, as well as people from marketing and advertising agencies, students, researchers, architects, engineers in general, and engineers from the space industry in particular.

The empirical material consists of interviews with key actors that have come and gone in the project, field notes taken during participative observation and during travels with key actors (for example, to NASA) as well as collected printed material about the Moon House. Moreover, the biography *Lunatic: Genberg and the Thousand Musketeers*, written by the journalist Anders Lif (2008), has been used as a source for tracing the history of the artist Mikael Genberg. This means that the empirical material is vast, encompassing dozens of folders with documents, numerous interviews and several books with field notes. In addition to this material the self-reflection of the entrepreneur himself has been valuable for our insight.

The ethnographic process behind the Moon House case is thus based on an almost decade-long participative observation encompassing times of rather passive observation as well as times of enactment (Johannisson, 2011) and highly interactive participatory research. To follow a person and different projects for such a long period of time, undertaking varying research roles, provides space for reflection, which is impossible when a study is built upon interviews (even if they occur in intervals) or normal ethnographic processes lasting a year or so. The longitudinal focus of the Moon House provides us with a unique opportunity to understand the entrepreneurial processes in situ – something that is rare in entrepreneurship research. Furthermore, the extent of the material makes it possible to not only focus on the entrepreneur, which is commonly the case in entrepreneurship research, but also on the actions that are undertaken and the way all actors involved together carry, create and recreate the ideas initiated in the Moon House process.

The IKEA case is based on two biographies about Ingvar Kamprad and a third book about Otto, a Jewish refugee in Sweden, where Kamprad is a subsidiary character. The first book has Kamprad himself as author and story-teller; it was however written down and commented on by Bertil Torekull. It is a book where Kamprad as practitioner reflects on his own life and tells the story of IKEA in his own way. The second book was written by Stenebo (2009), a former employee of IKEA, who painted a critical picture of Kamprad and IKEA. The third, by Åsbrink (2011), is a biography of Otto, who in his childhood was saved from Nazi persecution in Vienna during the Second World War and settled in Southern Sweden and became a personal friend of Kamprad's. Together these three books give a deeper, more nuanced account of Kamprad, as compared to the superficial view of the entrepreneur portrayed in the media.

The two cases – the Moon House and IKEA – thus differ in many ways. Both in terms of how they have been studied and of their stage in the entrepreneurial process (whilst the Moon House one is emerging, IKEA is clearly a success; no matter how much it is talked down in media, Kamprad remains an entrepreneur). However, considering the view of entrepreneurship discourse as polarized, the cases can be seen as complementary, as the effects of this polarization create a difference between the two. While both cases are located in the Swedish context, the Moon House project is contextualized according to contemporary institutionalized understandings of entrepreneurship, that is, embedded in prevailing societal structures where the three sectors (private, public and NPVO) are highly visible. This is complemented by IKEA with its much longer history. This temporal difference motivates a comparison, focusing on the process of becoming an entrepreneur, and how that has changed on account of how this is valued in society. While the Moon House entrepreneur is 'under construction', the IKEA entrepreneur has already been constructed. It would be difficult to question the kingdom built by Kamprad, who seems to have to live with this grandiosity for better or for worse. However, Genberg is not yet 'grandiose', but only promising to become one of the successors of successful entrepreneurs. At this point of time his position as an entrepreneur can however be called into question, and he even runs the risk of being positioned as a scam, as in the case of Bagger (compare Bill et al., 2010). From a contextual perspective (Welter, 2011) the cases are clearly complementary; reminding us that entrepreneuring may not just be a universal state, but also a result of historical and institutional conditions.

Central to the analysis is that both cases are built on stories, and the recognition that stories can be closed or open. It has been argued that entrepreneurial success stories have a tendency to be closed stories (Johansson, 2004). Thus, most entrepreneurial life stories could be expected to be closed. The opposite, an open story, indicates a plot which is unclear and under negotiation, as are the characters within the story. However, in our cases we find the opposite. While the story of the Moon House is in a phase of construction, mechanisms of closing this story according to the mainstream entrepreneurship discourse are at work. On the other hand, the story of IKEA seems to be open, both due to the entrepreneur himself as well as to media efforts in trying to depict a dark side of Kamprad. From the notion of the polarized discourse and the dark and bright sides of entrepreneuring the interpretation may be that Kamprad – put in an utmost position of success – seems to escape it. On the other hand, Genberg is oscillating between success and failure, moving in and out of polarized positions.

THE MOON HOUSE CASE

The House on the Moon project is an attempt at realizing the idea of 'building' a small red house which is to be placed on the surface of the moon and thereby creating a picture which communicates that the impossible is possible if we do it together. Moreover, the picture – or trademark – is also to be capitalized on with the aim of contributing to new projects (adventures), drawing attention to issues that address how we – together – can contribute to a better world. The project is formalized by the non-profit association Friends of the Moon House and the Luna Resort company, but it can above all be seen as an extensive network consisting of numerous activities involving actors from diverse spheres such as politics, business, art, science or technology development.

The inspiration and the birth of the Moon House can be traced years back in time to the artist Mikael Genberg's idea of creating a trilogy of housing projects, in which the House on the Moon makes up the third piece in his installations, the former two being known as the Hotel Woodpecker, a tree house in the city park of Västerås, inaugurated in 1998, which by accident became a hotel. This piece of art was followed by the Otter Inn Hotel in the summer of 2000, which turned into an underwater hotel in Lake Mälaren. The process of the Moon House was officially initiated in 2002 when the local newspaper reported the idea in a four-page coverage. However, a couple of years of thinking about the idea and then a year of intense preparation considering whether and how the idea could be realized preceded this moment.

Altogether, the idea of the house on the moon can be understood as a story told about entrepreneurship in the making, which describes how entrepreneurship is performed in situ. Moreover, Genberg, the artist, is recurrently addressed as the entrepreneur, the one who brought up the idea and from whom many people expect great achievements. While Genberg, being an artist, first and foremost views the images – both mentally as well as those that have been realized in concrete form – and the poetic vision they communicate of 'making something together' – as more important than the materialization of the project.

Nevertheless, the far-fetched idea of 'building' a Moon House has unleashed a great deal of creativity and collective work among a wide range of actors. One example is the informal team of engineers that volunteered to test some of the ideas that were brought up in a workshop gathering actors from various organizational settings – students, researchers, engineers, PR consultants, artists, small-business owners, architects, innovators, designers, politicians, and so forth. Since the house on the moon cannot be built by craftspeople on site, it needs to be transported there in an unpiloted lunar module. As the space of a module is limited, the box containing the house is thought of as comprising approximately six milk cartons with a maximum weight of 5 kilograms (about 11 pounds). The engineering team met in a follow-up workshop in the summer of 2009 and arrived at the conclusion that it would take a great deal of experimental work to move further and decided therefore to meet regularly in order to try out how the house could be 'built'.

This team, together with a number of enthusiastic co-workers from other areas, built for example a house using sailing-cloth in order to measure its weight and to see how it could be fitted into a package of the limited size that had been negotiated with Odyssey Moon, the spacecraft provider. The team also tested if the house could be filled with compressed air, as a first step in examining whether the inflation mechanism could be built, at least partly, by using gas. The engineers, spurred on by the possibility of testing new ideas and stretching the boundaries of their scientific knowledge, were fascinated by the Moon House idea and devoted plenty of time and effort to the creative process. Other examples of collective processes include a number of workshops taking place in the spring of 2008; one of them gathered about 20 people dedicated to developing an idea for how 'moon messages' (sending messages with the house to the moon) could be commercialized. This workshop, which featured finger paint, storyboarding, cutting, pasting, and story-telling, resulted in a concretized idea and a number of possible ways for how to move on. This aroused the interest of one of the big mobile phone and Internet providers to be part of the endeavour in setting up the service.

The artist himself has also made a living of telling about the 'Moon House entrepreneurship' as an inspirational speaker at different events, when being encouraged to tell a story about big plans, grandiose visions, highlighting important people (for instance, one of the pictures is always dedicated to the Swedish astronaut Christer Fuglesang, who is also the No. 1 member of the Friends of the Moon House association), key events (as for instance a castle dinner with powerful people from politics and industry), and international partners (such as NASA). In December 2011 he was even awarded the Speaker's Award at a Venture Cup gala. To be seen as 'the Entrepreneur' thus seems beneficial for the artist, who in the biography *Moonstruck – Genberg and his Thousand Musketeers* reflects on the usefulness of the entrepreneur symbol:

> Entrepreneur is also a good title – it sounds like something that people admire without really knowing what the practice of it is. (Lif, 2008.)

The 'everyday work' involving the togetherness, so much appreciated by the entrepreneur and an obvious ingredient for those involved, is however hardly ever narrated in media, and is also downplayed when the artist delivers the story on stage as the admired entrepreneur with a fantastic tale of entrepreneurship to tell. This, however, does not mean that the entrepreneur tries to break free from his own story-telling. The following episode took place during the opening of the House on the Globe, as illustrated in the prologue to this chapter, when a red house was placed on the spherical national arena The Globe in Stockholm. The week before this event Genberg had been working hard to tell a new story which really included everyone in the story – and the making of the House of the Moon.

About a hundred guests were invited to this opening and were all welcomed with a glass of champagne. The atmosphere created a sense of 'we made it' and people mingled, laughed, ate from the buffet and talked about their devotion and contribution to the project at large and to the house on the Globe in particular. In the middle of the room there was a stage which was entered by Håkan Wåhlstedt, a former mouthpiece of the Green party. As one of the people who have made invaluable efforts to communicate the idea to the political sphere, he was moderator of the day and welcomed everyone to the event of this evening taking place at the Globe arena. However, before the welcome speech, a film started to roll on a large screen behind the stage and a serious voice started the countdown to launching. The sequence was taken from the adventurous Apollo 13 launch in 1970. After that, another film took over – following how the small red metal house was placed on the top of the Globe. All people on the ground were made visible, the constructors of the house, the climbers who had arranged the points of attachment for the house, the management of the Globe, the students from the local university who had contributed in making workshops and many, many more, in other words, all of those who, according to Genberg, have made the idea possible. This was the central message in Genberg's talk, which followed the welcoming from Wåhlstedt after the two movies. Consequently, the old PowerPoint presentation was replaced with a new one in which a number of pictures were added which presented many of the people who had contributed to the project. Genberg concluded his speech with the words 'this is above all a project for people and about people – people who together contribute to something bigger'.

The next speaker was the chairman of the Friends of the Moon House. He was also the former minister of finance in Sweden. As he entered the stage he could not have contradicted the previous story more obviously. However, it seemed that no one noticed. Numerous adjectives were used by the chairman to describe this fantastic entrepreneur, one of the few that Sweden really needed – a man with great ideas, an idea that could even take the rest of us to the moon. The next speaker to enter the stage was the Stockholm commissioner of culture. She continued to applaud this marvellous entrepreneur. How lucky we were to have him there! And so it went on. The story of togetherness literally fell into pieces. Left on the pedestal was the entrepreneur – alone, 'fantastic', 'marvellous' and lots of other things. But, was he together with anyone else? In reality – yes indeed. But in the story told about the entrepreneur? Not at all.

Hence, the story of 'grandiosity', big plans and visions does not give room for the everyday practice (sometimes dull, but often fun), which in some respects has made the project dysfunctional, since it gives a confusing picture of 'what is really going on' and 'who is part of it'. Realizing this, the entrepreneur is trying to break with the story of the grandiose entrepreneur. But breaking out is obviously difficult since the surrounding context relates to the 'grandiose entrepreneur', re-constructing the importance of 'grandiose vision', neglecting the hard work it takes to realize an idea which comprises the involvement, dedication and hard work of many people.

In retrospect the Globe inauguration can be seen as one in a series of spectacular events in the Moon House history involving castle dinners with the county governor, NASA visits, journalists, television teams reporting on the Moon House, and meetings with politicians and renowned industry people and space engineers. However, there is also the everydayness consisting of meetings about how to make the spectacular happen: creating invitations, arranging scenes, enrolling sponsors, sending emails, posting Moon House members' letters, printing new Moon House friends' cards and updating the member register. Moreover, the mundane activity of creating solutions for – actually – being able to send an inflatable red house by a lunar module to the moon, where it can unfold due to some (not yet known) mechanism, makes up a vital, yet often silent part, of the project.

At the moment it is not clear what the next step in the process will be. The space industry in the US struggles with budget cuts, trying to allocate resources for maintaining the investment in space research and development by entering the commercial road. One of the engineers, heavily involved in the Moon House, has started a new company within this field of 'commercializing space', and more actors are still waiting to take the next step. However, they all seem to await the response from the entrepreneur, the person who remains the owner of the Moon House, symbolically (as the artist that has introduced the idea, painting and making sculptures, the Moon House remains his individual hallmark) as well as formally (he is still the only owner of Luna Resort Ltd).

Hence, from the position of the ethnographer, it is obvious how the social setting constructs the solitary entrepreneur. Since the entrepreneur (sometimes also referred to as the artist) simultaneously communicates the importance of relationships – or 'togetherness' – it becomes a process full of contradictions. The 'heroic' story of the Moon House is continuously narrated and pictured in magazines, emphasizing Genberg as a role model with new innovative ideas that this society is in need of. In the mundane this story is not beneficial; instead it has been made up by obstacles in the mobilization of actors, resources and new efforts in moving the house closer to the surface of the moon and dreams of endless opportunities to come true.

THE IKEA CASE

Next, let us take a look at IKEA and especially at its founder, Ingvar Kamprad. He was only 17 years old when he started IKEA as a mail order business. The first IKEA catalogue was distributed in 1951 and flat packages started in 1955. In spite of fierce competition from the furniture industry in Sweden he successfully developed the company, opening the first store in Stockholm in 1965. From the 1980s onward IKEA has expanded into international markets. Ever since the 1990s social and environmental concern has been a conscious part of the business strategy, which has been further developed in the new millennium. In 2010 IKEA had 313 stores in 37 countries. IKEA has created a unique interior design concept which has permeated Swedish society and been successfully marketed throughout the world. In 2004 a Swedish newspaper proclaimed him the richest man in the world, richer than Bill Gates. While he probably no longer is that, few would deny that he is a really successful entrepreneur.

In the middle of the 1990s a Swedish journalist found out that Ingvar Kamprad had been involved in Swedish pro-Nazi movements in his younger years. A big media hunt followed. Kamprad was, however, quite successful in handling this 'personal failure'. He admitted his mistake in a quite articulate way. This seems to be a main reason why the book, *The History of IKEA* (Kamprad, 2006) was written together with Bertil Torekull. Kamprad's 'confessions' about his past pro-Nazi sympathies are elaborated on rather than silenced. In Kamprad's own words, they are confessed as being the 'sins of youth'.

The History of IKEA has been viewed as a potboiler and has also been criticized for being too Kamprad-friendly. In 2009 a new book about IKEA was published, written by the former employee Johan Stenebo (*The Truth about IKEA*). Johan Stenebo wrote this book when he had left IKEA after 20 years in the company. The surface message of this book is to reveal the truth about IKEA, beneath layers of frontage. Stenebo argues, for example, that what is portrayed as personal weaknesses in

Ingvar Kamprad (alcoholism, word blindness and so on) constitutes an intentionally made up image which highly exaggerates the real situation. The intention, according to Stenebo, is to produce an image of an ordinary man, which will serve the purpose of managing the company and earning more money for himself.

Interestingly, while these two books can be described as contrasting pictures of Ingvar Kamprad, they definitely share certain similarities. The 'propaganda' book paints the picture of a very complex person, and so does Stenebo's book. Besides, the supposedly critical author cannot deliver his 'dark' story about Kamprad without revealing his fascination and admiration for Kamprad as a very capable entrepreneur. We think that a really insightful passage is articulated by Kamprad himself in *The History of IKEA* when he reflects on what happens when someone who starts a family firm with his own family and close friends as co-labourers finds himself running a big company:

> No matter how close you might think you are to people around you, in practice there is a distance. I was and am sitting in double hell, as I have both power and money. Even my CEO is much better off – he 'only' has power but on that top, too, the winds are icy. For sure, many of my other collaborators in the company would be ready to stand up for me and help me in an emergency situation. That has been proven. But from there, that they would dare to be completely open and frankly criticise me – 'How the heck can you do things this way?' – is a long way to take. With my authority I have been permitted to say a lot of stupidities without anyone reacting. I think this is the curse of leadership: people take care. Even when you invite them to be outspoken there is stratification in the selection – you choose people you expect something certain from, it can't be totally honest, not totally objective. (Translated from Kamprad, 2006, pp. 115–116.)

Kamprad's own words illustrate the other side of the coin of being a successful entrepreneur. As a person as well as being the leader of a big company you need closeness to and honesty from the people you work with. Success as an entrepreneur is what makes closeness and honesty impossible, not in a total sense, but success creates the distance which works against closeness and honesty.

In 2011 the journalist Elisabeth Åsbrink published a book about the Jewish boy Otto, who belonged to a group of 60 children that were given permission to leave Nazified Vienna in 1939 for Sweden. A few years later Otto came to the Kamprad family in Småland as a worker on their farm. Ingvar Kamprad and Otto, who were of the same age, became very close friends and Otto was later employed by IKEA in its infancy. Even if Ingvar Kamprad is a minor character in the book, Åsbrink provides information about his father and grandmother who were warm support-ers of the Nazis as well as describing Kamprad's own involvement with the Swedish Nazi movement. Åsbrink also portrays him as a close friend to one of the leading Swedish fascists, Per Engdahl. She asks the question how it can be possible to appreciate the ideas of Engdahl and still being a close friend of someone who has faced the consequences of some of these ideas. Ingvar Kamprad's own answer to this question in the book is that he sees no contradiction in these relationships. He has admitted his mistakes when it comes to Nazi philosophy, but maintains that he respects the personal qualities of Per Engdahl. While Åsbrink's book provides more details about Kamprad and his involvement with the Nazi movement in the past, the question we ask is whether Kamprad would at all have been a side character in this book, had he not been the founder of IKEA and had this company not had the success it has had. The grandiose side of the entrepreneurship discourse seems to call for the opposite side; that of not allowing the person to have friends whose values can be questioned.

While the story about IKEA as a company is so far a ceaseless success story, these three books have in common that they deal with some of the dark sides of the entrepreneuring process and of the entrepreneur himself. Great success as an entrepreneur brings with it an interest in the person behind and delimits the agency of the entrepreneur and those around him. What stands out is that Kamprad has acted by giving response to the dark sides that he has been confronted with.

THE BRIGHT AND DARK EFFECTS POLARIZING THE ENTREPRENEUR AND ENTREPRENEURING

A prominent feature of the polarizing entrepreneurship discourse is the idea of (constant) success, produced by a mythical entrepreneur. This is made visible, both in the Moon House and in the IKEA case, by enrolling the entrepreneurs in contemporary tales of successful entrepreneurship. However, the discourse creates different effects in the two cases. Following the story-making in – and of – the Moon House it is clear that the entrepreneur is struggling to gain the entrepreneurial position, which has consequences for the 'togetherness' and actions that form the ideal asked for. The episode from the Globe mingle illustrates how the artist Mikael Genberg is socially constructed as the mythical entrepreneur by the people around him. It is actually not only this episode, since he has been recognized as the 'grand entrepreneur' by other means, not least in magazines and through media coverage all around the world. In contrast, Kamprad seems to invite, rather than refuse, the accusations and smearing, elaborating and reflecting upon how the dark sides have been – and still may be – part of his and IKEA's life. While the Moon House case illustrates entrepreneuring that seems to show off the bright sides recreating the successful entrepreneur, the IKEA case indicates efforts to invite the dark sides, destabilizing the discourse. Now let us scrutinize this from the notion of the polarized entrepreneurship discourse.

Following the Moon House it is clear that this third piece in the trilogy of housing is much more demanding considering the time and people involved, which requires cooperation in other ways than asking for a favour. However, being put on the pedestal as the mythical entrepreneur makes it hard to ask people for favours, not to mention to go into prolonged cooperation, as the mythical figure brings with him the idea of being the one who does everything for himself. Symbolically, as well as legally, the artist has become equated with his work, a pattern that locks the entrepreneur in a destructive circle as the enterprising entrepreneur who is expected to do everything and who gains control, but who also needs other people to cooperate with who must be given scope of action. Thus, the entrepreneur continues to be in charge, but since this leadership is not exercised, actors remain at a distance. This has led to some actors initiating their own endeavours. Even if some of them touch upon the Moon House idea, these are new ideas, standing on their own, yet gaining interest within the space industry. How this is compatible with the efforts of mobilizing the Moon House is too soon to tell. Interestingly, the story told about the Moon House endeavour is a story of togetherness, which has enrolled numerous actors. But since they never received an equal part in the project their enterprising efforts are turned in other directions. So while Genberg continues to live up to the story of the 'mythical' entrepreneur, which casts him in polarized positions, entrepreneuring in terms of collective efforts is stifled. This resembles the discussion of the disconnection of the spectacular and the mundane, which has consequences for making the project viable while being on the move.

So, success is yet unclear in the Moon House case. While two endeavours have been successfully completed, the third is in progress or emerging. The Moon House, so far, seems to rest on the success of the spectacular event, attracting powerful people, which in turn gains attention in media, and thus legitimization. No one seems to ask what is really done in the project. Rather than acknowledging the hard work of inventing new materials, methods and ways of solving the problem of constructing a house, so that it can be placed at the surface of the moon (which has never been done hitherto), the enthusiasm calls for more of the spectacular. The entrepreneur and 'his musketeers' (see the title of Anders Lif's book about Genberg) continue to deliver what is asked for, namely spectacular events. However, everyday work is lagging behind. As in the case of Bagger (Bill et al., 2010), the spectacular is disconnected from the mundane everyday meetings, mail writing, coffee-making, sketching, problem-solving, material search, all the activities that get the project going in the first place. These activities are rarely stressed as important, even though attempts have been made to initiate voluntary workshops to find solutions for the construction of the Moon House. Hence, it is not this activity that has given legitimacy and attraction to the project in the first place. Consequently, in order to gain attention as an entrepreneurial project in contemporary society – attracting the necessary people (remember, placing a house on the moon is not a one-person job) entrepreneuring in the Moon House that can bring in the resources needed, disconnects the mundane in its search for the spectacular. Unfortunately, this kind of disconnection is counterproductive, since the routines and hard work – the mundane part of entrepreneuring – are suppressed into a state of non-existence. So, while as an entrepreneur Genberg symbolically portrays the spectacular, the efforts of recognizing and valuing the mundane are diminished. The spectacular is what is asked for, which leaves the mundane – and simultaneously the actors involved, entrepreneuring and 'togetherness' in the shadow.

A closer look at the history of Ingvar Kamprad, the founder of IKEA, makes it clear that success has been accompanied by mistakes and failures over the years. There have been several destructive elements, among them the discussion about Nazi involvement and alcoholism. These are also disclosed in the biographies of Ingvar Kamprad. However, today IKEA is described as one of the successful entrepreneurship stories, making Kamprad one of the grand entrepreneurs of our time. Becoming such a famous and mythical entrepreneur seems nevertheless to have a reverse side, as told by the entrepreneur himself. People suddenly start to relate to him, as the 'God-similar creature' that the discourse depicts. Kamprad becomes locked in a position where he has a hard time to meet opposition from which his ideas can be developed, which is neither desired by the entrepreneur nor is good for the development of the business. The books about Ingvar Kamprad also correspond to the two contradicting myths discussed by Nicholson and Anderson (2005) which separate the entrepreneur into, on the one hand, a God-similar creature and, on the other hand, a villain. There is one picture of Kamprad in the media as a very successful entrepreneur and another picture of the mistakes and personal characteristics that are put into question; one bright and one dark side of the entrepreneur. While the complex character of an ordinary human being is no surprise, the entrepreneurship discourse cannot tolerate this complexity. This means that the pictures are separated in the media, one day reporting the bright, and the other the dark sides. Hence, the very success of Kamprad could be understood as creating a demand for the dark side and the 'undercurrent' that Nicholson and Anderson write about. Once a dark side has been detected the two separate stories are told, but not at the same time. In the media, the bright and dark do not meet. In our interpretation of the books by and about Kamprad, we see efforts to combine the two sides in a coherent story that integrates the dark and bright sides of the entrepreneur.

While the spectacular is part of IKEA, in the company's performance at the global market, in its rewarding marketing, and the continuous improvements and inventions in furnishing, even inviting people to launch Facebook groups such as 'seek and hide at IKEA', the mundane is part of all this action. Shopping for a new chair, perhaps making a bargain of some product we suddenly realize that we must have, asking the personnel for a delivery receipt, having a hot dog afterwards, or taking part of the new catalogue; the mundane and the spectacular are both part of the story. We may create spectacular new homes, but carrying the boxes home, mounting the new piece of furniture, and having to go to the recycling centre with the empty boxes, are definitely not part of the spectacular. It is rather the mundane that integrates with the spectacular.

Summing up, the presence of a dark side of entrepreneuring is nurtured by the polarized entrepreneurship discourse. However, the discourse has different effects. In the case of the Moon House – a case of nascent entrepreneurship – the polarization results in continuous efforts to fixate the entrepreneur; disconnecting the entrepreneur from the collective efforts of entrepreneuring. Moreover, it disconnects and diminishes mundane entrepreneuring from the continuous investments in spectacular events. On the contrary, in the case of IKEA, Kamprad acknowledges the dark sides, both in response to the media and in the way they are reflected on by himself in the biography, which can be seen as efforts to admit and reconcile oneself with being neither a mythical God-similar creature nor a villain, but only a person that has been part of a great adventure. With respect to entrepreneuring, the mundane (in this case interpreted as all the routines that contribute to the organization of IKEA) and the spectacular are integrated, since we all become part of reconstructing IKEA as a successful venture.

THE PROSPECTS OF SOCIETAL ENTREPRENEURSHIP

In this chapter we have presented the entrepreneurship discourse as a polarized discourse. From discussing the polarized discourse in relation to the two cases, the Moon House and IKEA, some down sides of success and how they affect individuals and collectives in entrepreneuring endeavours have been illustrated. We can now pose the question of the relevance to societal entrepreneurship.

With the view of entrepreneurship as a discourse, 'societal entrepreneurship' cannot be seen as something completely new, but remains part of the entrepreneurship discourse, despite attempts (along with other prefixes, such as social, environmental, sustainable) to bring in counter-discourses. Thus, adding the prefix 'societal' can be perceived as a language game, with the potential of pointing towards enterprising practices that have hitherto been neglected by the entrepreneurship discourse, and also stimulating new entrepreneurial initiatives to be taken. If these practices counteract the tendency of the polarized entrepreneurship discourse to make even bigger leaps between 'heaven and hell', it cannot be proved by these two cases, but it remains a question to be addressed. However, if the polarization increases, we can expect entrepreneuring – no matter what prefix – to be scattered all over the place, leaving fragments of societal entrepreneurship, followed by disenchantment.

Paradoxically then, we live in a society which calls for entrepreneurship in each and every corner, fostering a discourse that seeks to promote entrepreneurship. However, this discourse is counterproductive in terms of creating sustainable conditions for societal entrepreneuring to unfold. While the entrepreneur remains on a pedestal (with the risk of falling down), mundane routinized activity-making processes may appear as trivial to the benefit of occasional spectacular events. This points towards the importance of integration, breaking with a traditional entrepreneurship discourse and its connotation of the mythical entrepreneur and the view of success. However, considering that the discourse is built on the idea of the enterprising human being, entrepreneuring may become completely incomprehensible, unless the entrepreneur remains included in the story. Instead of diminishing the agency of individuals, what is urged for here is the continuous need to reflect on how 'strong agency' is depicted. Just as there are many entrepreneurs playing vital parts in an entrepreneurial process, 'the entrepreneur' may still have an important symbolic role in order to communicate emerging entrepreneurial projects.

From this reasoning, societal entrepreneurship can be viewed as the kind of entrepreneuring that acknowledges the bright and dark sides of entrepreneurship, emphasizing the collective actions taken, resisting from pointing out one person as 'the entrepreneur' and working in the 'shadow' from spectacular events, yet getting attention for its efforts to create sustaining values. This can be seen in Chapter 6 by Schwartz about how the fair-trade entrepreneur struggles with what is bright and dark in different contexts. It is also discerned in the Macken entrepreneur's efforts to decentralize himself from the routines taking form, as illustrated in Chapter 3.

Finally, we permit ourselves a reflection on the prospects of the concept of societal entrepreneurship to transform the contemporary entrepreneurship discourse.

As human beings we not only buy furniture – furniture being part of how we create our homes. IKEA seems to be interacting with its customers from that perspective, which means taking part in how people create their homes, thus transgressing the traditional borders for customer interaction. As human beings we also relate to society at large. IKEA interacts with several NPVO organizations related to the social initiatives which not only aim to create our homes but also to create a better society. In this way IKEA enacts societal entrepreneurship and seems to combine commercial with non-commercial considerations in a way that strengthens both. The Moon House (with or without furniture from IKEA) is transgressing our preunderstanding of human life, indicating new possibilities for homes and humankind. In this way societal entrepreneurship transforms the kind of actions associated with the contemporary entrepreneurship discourse. But does that mean that societal entrepreneurship will not tend to be polarized? The Moon House case would rather suggest the opposite. The IKEA case, on the other hand, points to possible ways of dissolving the polarization by bringing the dark and bright sides together. Thus we argue for a concept – societal entrepreneurship – that acknowledges both the bright and dark sides of entrepreneuring, positioning it as human conduct – nothing more, nothing less.

REFERENCES

Abdukadirov, S. (2010), 'Terrorism: the dark side of social entrepreneurship', *Studies in Conflict & Terrorism*, 33: 603–617.

Ahl, H.J. (2004), *The Scientific Reproduction of Gender Inequality: A Discourse Analysis of Research Texts on Women's Entrepreneurship*, Stockholm: Liber.

Alvesson, M. (2006), *Tomhetens triumf: om grandiositet, illusionsnummer & noll-summespel*, Malmö: Liber.

Barringer, B.R. and R.D. Ireland (2006), *Entrepreneurship: Successfully Launching New Ventures*, Upper Saddle River, NJ: Pearson Prentice Hall.

Bauman, Z. (2001/2002), *Det individualiserade samhället*, Göteborg: Daidalos.

Baumol, W. (1990), 'Entrepreneurship: productive, unproductive, and destructive', *Journal of Political Economy*, **98** (5): 893–921.

Beaver, G. and P. Jennings (2005), 'Competitive advantage and entrepreneurial power: The dark side of entrepreneurship', *Journal of Small Business and Enterprise Development*, **12** (1): 9–23.

Berglund, K. and A.W. Johansson (2007a), 'The entrepreneurship discourse – outlined from diverse constructions of entrepreneurship on the academic scene',

Journal of Enterprising Communities: People and Places in the Global Economy, **1** (1): 77–102.

Berglund, K. and A.W. Johansson (2007b), 'Entrepreneurship, discourses and conscientization in processes of regional development', *Entrepreneurship and Regional Development*, **19** (6): 499–525.

Bill, F., A. Jansson and L. Olaison (2010), 'A duality of flamboyance and activity', in F. Bill, B. Bjerke and A.W. Johansson (eds) *(De)mobilizing Entrepreneurship – Exploring Entrepreneurial Thinking and Action*, Cheltenham, UK and Northampton, MA, USA: Edward Elgar Publishing.

Dahlvig, A. (2012), *The IKEA Edge: Building Global Growth and Social Good at the World's Most Iconic Home Store*, New York: McGraw-Hill.

Henreksson, M. and M. Stenkula (2007), *Entreprenörskap*, Stockholm: SNS förlag.

Johannisson, B. (2011), 'Towards a practice theory of entrepreneuring', *Small Business Economics*, 36: 135–150.

Johannisson, B. and C. Wigren (2004), 'Extreme entrepreneurs – challenging the institutional framework', in P.R. Christensen and F. Poulfeldt (eds), *Managing Complexity and Change in SMEs: Frontiers in European Research*, Cheltenham:, UK and Northampton, MA, USA Edward Elgar Publishing.

Johansson, A.W. (2004), 'Consulting as story-making', *Journal of Management Development*, **23** (4): 339–354.

Jones, C. and A. Spicer (2005), 'The sublime object of entrepreneurship', *Organization*, **12** (2): 223–246.

Kamprad, I. (2006), *Historien om IEKA. Ingvar Kamprad berättar för Bertil Torekull*, Stockholm: Wahlstrand & Widstrand.

Kets De Vries, M.F.R. (1985), 'The dark side of entrepreneurship', *Harvard Business Review*, **63** (6): 160–167.

Kets De Vries, M.F.R. (1996). 'The anatomy of the entrepreneur: Clinical observations', *Human Relations*, **4** (7): 853–884.

Khan, F.R., K.A. Munir and H. Willmott (2007), 'A dark side of institutional entrepreneurship: Soccer balls, child labour and postcolonial impoverishment', *Organization Studies*, **28** (7): 1055–1077.

Lif, A. (2008). *Mångalen: Genberg och de tusen musketörerna*, Sportförlaget, Västerås.

Lindgren, M. and J. Packendorff (2003), 'A project-based view of entrepreneurship: Towards action-orientation, seriality and collectivity', in: C. Steyaert and D. Hjorth (eds), *New Movements in Entrepreneurship*, Cheltenham, UK and Northampton, MA, USA, Edward Elgar Publishing, pp. 86–102.

Lockwood, F.S., R.T. Teasley, J.C. Carland and J.W. Carland (2006), 'An examination of the power of the dark side of entrepreneurship', *International Journal of Family Business*, 3: 1–20.

Nicholson L. and A.R. Anderson (2005), 'News and nuances of the entrepreneurial myth and metaphor: Linguistic games in entrepreneurial sense-making and sense-giving', *Entrepreneurship Theory and Practice*, **29** (2): 153–172.

Ogbor, J.O. (2000), 'Mythicizing and reification in entrepreneurial discourse: Ideology-critique of entrepreneurial studies', *Journal of Management Studies*, **37** (5): 605–635.

Rehn, A. and S. Taalas (2004), '"Znakomstva I Svyazi" (Acquaintances and connections) – Blat, The Soviet Union, and mundane entrepreneurship', *Entrepreneurship & Regional Development*, **16** (3): 235–250.

Schumpeter, J. (1934), *The Theory of Economic Development: An inquiry into profits, capital, credit, interest, and the business cycle* (transl. by Redvers Opie), Cambridge, MA: Harvard University Press.

Schumpeter, J. (1939), *Business Cycles*, New York Toronto London: McGraw-Hill Book Company.

Schumpeter, J. (1942), *Capitalism, Socialism and Democracy*, New York: Harper Publishing.

Shane, S. and S. Venkataraman (2000), 'The promise of entrepreneurship as a field of research', *Academy of Management Review*, **25** (1): 217–226.

Shepard, D. and M. Haynie (2009), 'Birds of a feather don't always flock together: Identity management in entrepreneurship', *Journal of Business Venturing*, 24: 316–337.

Stenebo, J. (2009), *Sanningen om IKEA*, Västerås: IKEA bokförlag.

Steyaert, C. (2007), '"Entrepreneuring" as a conceptual attractor? A review of process theories in 20 years of entrepreneurship studies', *Entrepreneurship and Regional Development*, **19** (6): 453–477.

Van Maanen, J. (1988), *Tales of the Field: On Writing Ethnography*, Chicago and London: University of Chicago Press.

Welter, F. (2011), 'Contextualizing entrepreneurship – conceptual challenges and ways forward', *Entrepreneurship Theory and Practice*, **35** (1): 165–184.

Åsbrink, E. (2011), *Och i Wienerwald står träden kvar*, 1. uppl. Stockholm: Natur & kultur.

PART III

Promoting societal entrepreneurship – an educational perspective

The third theme – *Promoting societal entrepreneurship – an educational perspective* – puts societal entrepreneurship in a learning perspective. Employing *promoting* as a key concept this theme seeks to address how societal entrepreneurship can be endorsed in society. The notion of learning usually relates to the educational system. With an increasingly overloaded agenda the educational setting makes up a key target for new topics being addressed. Information technology, sustainability and internationalization are just a few of the many 'concepts' that have been put forward. It is also the case for entrepreneurship, which nevertheless was included in the national curriculum for daycare centres, preschool and nine-year compulsory school in 2010. This can be seen as a result of a twenty-year-long process, which has oscillated between practice and policy, but had the effect that entrepreneurship now constitutes an unquestionable issue on the educational agenda in Sweden. Thus, as integrated in the curriculum entrepreneurship appears to have become more than a fly-by-night.

In the upcoming chapters we are introduced to how entrepreneurship has gained a position within the world of school, and how this emerging process can, strikingly, be perceived as societal entrepreneurship in the sense that it has invited cooperation between sectors. Furthermore, entrepreneurship education, as translated among teachers, goes in line with the conceptualization of 'societal entrepreneurship', as described in Chapter 1 by Berglund and Johannisson, depicting a kind of learning that mobilizes initiatives (among students and teachers), provides an innovative (pedagogic) force, and channels a value-creation power by way of inviting children, pupils, students and teachers to view themselves in a process of becoming societal entrepreneurs.

In the first contribution to this section, *Friends, feelings, and fantasy: the entrepreneurial approach as conceptualized by preschool teachers*, Karin Berglund reports how entrepreneurship has been made sense of in a preschool setting. By following the preschool teachers' meaning-making of what is addressed as 'an entrepreneurial approach' relational aspects of entrepreneurship are highlighted. Three relational features are especially emphasized: *Making friends* with yourself and others, *listening to one's feelings* and translating them into deliberated choices, and *using one's imagination*, not to escape the world, but to bring something better back to it. These relational aspects are proposed in analogy with 'glue', without which it may be difficult for entrepreneurial processes – for whatever purpose – to sustain. Hence, the preschool teachers' conceptualization of the entrepreneurial approach invites to relating to entrepreneurship in new ways, thinking new thoughts of how it is conducted and widening our perspective of how it can be socialized.

This means that the entrepreneurial approach is a broad concept used in everyday life in general, and in the world of schools in particular. It is brought in to perceive that entrepreneurship is 'here and now', rather than describing how (and how many) companies are started and developed. Accordingly, the entrepreneurial approach concept is part of all kinds of entrepreneuring, but may be more fruitful to apply in settings where entrepreneurship – in accordance with the business discourse – may be strange, or even awkward, to address. The point made in this chapter is that societal entrepreneuring is promoted in relations. Considering the relational aspects not only children but also adults turn into novices. While adults may be good role models, supporting development processes and inviting children to be part of constructing something meaningful in a familiar context, the situation is also the reverse, because children are a vital part of this relationship, contributing to opening the eyes of adults by pointing towards important questions, making visible possibilities and solutions which open up for how societal entrepreneurship can be enacted – here and now as well as in the future.

In the next chapter, *Translating entrepreneurship into the education setting – a case of societal entrepreneurship*, Carina Holmgren sketches the overall picture of how entrepreneurship has become an increasingly important topic with regard to policy. This political interest in entrepreneurship with accompanying funding has contributed to an expansion of external actors who, with different projects, concepts, tools and methods have positioned themselves within the entrepreneurial discourse for the purpose of developing education in primary and secondary schools. In this chapter the introduction of entrepreneurship into the educational system is discussed as a process of translation. Seeking to grasp the complexity of this process, discursive struggles of teachers' difficulties with – and resistance towards – the concept of entrepreneurship are examined. Furthermore, the governing dimension, in terms of the external actors' attempts to involve teachers in the translation process is analysed. The process of translating entrepreneurship education to the educational setting has thus involved all three sectors: the public sector, the domicile of schools in Sweden; the private, with influential actors that have different entrepreneurship learning models to offer; and also the NPVO sector, where fiery souls have organized, engaged to transform pedagogy and having found that entrepreneurship opens up for new possibilities to do so.

Hence, the conclusion drawn in this chapter is that the translation process can been seen as an expression of enacting societal entrepreneurship as it crosses over sectorial boundaries – in attempts by teachers, actors from the private sector and enthusiasts in the NPVO sector to solve societal problems by way of introducing entrepreneurship education. While the struggles are proposed as a way to fight for pedagogic development, the mainstream economic entrepreneurship discourse has been transformed in this process. This means that, in many cases, entrepreneurship education goes in line with the ideas of an entrepreneurial approach as presented in the first chapter of this part of the book.

The first chapter addresses the preschool setting, the second the primary and upper secondary school, while the last chapter emphasizes how to perceive of societal entrepreneurship at university and at a Folk High School. In this last contribution, *Academic and non-academic education for societal entrepreneurship*, Anders W Johansson and Erik Rosell discuss two cases of entrepreneurship education. While the first case, the EBD program, stems from an academic context, the other is an example of collaboration between a non-profit organization (the SIP Network) and a local Folk High School. The two education programs share the belief that entrepreneurial abilities are important for creating something new and changing old structures, regardless whether it is about starting a business or working with a publicly funded project in the non-profit or the public sector. The complexity in such processes, where all kinds of actors encounter different purposes, implies, however, that economic rationalities and social objectives have to be worked out simultaneously. As is illustrated, there are several similarities between the academic EBD program and the Folk High School education program. But there are also differences, which can be related to the different sector logics discussed in the introductory chapter. Moreover, the SIP Network appears to be a genuinely social space in which an entrepreneurial approach is promoted among students, focusing on personal development and encouraging action orientation. As a contrast, the academic program puts an emphasis on conscious reflection, which makes it difficult to pursue action and personal development in the way that it is done in the SIP Network. Still, the ideal of promoting an entrepreneurial approach among its students is nevertheless appreciated and visible in both programs.

Both of these education programs are in line with the examples given in the two previous chapters, in the sense that entrepreneurship has been translated into a progressive pedagogy, rather than being prescribed as a means towards profit (for individuals) and creating economic growth (for society). Common to all chapters is the ambition to encourage students' creativity, power of initiative and ability to reflect upon their situation in contemporary society. While the entrepreneurial approach is exclusively mentioned in preschool and the lower grades, entrepreneurship appears as a way of learning how to initiate a new organization in upper secondary school. Nevertheless, considering the view of entrepreneurial approach as glue, it remains a vital part whenever entrepreneurship is addressed in the educational context.

Following the reasoning on societal entrepreneurship in this chapter, the notion of promoting moves beyond education as a practice, instead emphasizing the learning processes of being part of introducing entrepreneurship (in many different ways) in the educational setting. This stresses the importance of processes that work against specialization and differentiation, separating sectors and actors from each other and thus making it difficult for common life spheres to emerge that cross boundaries and traditional subdivisions where each sector is permeated by its own rules, practices and language. Promoting societal entrepreneurship may therefore be better described as a process where actors from different sectors act together to create a common language that lays the ground for a sphere that is created in between the three sectors. Moreover, from both Chapters 9 and 10 we learn that this process is not as harmonious as it seems at first sight, but involves struggling with opposition and finding ways to break through resistance. Thus, entrepreneuring within the educational system unfolds the many facets of societal entrepreneurship.

8. Friends, feelings, and fantasy: the entrepreneurial approach as conceptualized by preschool teachers

Karin Berglund

PROLOGUE

Walking in the garden centre, looking for flowers to plant in early spring, I received a phone call from my ten-year-old daughter Tove:

> 'Hi mom, we have a new business idea! So . . . I wonder if I can take care of people's pets when they are on holiday.'
>
> 'Ok?', I answered but did not get the time to formulate a question as she went on explaining the set-up of their new organization.
>
> 'You see, Lollo will take care of dogs, Klara of bunny rabbits, and I will take care of the rest of the pets.'
>
> 'Hm, what will you do if someone brings a snake', I then asked her (knowing that she was not that fond of snakes).
>
> 'Well, I don't need to touch it, do I! I just have to give it food. Please, please, please, mom! We are just about to go to ICA (the local grocery store) and "Plantagen" (the local garden centre) to put up notes with information on who to contact and all that is needed.'
>
> 'Well it's ok with me', I answered (who wanted to support their creativity and power of initiative), 'but you better check with you dad first'.

As her father rejected the idea (considering the responsibility it would mean to take care of someone's pet – in case it ran away or went sick) she called me again (obviously both down and dejected) saying that there is no idea to do *anything at all* in this world. Half an hour later the sudden blues were completely vanished; Tove now adjusting to the new circumstances. Accordingly, she would take care of people's plants instead. Because if a plant died was not considered to be the same disaster as if a dog should pass away.

INTRODUCTION

So, why did I start this chapter with this story? Well, the moral is that this story has something to say about an entrepreneurial approach, which is being increasingly emphasized in policy texts as important to create conditions for throughout the Swedish school system. In the fall of 2010 'the entrepreneurial approach' even reached its way into the national curriculum for daycare centres, preschools and nine-year compulsory schools (Curriculum, 2010). This stems from a process going on for two decades, during which there has been an increasingly strong emphasis on the need of integrating entrepreneurship in the Swedish school system. Consequently, this has challenged teachers to find their ways of relating to entrepreneurship, a concept that has travelled from the private sector to the school system, an institution that is financed and controlled by the state and therefore constitutes a public sector. In this process, the entre-preneurial approach has grown strong as a concept that resonates with teachers seeking out new ways to relate to pedagogy, to students, to the surrounding community, and also to themselves. Likewise, an entrepre-neurial approach addresses, for both students and teachers, how to relate to themselves as creative, curious, initiative, and becoming human beings.

While the new curriculum primarily addresses entrepreneurship in primary and upper secondary school, this chapter presents a study from a preschool context in which it is argued that preschool pedagogy in par-ticularly highlights the entrepreneurial approach. A translation will be made of the meaning ascribed to the entrepreneurial approach by preschool teachers from the philosophical reasoning of becoming (for example Chia, 1995), which in entrepreneurship studies has been proposed to address the verb 'entrepreneuring' (Steyaert, 2007). The 'entrepreneurial approach' is thus related to as an empirical concept, which is further expounded from the theoretical framework of entrepreneuring. Vice versa, encountering preschool pedagogues, with their often implicit view of children as part of a process in which they become – or remain, as Johannisson (2010) proposes – thinking, learning, and creative human beings, insights can be made into how entrepreneuring is enacted. Not only in preschool, but also in wider society.

The preschool teachers encountered in this chapter suggest that they learn so much from their entrepreneurial children. This motivates elabor-ating on the lessons learned from children, since they may very well have a great impact on adults who are interested in exploring their entrepre-neurial selves (Achtenhagen and Johannisson, 2013). However, while the entrepreneurial approach infiltrates social life as a 'natural' way of becoming in the context of preschools, reading a book (addressed to preschool teachers) made it easier to defamiliarize myself from a culture I am very much part of and thus apprehend 'the entrepreneurial'. The lessons learned are labelled 'friends, feelings and imagination' and will be further developed in this chapter.

THE ENTREPRENEURIAL APPROACH FROM A BECOMING PERSPECTIVE

On the basis of earlier studies it is argued that a traditional understanding of entrepreneurship as a business activity has been, and still is, contested in many educational contexts (for example Skogen and Sjövoll, 2010). However, talking about an entrepreneurial approach seems to gain acceptance and legitimacy among teachers. Leffler (2006: 223) refers to an enterprising discourse, based on student activity, encouraging students to take initiative and responsibility, in contrast to a management discourse. In Sweden the enterprising discourse was verbalized in an early study by Johannisson and Madsén (1997: 17) referring to a citizenship that is fostered by an enterprising approach which calls for the same power of initiative and commitment as that which can be discerned among small business owners. Despite variations in how entrepreneurship education is organized, most teachers agree that entrepreneurship education deals with enterprising in the sense of creating conditions for an entrepreneurial approach, characterized by the vitality of creativity, the power of initiative and the importance of reflexivity (Berglund and Holmgren, 2007). This seems to have enabled teachers to translate the idea of entrepreneurship into the context of pedagogy in which it has turned into an umbrella for a progressive pedagogy, rather than a means for creating economic growth (Ahl and Berglund, 2008), a translation which seemed to have created considerable tensions between policy and practice (Berglund and Holmgren, 2013, see also Chapter 9). Hence, in the educational context the entrepreneurial approach has become a concept which has been implicitly accepted and agreed upon by teachers.

The term 'entrepreneurial approach' stresses the way individuals relate to themselves, to others and to the world. Thus, 'approach' should be understood as a way to relate, rather than as an attitude (which is in psychological terms often seen as stable, fixed and with minor variations, see Potter and Wetherell, 1987). In contrast, the entrepreneurial approach points to the variations by which individuals respond to another person, a situation, a thing, a meeting, or an incident. Thus, the contrast to stability, surprise, open-endedness and unfinalizability is acknowledged (Steyaert, 1997).

In an article that delves into two contrasting, yet interdependent, styles of thinking in social sciences 'becoming' is discerned as a way to understand movement, emergence and becoming (Chia, 1995). In such processes the ephemeral character of what is seen as 'there' or 'real' is accentuated. This style of thinking accentuates, and invites to, viewing the world in flux, in which both humans and things are 'moveable'. This has been recognized among entrepreneurship scholars as a vital way of perceiving entrepreneurial processes so the concept of 'entrepreneuring' has been suggested to describe the processual nature of entrepreneurship (Steyaert, 2007, Johannisson, 2011). It should be recognized that this research approach challenges a research tradition which has been guided by the idea of explaining, predicting and stabilizing the messy and ephemeral features of entrepreneurship. Entrepreneuring thus constitutes an epistemological alternative for researchers interested in engaging 'in studies that approach entrepreneurship as a creative process in which it is accepted that entrepreneurs are creators of new realities, walking on the boundary between destabilizing existing situations and actualizing implicit possibilities in new contexts' (Steyaert, 1997: 22).

Subscribing to this view, as well as to the belief that 'the entrepreneurial' will always escape us in some respect, it should be acknowledged that entrepreneuring is a theoretical concept. What is highlighted here is that the entrepreneurial approach shares many similarities with entrepreneuring, recognizing the becoming (of students, teachers, and pedagogical processes), a movement (of educational practices), an open-endedness (towards the surrounding community), and the destabilizing and questioning (of education as organized in terms of particular subjects and time slots, instead emphasizing themes, see Chapter 10). While entrepreneuring focuses on how to epistemologically relate to entrepreneurial processes as a research subject, the entrepreneurial approach addresses how to enact entrepreneurship in societal contexts.

Hence, the entrepreneurial approach story, shaped by teachers, promoters of entrepreneurship education, politicians and policy-makers goes in line with the conceptualization of entrepreneuring as part of a dull and mundane life. Taking a point of departure in the movement of the entrepreneurial approach in the education context can itself be seen as a result of a cross-border movement. While this study focuses on how to make sense of an entrepreneurial approach, Holmgren further elaborates in Chapter 9 on the translation of entrepreneurship from the private to the public sector.

Hence, the research reported in this chapter pays attention to how the entrepreneurial approach is made sense of in the preschool context, organizing thinking, learning, initiative and creativity. From an ethnographic study of a group of four preschools, which have all been preparing to introduce and work with entrepreneurship in their pedagogy, the concept of entrepreneurial approach is elaborated on further. Whereas the entrepreneurial approach has been promoted in policies and in the new curriculum, this study is made in a setting of four preschools that initiated an entrepreneurship project in order to further their pedagogy. The project they initiated thus did not stem from a policy directive, but from their own wishes to develop and further understand how an entrepreneurial approach could contribute to their pedagogy. The study is based on participative observations, interviews with teachers and children, as well as text studies of a particular book (Rossling, 2007), referred to as a key source of understanding an entrepreneurial approach.

The purpose of this chapter is to find out how the entrepreneurial approach is made sense of in a preschool setting and to translate this to the adult world in which societal entrepreneurship is called for. A further intention is to situate the entrepreneurial approach in a theoretical framework of societal entrepreneurship.

THE ENTREPRENEURIAL APPROACH AND SOCIETAL ENTREPRENEURSHIP

The entrepreneurial approach, as a way of relating to the world as becoming, is constructed in line with the broad understanding of societal entrepreneurship as something that imbues society and is part of transforming its structures, rather than a tool that adds another piece of company to the market settings that prevail (see Chapter 1). As stated in Chapter 1, it is an innovative power that creates value and mobilizes initiatives. Thus, societal entrepreneurship does not exclude traditional entrepreneurship, but includes so much more. However, even if the societal entrepreneurship discourse addresses the broader spectrum of values created in entrepreneurial processes, we still know little about what it means in various practices. In this section I will outline some theoretical inspirations for interpreting societal entrepreneurship from the perspective of people enacting an entrepreneurial approach.

The thoughts of Schumpeter (1934, 1942), stressing that entrepreneurship is about creative destruction, laid a foundation for re-interpreting entrepreneurship as a societal phenomenon. When something new is added (by something being improved or made considerably better than before) the old ways of doing things are destroyed. An easy example would be to take a classical market perspective and reflect on what happened with the market for typewriters and calculation machines when the electronic computer was introduced, first among enthusiasts, and later among businesses and private persons. Thus, one market was destroyed to the benefit of another. A more complex example would be to look at the values a company contributes to. From an economic perspective many businesses contribute to economic growth and also to social concerns, since they offer employment. From an ecological perspective, many companies, not least the ones in production (for example, producing new models of plastic or electronic devices), make their living from improving their products so that old models end up on the global garbage mountain, which is argued to be disastrous for the environment. Hence, the early thoughts of Schumpeter can be fruitful in discussions on societal entrepreneurship, since they not only emphasize how innovative initiatives are created, but also what values they create and destroy. This was stressed in the previous section on the bright and dark sides of societal entrepreneurship.

Another theoretical inspiration is the critique of the entrepreneurship discourse, favouring one person (the entrepreneur) before another. This is in particular emphasized in gender and entrepreneurship studies, where the entrepreneur has been constructed as a masculine human being (Ahl, 2004). However, it has also been suggested that the entrepreneur is not only a gender stereotype, but is constructed as the ideal human being that only exists in our imagination (Jones and Spicer, 2005). In this vein entrepreneurship is supposed to exclude in a more thorough way than previously imagined. The discourse – that is our common conceptions of entrepreneurship – oppresses the enterprising capacity among many people in contemporary society (Berglund and Johansson, 2007, see also Chapter 7). To break with the heroic and idealized view of the entrepreneur, a relational turn is suggested, focusing on how people relate to each other when being occupied with the 'doing of entrepreneuring' (Bruni et al., 2004, Steyaert, 2007).

The *Movements of Entrepreneurship* anthologies by Steyaert and Hjorth (for example. 2003, 2004) and the anthology *Demobilizing Entrepreneurship Discourse* (Bill et al., 2010) can be seen as efforts to contribute to the relational turn in entrepreneurship studies. Demobilizing the entrepreneurship discourse means starting out from the assumption that 'all human beings have an inherent entrepreneurial potential. This entrepreneurial potential is naturally released in the interplay between individuals if it is not prevented. Therefore entrepreneurial behaviour can be seen when children are playing' (Bill et al., 2010: 4).

Sarasvathy (2001) introduced the contrasting concepts of causation and effectuation, proposing that the latter describes how entrepreneurs 'do it'. Using the 'cooking' metaphor she explains the differences between causation, in which you follow a recipe without deviating from any of its instructions, and effectuation, where you open the refrigerator and try to make something out of what you already have at hand. This way of relating resembles play – to take what is at hand and make something out of it, which contrasts the view of entrepreneurship as an institutionalized form of a game, as depicted by the management discourse. Comparing entrepreneuring with creative children (Hjorth, 2004, Johannisson 2010) implies acknowledging that there are always spaces for play (Hjorth, 2005), even in institutionalized settings.

Play invites viewing entrepreneurship as an intersubjective activity. Instead of talking about the level of growth and/or the growing number of companies, rising productivity, a set of traits among entrepreneurs, play requires us to embrace entrepreneurship as an altogether human activity. It is in interaction with other people, symbols, pictures, or stories that entrepreneuring takes place. The way children constantly play – even though they do not think about it as fun play since play often includes serious matters to them – they can be seen to creatively imitate adults in ways that disclose new life-worlds (see Spinosa et al.'s 1997 discussion on disclosing new worlds, and Johansson's 2010 discussion on creative imitation). When children for instance do nursing (with a doll, a Barbie, a cuddle toy or anything else at hand), grocery shopping (using what they find to create a supermarket), or hospital (a pen becomes a needle and the kitchen towel a nursing outfit), they are entrepreneuring. Children thus imitate the adult world in their own creative ways, mixing, and transforming the ways we view things. However, they are also skilled learners, picking up what is 'right' and 'wrong', for example in relation to gender, learning how to do girlish things, as well as boys' stuff (see Thorne, 1993).

The entrepreneurial play among children is further developed by Johannisson (2010), drawing from studies in a preschool context. In the quotes from preschool teachers I can discern an enthusiasm about how they (the adults) learn from children, but also how easily they (as adults) can kill children's play in the ambition to introduce them to the world of grown-ups, socialized as responsible corporate citizens. An important point made by Johannisson is that the transformation from child to adult often means entering a world populated by 'homo traditionalis' and 'homo economicus' more than anything else. He suggests that being sensitive to this transition, learning from children, forms a productive context for the playing and curious human being which invites us all into a world where imagination and fantasy can be enacted. This, it is argued, fosters entrepreneuring.

Following Asplund (1987),[1] the ability of human beings to respond to each other is closely connected to the notion of 'play' and 'game'. Human responsivity, according to Asplund, creates the ability of the human being to relate to herself, as well as to others. With reference to Huizinga (1955), Asplund describes play as something undeniable, constituting a basic form of relating. Consequently, play as a form of social interaction cannot be contested but makes up an 'absolutely basic form of life' (ibid.: 62). In contrast, 'the game' refers to the kind of responsiveness that is restricted by being guided by rules and regulations, but also by norms and values. When we play according to the rules of the game we hesitate, but when we 'just play' we act unexpectedly, impulsively and unpredictably. Accordingly, even if play is restricted throughout life, human activity can never be predicted, even though it is often predictable. Considering the idea of the entrepreneur who 'breaks the rules', play is intriguing to look further into. Perhaps the fascination (and admiration, see Chapter 7) for the entrepreneur has to do with the notion that it visualizes human impulsivity – the space for playing around – with the thought of doing or realizing something. Trying ideas out differently, to see where they might lead. Taking this view, play is not exclusive to children; it is more of a basic form for understanding human relations. So, if we understand play as a basic form of human action, describing human creativity, we come close to how an entrepreneurial approach is enacted. The notion of *homo ludens* – playing humans – may thus be appropriate when studying how such an approach is made sense of in a preschool context. Besides, this may benefit the theorizing of playing humans in entrepreneuring.

Hence, play is proposed to be a fruitful theoretical concept to further our understanding of what it means to embrace an entrepreneurial approach, which from a theoretical perspective is translated as the enactment of entrepreneuring in the mundane. In addition, as suggested in this chapter, the context of preschools can teach us more about entrepreneurship if we are open to interpreting children's play as an instance of entrepreneuring. Or, as emphasized in the chapter, to relate to the world in a way that encourages human beings to act entrepreneurially.

STUDYING A PRESCHOOL CONTEXT: ON METHOD

Methodologically, this study is informed by the introductory reasoning, acknowledging societal entrepreneurship as a cross-cultural phenomenon (see Chapter 1). Pursuing an interest in entrepreneurship in a preschool context can be like walking from the legitimate private sector (in terms of how entrepreneurship is generally understood) to paying attention to how teachers (mainly in upper secondary and elementary schools) translate the concept of entrepreneurship into the public sector (see also Chapter 9) and/or to considering how entrepreneurship is made sense of by preschool teachers. The idea of multi-sited ethnography, tracing how emerging cultural phenomena unfold in different settings (for example Marcus, 1995), may support this kind of cross-sectoral movement, encouraging ethnographers not only to focus on one 'site' – whether it is one place, one organization, or one particular group – but to follow how a phenomenon unfolds. In this case an entrepreneurial approach has been followed, from teachers' obvious reflection that 'this is what we want to promote' (Berglund and Holmgren, 2007), to how the concept has been incorporated into the new curriculum, and further to studying the work of preschool teachers, who in the context of education are seen as entrepreneurial approach 'experts' (viewing children as becoming).

The school world in itself, and the preschool context in particular, can thus be seen as one 'site' among many others in society in which entrepreneurship forms a vital part in organizing activity. Following entrepreneurship in this 'site' cross-cuts a dichotomist understanding of entrepreneurship, like viewing people as either entrepreneurs or not, believing that entrepreneurship is about starting a company in contrast to being employed, or separating social value from economic gains. This study traces, in particular, how the entrepreneurial approach unfolds in the sites of four preschools. This leads to incorporating another fifth site – popular literature – which worked as a structuring tool, making it possible to interpret the common knowledge constructed with regard to the entrepreneurial approach in the four preschools. The empirical material instructing the reasoning in this chapter thus emanates from tracing where an entrepreneurial approach is seen to be promoted in society. This leads to the preschool setting where I found that they used the concept to create meaning for how to relate to each other in a way that promoted entrepreneuring among children as well as adults.

For six months I visited four preschools ten times, talking to children aged 1–6 years, preschool teachers, parents and the manager. The four preschools are all located in the same residential area and were chosen from my knowledge that at the time they worked with an 'entrepreneurship project'. Besides, they are all organized as a group, having the same manager, who is in daily dialogue with the head of each preschool. Even if each one of the preschools has its own profile, interests and background, they all participated in joint change projects. They were thus free to organize the activity according to the knowledge and experience of each preschool team, which made the four schools differ from each other in what they stressed as important in their pedagogy. When one preschool worked with recycling, another emphasized music, a third outdoor activities to encourage creativity, and the fourth saw 'the entrepreneurial' in all they did. At the time of the study the four preschools were in the midst of introducing entrepreneurship among their activities, which was the reason why this study was conducted in the first place. In the preschools' entrepreneurship project, the entrepreneurial approach was emphasized, viewing entrepreneurship as an output that could be discernible later in life. Accordingly, the entrepreneurial approach was viewed as a way to internalize relating to the world, which could later in life be enacted in realizing new ideas creatively.

The entrepreneurship project succeeded a long-term gender project in which the preschool teachers decided to make observations of their everyday practices in order to discern taken-for-granted, yet gendered, practices. The purpose was to learn about gender-biased practices that they were unaware of, and about how gender is 'done' in each and every corner (for example West and Zimmerman, 1987), as well as trying out innovative ways to adjust practices in order to create more equal conditions for boys and girls in preschool. In interviews they described in detail how this project contributed to developing their pedagogy and how they were trained to relate to the children in a way that endorsed human growth and maturity.

During the several times I visited the preschools I decided to be part of the activity at each preschool for a whole day in order to follow the activity; talking to children and staff to learn about how the entrepreneurial approach was integrated in the preschool activity. Each observation was different from the other. On one occasion I followed the whole group to the small forest in which the children played. Except for a break to have a fruit or a sandwich, the children were running around making up new games. Of course, as always during my visits in the preschools, I was invited to take part in the children's play. They always had something to show me, or some story to tell, and tried continuously to enroll me in their play. Often, I think, I was unconsciously part in their play even if I was talking to the staff. As a potential customer, a monster, a mushroom, a prince, or something else that would suit their play. On one occasion I was part of a secret exhibition, searching for a hidden treasure. But, we had to be careful, because there were evil creatures hiding that wanted to do bad things . . .

While I took time for the children during the first hour, the snack moment gave me an opportunity to talk to the teachers over a cup of coffee. This furthered my insight into how closely they conceptualized entrepreneurship and gender. Both concepts, in their view, dealt with being able to challenge taken-for-granted assumptions, which was perceived as a prerequisite for breaking with diminishing traditions, gender being one of these. Unveiling such traditions, seeing each person as he or she really is, making star eyes shine; vividly, being seen as how to bring about enthusiasm and activity. This was not the first time I heard the idea of 'lighting star-eyes'. The staff I met, the manager in particular, emphasized the need to 'let children's star-eyes shine' and, even more importantly, not to extinguish their sparkling eyes. To have 'star-eyes' was their view of being entrepreneurial, that is, the burning desire to want to achieve something, exploring it further, not listening to the rules of conduct, but keeping the spark and passion alive (see the discussion of immediacy in Chapter 3). Creating conditions for maintaining 'star-eyes to shine' seemed to be a way of making sense of the entrepreneurial approach as something that was already part (and indeed an important part) of the context of preschools.

All the talk of 'lighting star eyes' made me aware that the concept came from a book called *Tänd dina stjärnögon: vad barn har lärt mig* ('Light your star eyes: what children have taught me') by Lou Rossling (2007). This book seems important for the preschool teachers' understandings of the topic of entrepreneurial approach. Rossling is herself a preschool teacher, as well as a popular lecturer. All preschool teachers had been introduced to the book and had also been invited to attend one of her lectures. Since this book appeared as vital to how the preschool teachers made sense of the entrepreneurial approach I decided to incorporate it in the study. The reading of the book was done in two steps. The first reading was done without trying to analyse it, but instead I tried to get the message through of the book as a whole, which consists of 192 pages and 24 chapters, including a 'thank you' and literature references. The chapters all contain one lead anecdote from Rossling's experiences as a preschool teacher, and how she has learned from children. In the second reading each of the chapters was analysed and summarized in a table describing the title of the chapter, the point of the anecdote told and, in conclusion, given my knowledge of the entrepreneurship discourse, the moral of an entrepreneurial approach. After studying this table, with its condensed content of the book and possible translations into an entrepreneurial approach, the following three themes revolved around the anecdotes on lighting star eyes: Friends, Feelings and Imagination. Departing from these themes the work of introducing the entrepreneurial approach in the four sites of preschools stood out as clearer in its contours. Thus, this 'fifth site' of popular literature, addressing the relation between preschool teachers and children, worked as a way to interpret the commonalities shared with regard to an entrepreneurial approach between one preschool and another.

Since the entrepreneurial approach, judging by my observations, infiltrated social life as a natural way of 'becoming', many episodes probably passed by during my visits in the preschools, since it was difficult to apprehend a culture that I am very much part of myself. The themes of 'friends, feelings and imagination' that came out of my reading of Rossling made it easier to interpret the practice of the entrepreneurial approach. Next, these three themes will be elaborated on. They all start with an anecdote from the 'lighting star eyes' book, which is followed by episodes, situations and activities noticed during observations in the preschools, and then each of these concludes with a discussion of how the moral of each theme affects how entrepreneurship can be understood.

UNFOLDING THE ENTREPRENEURIAL APPROACH IN THE PRESCHOOL CONTEXT

The idea of learning from children in conceptualizing the entrepreneurial approach stems from recognizing that preschool teachers view children during a process of becoming. The purpose is thus not to view children as particular people with a right or wrong answer to how the entrepreneurial approach is enacted, but to recognize human curiosity in an organizational setting which acknowledges 'the becoming' of its members. Moreover, children's view of the world may remind us that there is always another way to approach life. This was emphasized throughout the different preschools I visited and exemplified in various ways.

In all chapters of this book this point is made, implicitly or explicitly. In one of the anecdotes in Rossling's book – *'There is an uncle and he has no legs!'* – we are introduced to a way of approaching life that may make us, if not abandon, anyway reflect on our prejudices. The setting of this anecdote was a local store that the preschool teachers visited with a group of children during an excursion. As they entered the store an old man in a wheelchair was waiting to be served. The children started whispering 'Lou, look – the man has no legs!' which embarrassed her and made her try to excuse the children and hush them up. When the man had done his business he turned to Lou and said: 'I'm very glad that children talk to me, otherwise no one would recognize me'. The man had lost one leg, but the missing leg also made people (adults) uncomfortable about how to relate to him. Instead he was met with polite nodding and silence. The moral conveyed is that having preconceived ideas is an obstacle for learning to know those people who appear different from what we are used to. However, seeing the world for what it is – in this case recognizing the old man in a wheelchair – we can make new friends.

However, visiting the preschools I had difficulties in seeing 'the entrepreneurial', because I was too locked in traditional understandings of the dichotomy of playing children and responsible teachers. After a while, subsumed in the new context, I became more and more able to grasp the idea of the entrepreneurial approach and how the story of a two-year-old girl was not a cute story, but an illustration of how the entrepreneurial approach was practiced. At the end of a day, about the time when children and teachers were about to go home, this girl came up to one preschool teacher saying (in a very firm and resolute voice): 'It's ok, you can go now; I will take out the garbage'. One can imagine a smile among the teachers, but the child's initiative was not diminished or laughed at. Instead, she was approached as an adult in a 'thank you, dear, please do that so that I can go home to my family now' way. Proudly she went outside with the bag of garbage. The point is that the adults did not diminish the child, but viewed her as an equal. Translating this from the view of an entrepreneurial approach means not to presume responsibility, but that such approach *fosters* responsibility. See also Chapter 4 and the basic values that the author Astrid Lindgren associates with children. Approaching children as responsible we can expect them to do the same: taking charge of their ideas, viewing other people's ideas as equally important, and acting upon them. Whether it is about taking out the garbage or initiating practices which 'disclose new worlds', as Spinosa et al. (1997) put it.

Next, the three themes are introduced in greater depth. Hereafter they are referred to as lessons, with the emphasis on lessons learned from children about how adults can (re)learn to relate to the world in a more entrepreneurial way.

The Lesson of Making Friends

Making friends with others, but also with yourself, is an important wisdom that adults can relearn from children, according to Rossling. In one chapter she tells an anecdote about the son of a friend who, before going to his first football training, took a huge bag with him. When his mother wondered why he took such a big bag, she got the following answer: 'Well, I need something to bring home the silver cup in'. This made Rossling ponder over how as children we see no limits, but how later in life we almost end up in the opposite corner where we do not believe in our capabilities any more, letting the feeling of doubt take over:

> How can we recapture the joy of being able to do things, the joy we had from the beginning? For me it is about daring to meet the little child within who was once abandoned, the one that was criticized and complained about. The thing I learned was not to show off. If I first and foremost take care of my inner child, and give myself what no one else gave me, then I reach the part of me that says I cannot . . . (Rossling, 2007, my translation.)

This small child that Rossling talks about was part of everyday practice in the preschool context. In one moment one of the children could come up to me, wanting to show something he or she had done, while the next moment the same child was devastated by the fact that he or she had failed in doing something else. One of the preschools had a routine of music gathering, where they could play and sing as part of calming down and coming together before lunch. On this occasion I was fascinated by the children's creativity in making up new songs, improvizing, and daring to sing in front of the whole group. However, whereas many children wanted to show their skills I remember a boy who looked down to the floor, facing away from the small music community. The teachers encouraged him to sing, but he continued to look away. Then, the girl next to her just took his hand, which made him look up and, after a while, he was also part of the song. Evidently I was the only one who had problems in following them, being unfamiliar with their songs. The children, however, continuously tried to get me into their community, correcting me and repeating the lyrics.

Thus, making friends does not lend itself to the rational idea of 'networking' (for example Johannisson, 2000), but is about acknowledging the relational, subtle yet important aspects of everyday life. Not laughing at and putting down someone who is so self-confident that he takes a bag with him to bring home the silver cup in, at the first football training, but instead reaching out a hand to a friend sometimes who may reveal a hidden talent. The lesson of 'friends' from the perspective of an entrepreneurial approach is thus as much about making friends with oneself, as with others. In reaching the part of us that says 'I cannot' and persuade this part to appreciate silenced, or hidden, abilities and talents, we can make friends with our flaws and mistakes, creating a script of 'I can', allowing us to try and take action. For, without taking the next step nothing happens and, as entrepreneurship is clearly about action and movement (Hjorth et al., 2003), viewing oneself as capable seems to be a vital condition for taking action. Taking this step, moving forward, requires reaching the protesting part of us – persisting in saying 'I cannot' – and persuading that part to say 'I can!' Accordingly, every person is seen as capable of initiating interaction, and therefore also as a potential entrepreneur. In addition, every person (including a much admired entrepreneur) is seen to carry a child within that occasionally struggles against the things we dream about achieving.

The first lesson then is that friends are made in relations, with us and with others. Looking for who the person is (including yourself), and not for the person you expect her or him to be is a good start to get grounded in yourself, trusting your view of something when it does not coincide with expected norms and beliefs. This means to not always trust authorities, but challenge their assumptions, and have faith in your own ideas. This is also the popular version of what entrepreneurs do, as they are people who believe in something and 'go for it'. However, from the perspective of the entrepreneurial approach, this 'going' is far different from waiting for another entrepreneur to enter the room. It may as well be about finding the entrepreneur locked inside you.

The Lessons of Listening to your Feelings

Making friends with yourself and others requires being sensitive to emotions. The word 'feel' recurs frequently in Rossling's anecdotes and also in the vocabulary among preschool teachers. Listening to your body and developing an emotional repertoire to enhance the interpretation of what it tells you are emphasized. In the following quote Rossling writes about how she learned to deal with her fear of spiders from seeing how a little girl related to this little creature:

> . . . escaping from the fear makes it even stronger. It is about discovering it, acknowledging it, viewing it, feeling it and, once you feel it, choosing not to be stuck with it. Physical activity helps you to remember that you have an opportunity to make that choice. That is a completely different way of thinking than escaping your fear. . . . When the little girl with the spider showed me her lack of fear I realized that I could choose that myself. (Rossling, 2007: 160–162, my translation.)

Similar situations occurred during my visits to the preschools when children played with bugs of all kinds. Some children avoided the small creatures, but as the play went on – creating small roads for the ants in the woods, helping them to find their way to the haystack – they were soon all involved. Another example was when a group of small children discovered a tree to climb in. Instead of rushing there, saying no in a voice that responded to feeling fear instead of excitement, the teachers observed the children and were ready to assist if something went wrong. The most obvious example I recall is the episode of dressing up as someone else. One of the boys longingly looked at the girls playing princesses, but also cowboys, doctors and hippies (they had collected all sorts of leftover clothing from parents and relatives). This was noticed among the teachers, who interpreted the boy's hesitation as a struggle with his feelings to be part of the play, perhaps having learned about the princess/prince divide. One of the teachers then approached in a gentle way with a scarf, asking, 'Have you seen this?' and then 'Do you want to try it on?' Nodding yes, he was soon part of the play, assisted by the other children and enrolled in their play trying out various clothes, ending up as a pink and purple princess and glancing appreciatively at his new look in the mirror. Later one of the teachers briefly commented on this situation from the perspective of the entrepreneurial approach – how the children were encouraged to discover their many dimensions and made to acknowledge a range of feelings they sense. 'It is never wrong to *feel* something, but it is wrong to act in a way that hurts others. This is what we try to create conditions for. Trying out yourself in various ways, and simultaneously developing a sense for other ways to do the same.'

It is argued that fears shrink our world, making it smaller and less 'potential' in the sense of viewing opportunities, which is held forward as a critical competence for entrepreneurs (Nilsson, 2003). In mainstream understandings of entrepreneurship fear is attached to 'non-entrepreneurs', as compared to brave and fearless entrepreneurs. However, acknowledging that fear is part of the emotional repertoire of every human being, the lesson here is rather to accept that we are controlled by (un)conscious fears. Instead of viewing entrepreneurs as 'brave' we may look upon them as people who have learned a state of 'unfear'. Whether it is about touching the spider, climbing the tree, being part of a play, or giving voice to an (outrageous) idea enrolling people in the realization of it. How we perceive risks is also a matter of our standpoint. In the eyes of the outsider (for example a banker or business angel) an idea may be seen as highly risky (causing feelings of fear), but in the eyes of the 'entrepreneur' who has internalized the idea working to unlearn the fear, the idea is constructed as an opportunity to be enacted (compare Hjorth et al., 2003). To 'unlearn fear' can thus be described as another way of expressing opportunities and taking risks.

The lesson on feelings is that reading what the body tells you requires subtle intuition, and an emotional repertoire. Not to stop listening to what your body tells you, but staying intuitive. Decisions are much easier then. Making decisions is considered a key feature in entrepreneurship research (see for example Casson, 1982) but it takes more to initiate entrepreneurial processes. To constantly be on the edge, making another move, is easier unless we have forgotten to read our body. We all have this from the beginning, perhaps this is all we then have, but learning to suppress our emotions and body signals is done more or less efficiently as adults. This can be connected to the vocabulary of those who entitle themselves entrepreneurs in contemporary society. Having the right 'gut feeling' is a popular description of how decisions are made. This assumes the ability to interpret our emotional repertoire, but also to interpret other people's emotions. Emotions have been an understudied area in entrepreneurship research, even if this has recently been paid attention to (Cardon et al., 2012). Moreover, Goss (2005) makes an exception in elaborating on how emotional energy relates to feelings of pride and shame, illustrating how emotions shape entrepreneurial action in different ways.

The reasoning of friends and feelings pictures a human being in stark contrast to the idea of the entrepreneur as an autonomous person with unique qualities. We do not become who we are only because of some intrinsic traits, but we are constantly shaped in relations with other people. The vision of 'star-eyes' seen in us as children is a feeling we can hold on to and, later in life, learn to recreate it ourselves and bring out our passions. Lighting star-eyes is supposed to be contagious since it describes an inter-relational activity. When we are around passionate people we are easily carried away, perhaps ending up in the state of the girls in the introductory prologue: with excited voices, warm cheeks and shining star-eyes.

The Lesson of Using Fantasy or Imagination as a Means to Disclose New Worlds

The entrepreneurial approach is also related to imagination, sometimes more appropriately referred to as *fantasy*. Perhaps this is the most impor-tant part in *societal* entrepreneurship. Without fantasies of a better society – in particular in terms of social and ecological standards – how can entre-preneurship for a better society flourish? When we play with our minds, visions are created and star-eyes are lit:

> Einstein says that imagination is more important than knowledge. He states that imagination is never limited, but with that you can go any length. I believe that people who lack imagination also lack the ability to have visions for how we may be able to develop. I often hear that I have to come down on the ground and be realistic. Of course, we need to be realistic but most of us are already realistic enough to manage. However, many have not yet developed their imagination enough to create change. Without imagination the world stops. We won't get any development but will keep on doing what we already do. Since there are quite extensive scarcities in the world it may be time to let loose fantasies) of a new world. (Rossling, 2007, p 174, my translation.)

During the visits to the preschool I witnessed numerous fantasies. In the woods, hunting for the treasure, dressing up as someone else, playing a superwoman in a tree, on a secret expedition with dangerous animals (ants), or something far-fetched (at least from my adult view of things). However, the teachers, creating conditions for new worlds to be created, also encouraged fantasy. In one of the preschools they were working on a project of making 'something new of old things' in which children had brought recyclable products from home for the purpose. These arti-facts were not only illustrative – a monster mobile, a thrash destroyer, or a space rocket – but also carried fantastic stories that were told and sometimes staged in the play afterwards. In these plays children acted 'as if' (compare Gartner et al., 1992) they were in outer space, in deep sea, or at some other place where only fantasy could take them. From the perspective of an entrepreneurial approach, the point is not to slip away from the 'real' world, but to return to it and make changes.

However, the notion of imagination or fantasy is not only applicable to children's play, but also to the reasoning of teachers and how they may come to modify their view of relating to children. A story which was told in all preschools, about an incident taking place in another preschool working with gender and entrepreneurship, described how teachers came to view their activities in a new perspective. From studying their own workplace they concluded that the localities were decorated with 'a nook with dolls' and 'a corner with cars'. Furthermore, whereas girls sometimes played in the corner with cars, boys seldom appeared in the nook with dolls. Hence, they had been part of constructing a gendered environment, one that obviously reproduced patriarchal gender structures instead of inviting the children to a world where they could discover themselves in play. They agreed on changing things but, considering their new interest in promoting the entrepreneurial approach, they decided not to try out their own fantasies about how to create a new arrangement. Instead they invited the children to a dialogue of how to redecorate the two corners. The children quickly responded that they wanted a pizzeria, a grocery store, a school, a hospital... They wanted to play the game of adults! Hence, the premises were redecorated (more often) and turned into different stages where the children were able to try out different adult games in their own way, of course. Mixing things up, inventing diseases (but also cures), new products, new ways of shopping, of posting mail, of travelling, and all sorts of creative combinations. Presumably some of them can, in time, be enacted in the adult world.

SOCIETAL ENTREPRENEURSHIP FROM THE PERSPECTIVE OF AN ENTREPRENEURIAL APPROACH

Taking part of preschool work with entrepreneurship, I participated in the translation they made of the entrepreneurial approach, which can be summarized as follows:

- Friends – make friends with yourself and others.
- Feelings (heart) – listen to them and translate them into deliberated choices.

● Imagination – use it, not to escape the world, but to bring back something better to it.

These three relational aspects found in this preschool study may give a new perspective to entrepreneuring, from a relational point of view. The preschool teachers' conceptualization of the entrepreneurial approach invites us to relate to entrepreneurship in new ways, thinking new thoughts of how it is conducted and widening our perspective of how it can be socialized. From being part of the preschools, and also with reference to the introductory anecdote and the research by Johannisson (2010), we learn that when children play they are thinking in unexpected ways and are flexible in their play. The moral is that it would be good for us (adults) to stop hiding behind rules and regulations and fears, in particular when common sense tells us that some rules, more than anything else, function as 'star-eye' destroyers. Instead, negotiating rules can also be seen as taking responsibility and giving priority to common sense. Breaking with rules and the 'circle of conduct' is emphasized as a vital attribute of entrepreneurship (for example Schumpeter, 1934). The proverb 'it's better to ask for forgiveness than permission'[2] is expressed among entrepreneurs as a way to allow the breaking of rules and going against the stream (Berglund and Gaddefors, 2010). Consequently, it seems important to not forget how to learn, but instead unlearn and relearn.

The relational aspect can be seen as glue, without which it may be difficult for entrepreneurial processes – for whatever purpose – to sustain. The focus on business plans, economics, accounting and so forth, which many associate with entrepreneurship (starting a company), may very well be part of entrepreneurship education. However, such focus may backlash in an instrumentality that neglects and, even derides, the relational aspects emphasized in the perspective of the entrepreneurial approach.

This study indicates that the entrepreneurial approach in the preschool context is constructed as 'lighting star-eyes', which opens up for a theoretical development of entrepreneuring, in particular its social-psychological aspects, focusing on creating knowledge of how entrepreneurship is practiced in social settings. Not only in the context of schools, but also in the context of societies. Taking a point of departure in the assumption that there is no entrepreneurial DNA, the knowledge of what an entrepreneurial approach means, as well as how it can be learned, is important for a society that seems to crave this competence in each and every corner of organizational life. This study also adds to the content of the entrepreneurial approach, frequently emphasized in contemporary policy texts, and to how entrepreneurship education can develop and be promoted.

Hence, the entrepreneurial approach is a broad concept used in everyday life in general, and in the world of schools in particular. It is used to perceive that entrepreneurship is 'here and now', rather than describing how (and how many) companies are started and developed. Accordingly, the concept of the entrepreneurial approach includes how ordinary people contribute to the development of society from a sustainable perspective in the mundane (see Steyaert and Katz, 2004). By talking of an entrepreneurial approach the traditional idea of the entrepreneur (often a man) who creates a successful company which contributes to economic growth becomes something completely different. The entrepreneurial approach is translated into being of concern to all of us. At least if we are interested in the kind of entrepreneurship/s that may have an impact in society, it moves beyond traditional understandings of business-making in the market place. This unquestionably goes with the discussion of societal entrepreneurship.

Moreover, the entrepreneurial approach conceptualized as lighting star-eyes is something that both teachers and students can relate to in education. Following the preschool teachers in this study, the concept of the entrepreneurial approach can be seen as the force that is mobilized when people become passionate. In addition, the study gives some idea of how we can become passionate and inspire others to become passionate, thus creating conditions for an entrepreneurial approach to flourish.

From the perspective of an entrepreneurial approach both adults and children are carriers of entrepreneurship. While adults can be good role models, supporting development processes, inviting children to be part of constructing something meaningful in a familiar context like school, the situation is also the reverse, because children also contribute to opening the eyes of adults – including teachers! – by pointing towards important questions, making visible both possibilities and solutions for how to deal with the problems that they perceive. Here and now as well as in the future.

NOTES

1. Asplund's work has been influential in Scandinavian social and organizational research (see for example Alvesson, 1994) and has also been translated to English in the field of sociology (Israel, 1988).
2. The quotation 'It's easier to ask for forgiveness than it is to get permission' has been attributed to Rear Admiral Grace Murray Hopper, a pioneer in computer programming (see Hamblen, D. 'Only the Limits of Our Imagination: An exclusive interview with RADM Grace M. Hopper', Department of the Navy Information Technology Magazine).

REFERENCES

Achtenhagen, L. and Johannisson, B. (2013), 'The making of an intercultural learning context for entrepreneuring', *International Journal of Entrepreneurial Venturing* (forthcoming).

Ahl, H.J. (2004), *The Scientific Reproduction of Gender Inequality: A Discourse Analysis of Research Texts on Women's Entrepreneurship*, Stockholm: Liber.

Ahl H. and Berglund, K. (2008), 'The introduction of entrepreneurship in contemporary Swedish education policy: Ugly duckling or beautiful swan?', Presented at: ECER 2008 in Gothenburg, The European Conference on Educational Research in Gothenburg, Sweden, 10–12 September.

Alvesson, M. (1994), 'Talking in organizations: Managing identity and impressions in an advertising agency', *Organization Studies*, **15** (4): 535–563.

Asplund, J. (1987), *Det sociala livets elementära former* (The Fundamental Forms of Social Life), Göteborg: Korpen.

Berglund K. and Gaddefors, J. (2010), 'Entrepreneurship requires resistance to be mobilized', in Bill F., Bjerke B. and Johansson A.W. (eds), *(De) mobilizing Entrepreneurship – Exploring Entrepreneurial Thinking and Action*, Cheltenham, UK and Northampton, MA, USA: Edward Elgar Publishing, pp. 140–157.

Berglund, K. and Holmgren, C. (2007), 'Entreprenörskap & Skolan – Vad berättar lärare att de gör lärare när de gör entreprenörskap i skolan?' ('Entrepreneurship & School – What do teachers do when they do entrepreneurship in school?'), Örebro: FSF Förlag 2007: 17 i FSF:s report series.

Berglund, K and Holmgren, C. (2012), 'Entrepreneurship education in policy and practice – on tensions and conflicts in processes of implementing entrepreneurship education', *International Journal of Entrepreneurial Venturing* (forthcoming).

Berglund, K. and Johansson, A.W. (2007), 'Entrepreneurship, discourses and conscientization in processes of regional development', *Entrepreneurship and Regional Development*, **19** (6): 499–525.

Bill F., Bjerke, B. and Johansson, A.W. (eds) (2010), *(De)mobilizing Entrepreneurship – Exploring Entrepreneurial Thinking and Action*, Cheltenham, UK and Northampton, MA, USA: Edward Elgar Publishing.

Bruni, A., Gherardi, S. and Poggio, B. (2004), 'Doing gender, doing entrepreneurship: An ethnographic account of intertwined practices', *Gender, Work and Organization*, **11** (4).

Cardon, M.S., Foo, M-D., Shepherd, D. and Wiklund, J. (2012), 'Exploring the heart: Entrepreneurial emotion is a hot topic', *Entrepreneurship Theory and Practice*, 36: 1–10.

Casson, M. (1982), *The Entrepreneur: an Economic Theory*, Aldershot: Gregg Revivals.

Chia, R. (1995), 'From modern to postmodern organizational analysis', *Organization Studies*, **16** (4): 579–604.

Curriculum, Lgr 11 (2010), Del ur Lgr 11:Läroplan för grundskolan, förskoleklassen och fritidshemmet: chapters 1 and 2, National Agency for Education.

Gartner, B, Bird, B.J. and Starr, J.A. (1992), 'Acting as if: Differentiating entrepreneurial from organizational behavior', *Entrepreneurship Theory and Practice*, **16** (3): 13–31.

Goss, D. (2005), 'Schumpeter's legacy? Interaction and emotions in the sociology of entrepreneurship', *Entrepreneurship Theory and Practice*, **29** (2): 205–218.

Hjorth, D. (2004), 'Creating space for play/invention – concepts of space and organizational entrepreneurship', *Entrepreneurship & Regional Development*, **16** (5): 413–432.

Hjorth, D. (2005), 'Organizational entrepreneurship: With de Certeau on creating heterotopias or spaces for play', *Journal of Management Inquiry*, **14** (4): 386–398.

Hjorth, D., Johannisson, B. and Steyaert, C. (2003), 'Entrepreneurship as discourse and life style', in Czarniawska, B. and Sevón, G. (eds), *The Northern Lights – Organization Theory in Scandinavia*, Malmö: Liber ekonomi, pp. 91–110.

Huizinga, J. (1955), *Homo Ludens: A Study of the Play-element in Culture*, Boston, MA: Beacon Press.

Israel, J. (1988), 'Social responsivity as elementary human action', *Acta Sociologica*, 31: 231–240.

Johannisson, B. (2000), 'Networking and entrepreneurial growth', in: Sexton, D and Landström, H. (eds), *Handbook of Entrepreneurship*, London: Blackwell, pp. 368–386.

Johannisson B. (2010), 'In the beginning was entrepreneuring', in: Bill F., Bjerke, B. and Johansson, A.W. (eds), *(De)mobilizing Entrepreneurship – Exploring Entrepreneurial Thinking and Action*, Cheltenham, UK and Northampton, MA, USA: Edward Elgar Publishing.

Johannisson, B. (2011), 'Towards a practice theory of entrepreneuring', *Small Business Economics*, **36** (2): 135–150.

Johannisson, B. and Madsén, T. (1997). 'I entreprenörskapets tecken – en studie av skolning i förnyelse', Stockholm: Närings och handelsdepartementet, Ds 1997: 3.

Johannisson, B. and Nilsson, A. (1989), 'Community entrepreneurship – leadership for local economic development', *Entrepreneurship & Regional Development*, 1 (1): 1–19.

Jones, C. and Spicer, A. (2005), 'The sublime object of entrepreneurship', *Organization*, **12** (2), 223–246.

Leffler, E. (2006), 'Företagsamma elever – diskurser kring entreprenörskap och företagsamhet i skolan ('Enterprising students – discourses of entrepreneurship and enterprising in the school'), Doctoral thesis in pedagogic work No.8, Umeå: Umeå Universitet.

Marcus, G.E. (1995), 'Ethnography in/of the World System: The emergence of multi-sited ethnography, *Annual Review of Anthropology*, 24: 95–117.

Nilsson, N. (2003), 'Entreprenörens blick: om förståelse, identitet och handling i det mindre företaget ('The eye of the entrepreneur: on understanding, identity and action in the small company'), Doctoral thesis, Business School of Gothenburg.

Potter, J. and Wetherell, M. (1987), *Discourse and Social Psychology: Beyond Attitudes and Behaviour*, London: Sage Publications.

Rossling, L. (2007), *Tänd dina stjärnögon: vad barn har lärt mig* (Lighten your star eyes: what children taught me), Nacka: Efron och Dotter AB.

Sarasvathy, S.D. (2001), 'Causation and effectuation: Toward a theoretical shift from economic inevitability to entrepreneurial contingency', *Academy of Management Review*, **26** (2): 243–263.

Schumpeter, J.A. (1934), *The Theory of Economic Development: An Inquiry into Profits, Capital, Credit, Interest, and the Business Cycle* (transl. by Redvers Opie), Cambridge, MA: Harvard University Press.

Schumpeter, J.A. (1942), *Capitalism, Socialism, and Democracy*, New York and London: Harper & Brothers.

Skogen, K. and Sjövoll, J. (2010), *Creativity and Innovation: Preconditions for Entrepreneurial Action*, Trondheim: Tapir Academic Press.

Spinosa, C., Flores, F. and Dreyfus, H.L. (1997). *Disclosing New Worlds of Entrepreneurship, Democratic Action, and the Cultivation of Solidarity*, Cambridge, MA: The MIT Press.

Steyaert, C. (1997), 'A qualitative methodology for process studies of entrepreneurship', *International Studies of Management and Organization*, **27** (3):13–33.

Steyaert, C. (2007), '"Entrepreneuring" as a conceptual attractor? A review of process theories in 20 years of entrepreneurship studies', *Entrepreneurship and Regional Development*, **19** (6): 453–477.

Steyaert, C. and Hjorth, D. (eds) (2003), *New Movements in Entrepreneurship*, Cheltenham, UK and Northampton, MA, USA: Edward Elgar Publishing.

Steyaert, C. and Hjorth, D. (eds) (2004), *Narrative and Discursive Approaches in Entrepreneurship: A Second Movements in Entrepreneurship Book*, Cheltenham, UK and Northampton, MA, USA: Edward Elgar Publishing.

Steyaert, C. and Katz, J. (2004), 'Reclaiming the space of entrepreneurship in society: Geographical, discursive and social dimensions', *Entrepreneurship & Regional Development*, **16** (3): 179–196.

Thorne, B. (1993), *Gender Play: Girls and Boys in School*, Buckingham: Open University Press

West, C. and Zimmerman, D.H. (1987), 'Doing gender', *Gender & Society*, **1** (2): 125–151.

9. Translating entrepreneurship into the education setting – a case of societal entrepreneurship

Carina A. Holmgren

PROLOGUE

The year was 2004 when, in my new role as a research assistant at a Swedish foundation for small business research, I was confronted with the concept of 'entrepreneurship' and made my first stumbling efforts to learn about the entrepreneurship field. As responsible for mapping initiatives concerning entrepreneurship among young students I was working with a comprehensive survey study comprising nearly all the Swedish primary and secondary schools (Lundström, 2005). The response rate was not overwhelming and some of the schools made comments and even questioned their participation in the study – they could not see any connection between what they were doing and the entrepreneurship concept. 'Why us?' one confused headmaster asked, 'Don't you know we are a humanistic school?' To ask the staff at this school if it was using the words 'entrepreneurship' or 'enterprising' as a description of some of their pedagogic activities would not render any answer.

However, I also met and interviewed several inspiring actors who were involved in the process to stimulate teachers to work with entrepreneurship. These actors were often external to the schools as well as to the whole traditional educational system, representing for example private firms, non-profit interest organizations, and EU-funded projects. Recurrently, these actors described their difficulties with using the 'entrepreneurship' and 'enterprising' concepts when trying to offer activities to sceptical teachers and principals. One of these actors I met for an interview in the late summer of 2003. As we sat in the warming sun he told me the project's stories of success but also about the problems they had encountered when using the concepts. 'The words enterprising and entrepreneurship have made many [of those who work in the schools] afraid and there are still many who don't know [that it is not only about business]. The problem has been to reach out with the meaning of the words. There is this "Jante Law" that permeates the Swedish community that says "Don't ever believe that you are someone"'.

Accordingly, the travelling of the entrepreneurship concept from the economic and business setting to the educational one does not only concern whether entrepreneurship is about business or not. It also raises concerns about Scandinavian culture, where the 'Jante law', made known by the Danish-Norwegian author Aksel Sandemose for criticizing individual success and achievement as unworthy and inappropriate, is brought up. Hence, the integration of entrepreneurship into education practice should by no means be seen as a simple process. These associations may create tensions, conflicts and even resistance among teachers (Berglund and Holmgren, 2012). Trying to handle these reactions some of the actors tried to avoid the concept altogether by inventing the word 'ta-sig-försam-het' (meaning, roughly, 'undertaking something'). By 2004 I had no idea that those stories concerning the integration of entrepreneurship into education practice could be viewed as expressions of a societal entrepreneurship process. I had not even heard anyone talking about entrepreneurship in these terms.

INTRODUCTION

In 2004 the interest in entrepreneurship in Swedish schools on the national level was mainly expressed in industrial and entrepreneurship policy terms. Locally, only a few municipalities made this an education-policy issue. On the EU level, though, the importance of entrepreneurship was made explicit and seen as a major road to economic growth (European Commission, 2004). In line with this interest all member states then agreed to integrate entrepreneurship education into all school curricular (European Commission, 2004). However, to integrate entrepreneurship into national Swedish school curriculum became a challenge. Some politicians presented proposals for entrepreneurship in primary and secondary schools, while others claimed that there was already enough support for working with entrepreneurship in the existing curriculum – even if the concept was not mentioned in the texts.

Eight years later the integration of entrepreneurship with education practice is still going on, even though its character has changed. In 2011 entrepreneurship became an explicit part of the national curriculum, focusing on the entrepreneurial approach (see Berglund, Chapter 8 this volume). The idea of entrepreneurship as part of the educational system has thus become more difficult to question. The integration process has hooked on to educational practices, and is now mandatory in all primary and secondary schools. The questions posed in this process have changed from being concerned with the issue *whether* entrepreneurship should be part of the educational system at all into dealing with the issue of *how* entrepreneurship can form part of the system.

In May 2011 I met three teachers working at a lower secondary school who had embarked together on the entrepreneurship journey and actively tried to integrate the ideas of entrepreneurship education brought forward by one external actor, a company in the growing 'market' of actors offering the schools different methods and ideas about teaching. In this specific case a leading company at what may be seen as an emerging 'market' for concepts and tools promoting entrepreneurship education was involved. The ideas offered were labelled entrepreneurial learning and were proposed to be a pedagogical form of training *for* entrepreneurship (see also Chapter 10). This pedagogical form presupposed a framework of cross-curriculum projects, long-time slots and cooperation between teachers, claiming to promote the training of 22 competencies (Peterson and Westlund, 2007). One of the teachers argued that entrepreneurial learning was not very different from how she already worked. She also explained that this kind of pedagogy was not so much about a particular method or working form, but more about her attitude as a teacher. She then told me that entrepreneurial learning deals with an approach not just focusing on knowledge feeding but also on developing students' faith in discerning and appreciating their own abilities. She wanted the students to be confident about accomplishing whatever they want, and about seeking and gaining the knowledge needed. This way of viewing entrepreneurship can be related to an entrepreneurial approach, as it is discussed in Chapters 8 and 10. She explained that the students should feel safe to stand on their own, after which she needs to give them the conditions for taking action and testing ideas. Her colleague explained that this requires seeing the whole person, finding the spirit and also making a connection to 'reality'. But she ended up, after reflecting on the definition, puzzled by her own thoughts, 'I can't put into words what it really is'.

In the process of dealing with entrepreneurial learning these teachers do not only participate in a struggle to ascribe meaning to the entrepreneurship concept that makes it relevant in their setting, but also to find out how to integrate it into their practice. They try, for example, to find a balance between giving the students responsibility adapted to their maturity and individual abilities. They have realized that some students are too immature to carry the responsibilities given in big cross-curriculum projects they have arranged where several different subjects and teachers were involved. Cross-curriculum projects are a popular method proposed and used to respond to the call for integrating entrepreneurship in education, as illustrated by Johansson and Rosell in Chapter 10 (see also Johannisson and Madsén, 1997). One of the teachers told me that the focus on big cross-curriculum projects for some students ended up in a lack of knowledge in some of the subjects being covered.

This chapter investigates the process when a concept – entrepreneurship – originating in the business sector, where its meaning has become institutionalized, imposes itself upon another sector, the public one and its educational context. When a concept travels between sectors, organizations and actors it involves a complex process of translation. The complexity of translation concerns making the concept travel (Rose, 1999) at all as well as difficulties in understanding how to make use of entrepreneurship in the new context. From a social constructionism perspective the concept is not just a word, as it brings along meanings, stories and pictures that may be incomprehensible in the new setting. The actors involved in this process have to translate and change the understanding and use of the concept from their own unique needs (Czarniawska and Sevón, 1996). The purpose is to analyse how the translation of entrepreneurship from the private sector, by way of policy, to the public sector and educational practice in the Swedish context can be understood as societal entrepreneurship. Actors like politicians and researchers in the business setting have a priori ascribed meanings to entrepreneurship which are strongly associated with business. This focus can be expressed by, for example, research interests in new companies (Reynolds et al., 1994), their fundamental importance for increased employment and economic regeneration (Audretsch and Thurik, 2001; Kirchhoff, 1994), the connection between entrepreneurship and economic growth (Kirzner, 1982), and by policy statements where entrepreneurship is held forward as a major driver of innovation, competitiveness and growth (European Commission, 2004; Swedish Government, 2004). When teachers and external actors are to translate entrepreneurship into practice this backpack of associations which the concept brings from the business setting constitutes a challenge (Gibb, 2008; Backström-Widjeskog, 2010).

The prologue and the introduction contain small fragments from the process of translating entrepreneurship from policy to practice and indicate the different actors involved in the process: politicians, researchers, external actors, teachers and students. The fragments also express how the translation process has changed over the last decade, from external actors' efforts of convincing teachers and other actors in the educational system that entrepreneurship is something belonging to the educational setting at all to shifting focus on to teachers' and external actors' struggle with how to ascribe meaning to and make use of it in educational practice. In this chapter I view the translation process as a societal entrepreneurship process where both the external actors and the teachers can be regarded as societal entrepreneurs. The translation process of entrepreneurship education is boundary-crossing, involving the private, public and non-profit/ voluntary (NPVO) sectors, with both external actors offering different programmes of entrepreneurship education for the purpose of solving societal problems and with teachers working to develop pedagogy being active in the process (see Chapter 1). Translating expresses societal entrepreneurship, as it involves long-term processes with the focus on developing society and societal change through the students during their stay at and after school.

ON METHOD

Over the years I have been part of national research mapping and studying the use of entrepreneurship in Swedish primary and secondary schools. I have also been involved in studies that have focused on different regional and local projects where processes have been followed in-depth through observations of teacher training and listening to teachers' stories. The multifaceted character of my studies has given me the opportunity to access the translation process from different perspectives, from policy, external actors' and teachers' perspectives. The external actors and their ideas have been focused upon in studies of different projects and initiatives concerned with stimulating schools to work with entrepreneurship (Lundström et al., 2005), and yet in other studies the focus has been on understanding what teachers are doing when they do entrepreneurship education; in sum, how the concept is translated into education practise (Berglund and Holmgren, 2007).

Throughout my encounter with this translation process I have frequently met with external actors and teachers at seminars, courses, conferences and interviews. The external actors and teachers that I have met have all had a commitment to developing education and society and it has not been difficult to become fascinated by them. Early in the process I was enthusiastically focusing on the progress of entrepreneurship education in terms of the growing body of active schools and stories of success concerning proactive and creative students. But during the process I have also travelled in my own mind, and by internalizing a social constructional epistemology I have been able to critically reflect on the translation process and see new aspects. By taking the starting point in theories based on social constructional ideas in this text, I view facts and truths as socially produced, reproduced and transformed, conditioned by a certain historical time or context (Berger and Luckmann, 1966; Burr, 1995; Foucault, 1993). I also understand entrepreneurship as a discourse, that is, the sets of meanings, metaphors, representations, images, stories and so on that together produce entrepreneurship and entrepreneurship education (Burr, 1995).

Characteristic for the traditional entrepreneurship discourse is the lack of unambiguity – instead dominating meanings of entrepreneurship are associated to business start-ups and economic growth. However, this has in the research community also come to be challenged with new meanings of entrepreneurship, as channelling a value creation power in all spheres of society (Berglund and Johansson, 2007). The dominating meanings of the entrepreneurship discourse have also been shown as all-inclusive, being gender-biased and ethnocentrically determined, where the Western man is taken for granted (Ogbor, 2000). In education practices the different meanings are also present, analysed by Leffler (2006) in term of the business and the enterprising discourses. The former refers to the dominating meanings of entrepreneurship as business activities while the enterprising discourse refers to a broader definition focusing on the general abilities development of an entrepreneurial approach, with the emphasis on stimulating students' curiosity, creativity, confidence and ability to make decisions (see Chapter 8 for an elaboration on these issues).

What entrepreneurship will be translated into an education practice is from this point of departure an ongoing construction process. In analysing the translation process I will relate to five of the studies that I was involved in between 2003 and 2011, covering different time periods as well as different research objectives and scopes (see Table 9.1).

Both the studies 'Entrepreneurship in school' (Berglund and Holmgren, 2007; Holmgren 2007) and 'Creating opportunities for young entrepreneurship' (Lundström et al., 2005) are national, covering mapping studies with the purpose of studying the use of the words enterprising and entrepreneurship in Swedish schools in terms of frequency. The second study also included mapping different initiatives and projects with the aim of supporting young entrepreneurship. The other three are studies of specific projects with the purpose of stimulating entrepreneurship in education. The Open for Business study (Holmgren, 2004) focused on the effects of an initiative imported from Canada, the Entrepreneurial Learning in Västra Götaland (Holmgren, 2010) on how teachers translated entrepreneurship into their practice, and the last, the PELP study (report forthcoming in 2012), was concerned with conditions for entrepreneurial learning, comparing the translations of a Swedish and an English school.

Table 9.1　Interactive research projects

Project (Time period)	Connection to Entrepreneurship Education	Empirical material
Open for Business (2003)	An evaluation of the Canadian Open for Business concept that was imported to Sweden in 2000 to stimulate young people to become entrepreneurs.	35 interviews with 39 persons involved in the project: project leaders, initiators, financers, competitors and teachers.
Creating Opportunities for Young Entrepreneurship – Nordic examples and experiences (2004)	A study of young entrepreneurship in the Nordic countries. The objective was to structure experiences from ongoing activities in the Nordic countries to stimulate young entrepreneurship, both inside and outside the educational system, to evaluate these experiences, to find good examples and to analyse possibilities and limitations with different types of measures and to relate this to existing theory.	Two seminars with actors, observations at conferences and hearings, document analysis of regional documents (21 Regional Agreements for Growth and 21 Regional Programmes for Growth), and a survey concerning 90% of the Swedish elementary schools and 98% of the upper secondary schools. The response ratio was 32% and 43% respectively, which corresponds to 1434 elementary schools and 322 upper secondary schools.
Entrepreneurship in school (2006–2007)	A study launched in autumn 2006 in Sweden with the purpose of mapping the progress of entrepreneurship at the lower levels of the educational system and develop the understanding of what teachers do when they do entrepreneurship education.	A web survey where the response ratio was 31% and 51% respectively, which corresponds to 1409 elementary schools and 394 upper secondary schools. 37 interviews with 95 people. 17 of them were actors outside the educational system actively involved in efforts to stimulate schools to work with entrepreneurship and the remaining 78 represented schools, mostly teachers but also some principals/headmasters, career advisors, parents and students.

Table 9.1   (continued)

Project (Time period)	Connection to Entrepreneurship Education	Empirical material
Entrepreneurial learning in Västra Götaland (2009–2011)	A study launched in 2009 with the purpose of studying the implementation of one concept of entrepreneurial learning. The concept was proposed by a regionally initiated project.	24 days of observations of teachers training in an entrepreneurial learning concept, 11 focus group interviews and 62 in-depth interviews with teachers and headmasters.
Pan European Entrepreneurial learning partnership, PELP (2010–2012)	A study launched in 2010 with the purpose of studying the implementation of entrepreneurial learning in a Swedish and an English case.	The study is ongoing and includes so far six interviews with nine teachers, headmasters and actors, one teacher questionnaire and one student questionnaire.

ANALYSIS OF THE ENTREPRENEURSHIP EDUCATION TRANSLATION PROCESS

With the purpose of analysing how the translation of entrepreneurship from policy to educational practice in the Swedish context can be understood as a societal entrepreneurship process, the teachers' and external actors' involvement in the process will be analysed. Taking a point of departure in the introduction of entrepreneurship education in policy, two analyses of the translation process will make up the central part of this chapter: (1) teachers' struggle to grasp entrepreneurship education, and (2) external actors' attempts to involve teachers in the translation process.

The continuing chapter starts out with *the introduction of entrepreneurship education into policy*. This serves as a setting for the forthcoming analyses of the translation process. The analysis of policy documents is focused on policy texts both on the supra level (EU) and on the national Swedish level (see Table 9.2). The understanding of entrepreneurship education is analysed in terms of the business and the enterprising discourse (Leffler, 2006). The analysis shows that when the lower levels of the educational system are in focus, the enterprising discourse is the dominant one,

Table 9.2   Analysed policy documents

EU level	Time period/year
Action plan for entrepreneurship, European Commission	2004
The concrete future objectives of education and training systems, Education Council	2001
Final report of the Expert Group on Education and Training for Entrepreneurship Education, European Commission	2002
Swedish national level	
Bill to the Swedish Parliamentary Education Committee	1998/99:UbU3
	1998/99:UbU7
	1999/2000:Ub268
	1999/2000:Ub206
Project plan Entrepreneurship programme, Swedish Agency for Economic and Regional Growth	2005–2007
Strategy for entrepreneurship in the educational area, Swedish Offices of government	2009
Curriculum for compulsory school, pre-class and leisure-time centres 2011. National Agency for Education	2011

in contrast to outside the educational sphere, where the business discourse – the traditional entrepreneurship discourse predominates.

With the policy of entrepreneurship education as a platform the first analysis concerns *teachers' struggle to grasp entrepreneurship education.* When the concept travels into the public sector and its educational setting, the a priori ascribed meanings and taken-for-granted assumptions of entrepreneurship are made visible and create tensions, conflicts and resistance among teachers. By taking a point of departure in Laclau and Mouffe's (2001) discourse theory these tensions, conflicts and resistance can be traced from the different views of what meanings should be ascribed to the concept in pedagogy and to previous meanings ascribed to the entrepreneurship discourse. As the a priori ascribed meanings contrast to pedagogical reasoning, the teachers are challenged to ascribe new meanings to the entrepreneurship concept. Laclau and Mouffe emphasize, in contrast to other thinkers (for example Foucault, 1980), that a discourse can always be contested, as it exists in a social field where other discursive resources can be employed. The created tensions, conflicts and resistance can in terms of Laclau and Mouffe be understood as a discursive battle – a process of change where the meanings ascribed to the entrepreneurship concept are contested by already existing discourses in the educational setting.

The second analysis focuses on how, despite the tensions, conflicts and resistance that the concept awakens, the concept of entrepreneurship is imposed upon the educational system. Here *the external actors' attempts to involve teachers in the translation process* are made visible and analysed. By taking a point of departure in theories concerning governmentality the translation process is enhanced as part of the complex process needed to govern at a distance, to realize and implement political decisions (Rose, 1999). The external actors are important in this process as they create links to the teachers. In making these links actors representing the NPVO, the private as well as the public sector cross the sector borders with the purpose of solving societal problems like the lack of businesses, the lack of engineers, and problems with unsuccessful studies, including the role of the school and how we (should) view education in contemporary society.

THE INTRODUCTION OF ENTREPRENEURSHIP EDUCATION INTO POLICY

Since the mid-1990s there has been a growing interest in stimulating entrepreneurship and entrepreneurial behaviour at all levels of the Swedish educational system. The efforts carried out derive from theories and beliefs in the importance of entrepreneurs and entrepreneurship as drivers of societal development with the emphasis on economic values (Schumpeter, 1961). The initially industrial and entrepreneurship policy interest in entrepreneurship in primary and secondary schools was expressed in national and various regional programs focusing on economic growth (Nutek, 1999; 2000; 2004), cheered by private organizations and non-profit organizations with a common interest in business and economic growth.

In the first few years after the turn of the millennium there was a slowly emerging trend where policy interest in entrepreneurship in schools locally gradually grew to become an education policy issue (Mahieu, 2006). In May 2009 entrepreneurship became an education policy interest at the national level and the National Agency for Economic and Regional Growth, previously responsible for stimulating entrepreneurship in Swedish schools, handed the responsibility over to the National Agency for Education, responsible for managing, supporting and monitoring schools (Swedish Cabinet Office, 2009). This policy change was expressed by a strategy covering the whole Swedish educational system in 2009 and two years later by integrating entrepreneurship in the national curriculum. As mentioned in the introduction, the process of integrating entrepreneurship into the national curriculum was not without political dissent. This was proposed to the Parliamentary Standing Committee on Education, as early as before the turn of the millennium, some of which proposals had strong links to the traditional meanings of entrepreneurship. They proposed, for example, the establishment of a national program for upper secondary school focused on business and entrepreneurship (1998/99:UbU3), and that knowledge about entrepreneurship and managing business should be integrated as early as possible in primary school and then be developed increasingly during the school years (1999/2000:Ub268). The latter bill was rejected with reference to the fact that the national curriculum for primary and lower secondary schools, preschool and leisure centres all included the abilities to solve problems, take initiatives, and the ability to be flexible and creative, aspects that the Education Committee emphasized was important for all individuals, not just the self-employed.

The introduction to the Swedish Government's strategy for entrepreneurship in education presented in 2009 made visible the strong links to businesses, in particular focusing on the necessity of opening up for self-employment:

> Self-employment needs to become as natural a choice as employment. To achieve this, the educational system can play an important role by helping pupils and students to develop and use the knowledge, skills and attitudes needed. (Swedish Cabinet Office, 2009.)

The strategy also made visible an idea of entrepreneurship in the educational system consistent with the idea advocated by the European Commission (2002). The Swedish government has emphasized that entrepreneurship should be a continuing theme through all the levels in the educational system, and that the lower levels should focus more on the development of an entrepreneurial approach, with the emphasis on stimulating students' curiosity, creativity, confidence and ability to make decisions. The European Commission expresses this in the same manner:

> At the level of primary education, entrepreneurship teaching will aim to foster in the pupils those personal qualities such as creativity, spirit of initiative and independence that contribute to the development of an entrepreneurial attitude, which will prove useful in their life and in every working activity. (European Commission, 2002.)

In upper secondary school and at the higher levels of the educational system, the Swedish government instead wants to emphasize special knowledge and competencies needed to start and manage a company. Following this ideal, entrepreneurship was explicitly integrated in the national curriculum in 2011 for primary and lower secondary school as one of the school's missions. Entrepreneurship at these levels was explicitly defined as problem-solving, creativity, curiosity, confidence, initiative and having the ability to work alone and in a group:

> An important mission for the school is to give an overview and context. The school should stimulate students' creativity, curiosity and confidence, and the will to test own ideas and solve problems. The students should get the opportunity to take initiative and develop their ability to work, both alone and together with others. The school should then contribute to students developing an attitude that promotes entrepreneurship. (Swedish National Agency for Education, 2011.)

Texts concerning the will to test students' own ideas, and some competencies and abilities previously included in the former curriculum (National Agency for Education, 1994) were now explicitly connected with entrepreneurship.

The outcome of the introduction of entrepreneurship as a concept in education is that Swedish policies do not ascribe meanings connected with business to entrepreneurship in primary and lower secondary school; instead the enterprising discourse dominates the policy – the discourse that is more about an entrepreneurial approach (see Chapter 8) that can be expressed in many different arenas in society. Starting and managing businesses, the business discourse, does not predominate until in upper secondary schools. Even if policy texts do not define entrepreneurship at the lower levels of the educational system as starting and managing a business, the translation process going on in Sweden since the 1990s has been permeated by struggles due to such associations. In the next part of the chapter these struggles will be analysed by framing the discursive battle going on within the translation process as the concept of entrepreneurship is contested by the pedagogical discourses in the educational setting. Teachers employ these pedagogical discourses to describe meanings to entrepreneurship that make it meaningful for them.

TEACHERS' STRUGGLE TO GRASP ENTREPRENEURSHIP EDUCATION

In 2007 I met two teachers and a headmaster from a compulsory school. The headmaster had answered in a survey that they used the word entrepreneurship as a description for some pedagogical activities and we wanted to explore this further (Berglund and Holmgren, 2007). On the spot the headmaster almost immediately confessed that they did not work with entrepreneurship, but that they saw this interview as a possibility to learn more about it. One of the teachers working in a primary school really wondered why she should participate in the interview, because she could not see any connection between entrepreneurship and her work with teaching her pupils to read and write:

> I feel totally locked in my way of thinking, I find it very difficult to see entrepreneurship connected to the small pupils I work with. When you say entrepreneurship I am thinking of services that you buy from outside school. That it is a service and that they communicate and that we can make use of it in school. (Quote from an interview, 5 May 2007.)

To make use of entrepreneurship in pedagogical work was totally incomprehensible to the teacher since she refers to entrepreneurship as business. Four years earlier in another part of Sweden we attended a presentation where a mapping of entrepreneurship education in a Swedish county was presented, and in line with the above example one of the most common comments made by teachers during that study was that they did not think that the entrepreneurship concept belonged in schools or 'I don't understand what you mean, this is a primary school'. One external actor working actively to stimulate teachers to work with entrepreneurship expresses similar thoughts in an interview:

> In schools the problem was that they [the teachers] viewed entrepreneurship as business: 'So, now they are going to make capitalists out of everyone.' (Quote from of an external actor in an interview, 20 August 2003.)

These comments can be viewed as a resistance among teachers to at all position themselves in accordance with entrepreneurship as a business concept, as this is for them associated with economic values and meanings like business or economic growth and even with being gender-biased (Berglund, 2007; Ahl, 2002). Such values are incomprehensible to teachers embedded in pedagogical discourses. They actually refuse to be at all involved in the translation process of entrepreneurship from policy to practice. This defence is not against entrepreneurship per se, rather against entrepreneurship in the pedagogical setting, as they are protecting pedagogical values.

The struggle in the translation process offers opportunities for external actors to market well packaged solutions for how to understand and deal with entrepreneurship in the educational system. As the following example shows, part of the struggle is teachers' resistance to such solutions offered. This teacher and his colleagues were participating in an EU-funded project organized by the county authorities working with regional development. They were attending a course where they were trained in a specific solution for entrepreneurship education labelled entrepreneurial learning. Most of the teachers had heard of the concept before, since the course lecturer was co-author of a book on the topic. Some of the teachers had also visited a lecture where students trained by the course lecturer had acted as speakers marketing the entrepreneurship education solution by reflecting on how it had contributed to their development. These teachers were told that they should now start working with entrepreneurship education at their schools. There were about 40 teachers in the course, but this very teacher stood out. In front of all the teachers and the course leader, he was one of the few arguing that he did not know whether he would later embark on the entrepreneurship journey.

The teacher explained to me in an interview that the course strongly advocated a specific conceptualization of entrepreneurship education that he first wanted to relate to before making a decision. To start with he wanted to know what this would mean to them in their personal teaching style and in the working team's teaching style, how they could sew the threads together; 'and have we evaluated what we do first?' he wondered. 'Does our teaching have shortcomings, or perhaps it is very good in many ways, I think'. He continued: 'The best way to teach today is to have a lot of careful briefings which capture the students' attention, where the students are aware of the development, but it is also important to involve students in the process where they learn how to achieve the goals together; it is together that we shall manage the teachers' mission today.' The teacher told me that he missed the generic discussion about traditional versus entrepreneurial education in the course, and that entrepreneurial learning was held forward as the mantra for learning. 'And of course', the teacher went on, 'the author (lecturer in the course) he sells an idea that he believes in, but then I want to reflect upon this idea, do I want to work like this? Is it so obvious? Is this the optimum way? I don't see one door to learning; for me there are many doors to walk through, and you come to the same room anyway, but all the doors are needed. And it is important to see through all these doors how you learn, and how the students learn.' The teacher was convinced that both entrepreneurial learning and traditional education are needed, where traditional education is associated with knowledge transfer, safe routines, and very concentrated briefings, but all merged together, and he is already working like this. 'Right now', he ended, 'it is very much entrepreneurial learning, go for it, this is the future of learning, and I can buy it partly, but not all of it'. After the course he decided not to embark on the entrepreneurial journey and implement the offered solution together with his colleagues. Instead he remained satisfied with the entrepreneurial elements he had already incorporated in his teaching.

Other teachers that I have interviewed over the years express in a similar way that this (entrepreneurship) is nothing new, that they are already doing this:

> The course (a teacher course about entrepreneurial learning) disappointed me, 'cause I already do this . . . I have been doing this for 6–7 years. (Quote from an interview with a teacher in lower secondary school, 9 February 2009.)

> I partly work like this today. (Quote from an interview with a teacher in lower secondary school, 27 February 2009.)

Still, other teachers and headmasters see the entrepreneurship concept as an opportunity to develop their pedagogy and also to benefit the process to organize school activity in novel ways (Berglund and Holmgren, 2007). Their stories about how they use this opportunity concern how entrepreneurship becomes the continuation of an already started process, often expressed in enhanced collaboration among teacher colleagues with cross-curriculum projects and (or) collaboration with external organizations in focus, creative organization concerning the time table to obtain longer time slots, and a stronger emphasis on students' competencies like initiative, problem solving and responsibility (like the teachers' stories from the introduction).

These teachers can be seen, together with external actors, as involved in a discursive battle (Laclau and Mouffe, 2001) about ascribing meaning to the concept of entrepreneurship in the pedagogical setting, but where the teachers are those who deal with it in their classrooms. The struggles presented above emphasize the need to ascribe new meanings to the entrepreneurship concept when translating it to the pedagogical setting, since the business association would be totally incomprehensible for teachers at the lower levels of the educational system. However, when the traditional entrepreneurship discourse is challenged by pedagogical discourses in the pedagogical setting, the entrepreneurship concept also offers a possible opportunity for a creative development of pedagogy.

THE EXTERNAL ACTORS' ATTEMPTS TO INVOLVE TEACHERS IN THE TRANSLATION PROCESS

Despite the tensions and conflicts the concept of entrepreneurship diffuses into the educational system. Leaving the discursive battle for ascribing meaning to the entrepreneurship concept to analyse the governing dimension of the translation process, the analysis now focuses on how entrepreneurship is diffused into the educational system. Now the external actors' creative work to explore different ways to involve teachers in the translation process is in the spotlight.

From a governing perspective the translation process concerns the creation of links between the objectives of authorities that wish to govern and the personal projects and objectives of organizations and individuals who are governed (Rose, 1999). The links needed between, in this case, policy agencies and programs on supra, national, regional and local levels, school authorities, business organizations, non-profit organizations like inventors and business associations, private educational companies, teachers, headmasters and so on are crucial for the translation process. The creation of these links is of particular importance to liberal government mentalities, like the one that pervades the Swedish government. Liberal political rationalities are committed to the twin project of respecting individual freedom and at the same time being involved in shaping the conduct of the citizens to fit the prevailing perceptions of how citizens should act (Rose, 1999). The entrepreneurship discourse in the business setting is in itself an example of this liberal rationality expressed by emphasizing the individual. Entrepreneurship is also associated with freedom, in that people should be stimulated to realize their own ideas, free themselves from mental structures and norms, and create something that manifests their existence in the world (see Peters, 2005). In their creative attempt to involve teachers in the translation process the external actors are involved in this complex process of governing at a distance.

The creation of links has been an especially important part of the early translation process when there was no explicit legitimacy in the national curriculum. Since the late 1990s many of the external actors, guided by their own projects and objectives, have been involved in extensive efforts to stimulate entrepreneurship in schools. These efforts have been expressed in inspiration, information and knowledge production activities as well as in the development and dissemination of pedagogic concepts. Due to the lack of interest from the educational sphere (such as teacher education programs at Swedish universities) in dealing with the concept, the development and the translation have been driven by different interest organizations, private companies and business stakeholders in the public sector, where the possibility of financing and the management of EU projects have had a great impact (Mahieu, 2006).

Creating links between entrepreneurship policy and external actors has not been a major problem, since these actors' own goals have often harmonized with the policy objectives. One category of external actors includes those representing initiatives and solutions that were active in the educational system before the entrepreneurship concept made its entrance. The first example is an innovation contest aimed at students in years 6–9, with the purpose to 'stimulate young people's creativity and awaken an early interest in science, technology and innovation.' The contest was initiated by an engineering association, whose reason claimed to be the lack of students in engineer education:

[In]1979 when the engineering association started the contest, the number of applicants for engineering courses started to decrease. The idea was to renew the interest by stimulating students and school staff to work with creativity, problem solving and technology. (Ingenjörsamfundet, 2010.)

The societal problem from which the organization takes its point of departure is the shortage of engineers, as well as a modernist discourse where technology is ascribed great importance for the development of society. When the actors responsible communicate why the association started the innovation contest they position themselves within the traditional entrepreneurship discourse by referring to the inspiration of a new generation of entrepreneurs.

The engineering association started 'the innovation contest' in 1979 to stimulate young people's creativity and early awaken an interest in natural science, technology and innovation. The purpose of the extension was to inspire a new generation of inventors and entrepreneurs. (Finn-upp, 2010a.)

With the focus on problem-solving and creativity the actors could easily position the innovation contest within the entrepreneurship discourse. Even if the actual objectives of starting the innovation concept differ from that of entrepreneurship policy, they harmonize, and the actors responsible for the innovation concept can act as necessary actors in the translation process. Among other established initiatives that these actors could easily position within the discourse is Young Enterprise.[1] With the focus of the initiative on starting and managing a business it can be seen as a manifestation of the traditional meaning ascribed to entrepreneurship, representing what Leffler (2006) refers to as the business discourse of entrepreneurship education. Many of the established initiatives that are positioned within the entrepreneurship discourse actually take a point of departure in various problems like the lack of interest in natural science and technology, the lack of businesses or of connection between schools and external organizations. To be able to position solutions and initiatives within the discourse gives external actors the possibility to access funding and to work with the problems they focus on.

Before entrepreneurship was included in the national curriculum, the creation of links between the initiatives and the teachers was more challenging than creating links between the initiatives and policy. As the association to entrepreneurship and business creates tensions and resistance among teachers, one way was to avoid using the word entrepreneurship and instead invent a new word. The word has now been in use since the first decade of the millennium. Other ways of creating these links with the teachers was to relate to already existent discourses in the pedagogical setting. In the following example one external actor thus relates to pedagogical method, problem solving and learning:

> The innovation concept is an educational method, a tool for all teachers in lower secondary school who want to encourage students' desire to discover. In the innovation concept invention is used as a way of learning. Students will identify a problem in their daily lives and may then try to solve the problem by their own invention. On the way there is much to learn: about our history, about society, about technology and not least about ourselves! (Finn-upp, 2010b.)

As external actors take their point of departure in specific challenges they also represent different themes within the entrepreneurship education discourse: innovation, business, collaboration school/working life, technology and natural science. Apart from these, there is a growing theme, in the last four years referred to as entrepreneurial learning or, as Leffler (2006) would call it, the enterprising discourse. This is also the theme which the teachers described in the introduction to this chapter referred to and which is further analysed in terms of entrepreneurial approach in Chapters 8 and 10. When referring to it as entrepreneurial learning it is viewed as a pedagogical approach that will encourage students to take initiative and responsibility regardless of what subject is on the timetable.

When one actor offered solutions for entrepreneurial learning it was communicated as a solution to implement the national curriculum for primary and secondary schools as early as 1994. Entrepreneurial learning is then associated with objectives and themes like an objective-oriented school, individualized education, striving for making every student develop an individual way to learn and adapted to individual conditions and needs, as well as with students taking responsibility and students that are active (Holmgren, 2010). These objectives and themes can all be found in the national curriculum from 1994, as pointed out as early as 1997 in a report to the Swedish government (Johannisson and Madsén 1997). This way of communicating entrepreneurship and entrepreneurial learning as a solution to problems that differ from those ascribed to the concept in the economic setting is not unusual. Entrepreneurial learning is for example claimed, by the above-mentioned actor, to be a solution to the problem labelled 'learned helplessness'[2] – a technical term in human and animal psychology. This is done in a widely distributed book, *Så tänds eldsjälar – en introduktion till entreprenöriellt lärande* ('This is how genuine enthusiasts are lit – an introduction to entrepreneurial learning') by Peterson and Westlund (2007). The book was published by the Swedish National Agency for Economic and Regional Growth[3] with the purpose of giving teachers information about and suggestions for how entrepreneurial learning can be initiated as well as taught. The actors describe that learned helplessness characterizes individuals who do not dare to take initiatives because they are afraid to fail. This is said to be caused when individuals fail to see the relationship between their own acting and consequences in their environment. The actors also describe that the higher demands on people to constantly choose as well as the constantly increased range of choices combined with media's external demands pouring over mankind cause children and young people to develop symptoms that can be traced to learned helplessness.[4] Entrepreneurial learning is then communicated to teachers as the solution for this learned helplessness:

> Entrepreneurial learning is an excellent educational form to create opportunities for the students who have started to develop learned helplessness to bring their own driving force to life. (Peterson and Westlund, 2007: 17.)

The construction of entrepreneurship as a solution to various problems in order to create links with the teachers is also visualized in the strategy for entrepreneurship in the Swedish educational system presented in 2009. According to this, entrepreneurial skills, apart from strengthening the individuals' possibilities to start and manage a business, can also contribute to students managing their studies better:

> Entrepreneurial skills will increase opportunities for individuals to start and manage a business. Skills like seeing possibilities, taking initiative and transforming ideas into action are also valuable for the individual and society in a wide sense . . . Other entrepreneurial skills such as learning to solve problems, planning the work and cooperating with others can also help young people to carry out their studies more successfully. (Government Offices of Sweden, 2009: 5.)

Finally, links are also created by means of dichotomies. This is done in the efforts to emphasize and highlight where the objectives and guidelines of the 1994 curriculum and the traditional entrepreneurship discourse harmonize. A common tendency is to set the 'traditional school' in direct contrast to the 'entrepreneurial school', while the objectives of the curriculum are held forward as being associated with the entrepreneurial school. There thus arises a struggle between those two discourses about the legitimacy to represent the true and correct education (Leffler, 2006).

Summarizing the governing dimension of the translation process, the analysis shows that external actors' link-making is part of the process of how the concept of entrepreneurship is governed into the educational system. The external actors' link-making in the translation process is both creative and innovative, expressed in the making of entrepreneurship education as the solution to various problems, the innovation of new words, and the use of pedagogical discourses. By this work the external actors are involved in the process of governing at a distance at the same time as they use the entrepreneurship concept to work with various societal problems, which is their mission.

CONCLUSION – THE TRANSLATION PROCESS AS AN EXPRESSION OF SOCIETAL ENTREPRENEURSHIP

In this chapter, taking a point of departure in the entrepreneurship education policy discourse, I have made two analyses of the translation process of entrepreneurship from policy to educational practices in the Swedish context: the discursive battle – teachers' struggle to grasp entrepreneurship education and the governing dimension – external actors' attempts to involve teachers in the translation process. The analysis of the discourse shows that there is an agreement in policy on the importance of implementing entrepreneurship in the educational system and also that there should be more focus on the development of an entrepreneurial approach among younger children and from upper secondary school, including the knowledge and competencies needed to start and manage a company. Despite this, the traditional meanings that actors in the business setting have previously ascribed to entrepreneurship create tensions, conflicts and even resistance when the concept travels into the education setting.

When a concept travels into a new setting governed by political intentions for future welfare there are challenges. First, such travel is dependent on translators as private organizations, associations and teachers, these translators all having their own agendas and being involved in their own projects. Secondly, translation processes do not occur without changing the ideas, as translators do it from their own unique needs (Czarniawska and Sevón, 1996). One conclusion from the analysis of the translation process is also that the travelling of the concept of entrepreneurship to the education setting has been used as an opportunity where both external actors and teachers have been mobilized. In this process both external actors and teachers act as societal entrepreneurs since they have been (and still are) involved in the creation of pedagogical values. For the external actors, the entrepreneurship concept is an opportunity to deal with a diversity of problems: the lack of businesses, the lack of engineers, learned helplessness, problems with implementing the old national curriculum, problems with unsuccessful studies, earning a living and so on. In their cross-sector task to solve problems and secure future welfare they have challenged the resistance among teachers to make them position themselves within the entrepreneurship discourse. This mobilization is also expressed by a non-profit network that external actors have initiated to support the translation process.[5] For the teachers the entrepreneurship concept is an opportunity to develop their pedagogy and schools. In this task they employ already existing pedagogical discourses to describe new meanings to the concept. The conclusion is that the translation process can been seen as an expression of enacting societal entrepreneurship since in order to solve societal problems it crosses boundaries and involves the private, the public as well as the non-profit/voluntary (NPVO) sectors. The struggles to ascribe meanings to entrepreneurship in the educational setting and the external actors' attempts to involve teachers in the translation process are simply two expressions of societal entrepreneurship in the translation process of entrepreneurship from policy into the educational setting.

During the translation process teachers' resistance has changed. In the early process they resisted dealing with the economic discourse at all. However, since entrepreneurship was explicitly integrated in the national curriculum in 2011, this kind of resistance is more difficult to state. By including the word in the curriculum all teachers need to relate to the concept of entrepreneurship. Even the teacher I met at a major school fair in 2011, when I was acting ambassador for women in entrepreneurship and told him that is was an initiative of the business minister to highlight women managing businesses, immediately made the association to the curriculum: 'It is she that has dragged this entr . . . oh I can't pronounce it, into the curriculum', looking not too happy about it. But as it is included in the national curriculum he has to do more than pronouncing the first letters; he has to relate to entrepreneurship in his practice, and instead he can, as the teachers cited in this chapter, resist the economic discourse by participating in the discursive battle, ascribe new meaning to the concept and enact societal entrepreneurship.

NOTES

1. Young Enterprise is a worldwide concept where students in upper secondary school start, manage and close down a business.
2. Seligman (1975) describes helplessness as when an animal or a person is placed in a situation where a particular outcome is – or appears to be – independent of his responses, he learns that his responses are ineffective. The affected individual may conclude that any responses he makes will be powerless to affect the outcome. The number of responses

decreases; a 'what's the use' syndrome develops; and helplessness becomes a self-fulfilling prophecy. If the outcome is a traumatic event – if it involves physical or emotional pain – the helpless subject may progress through successive stages of fear and anxiety to a deep depression and, in some instances, death. In 1965 Seligman experimented with dogs and by the use of chocks, the dog learned that is was futile to run away from the chocks and developed learned helplessness.

3. Only in 2007 were 39, 000 copies handed out for free, down-loaded copies not included. Information obtained from the agency by mail 22 January 2008.

4. In Chapter 8 and in Johannisson (2010) it is rather the teachers that learned helplessness is ascribed to.

5. The network is called Nelis (Network for Entrepreneurial Learning in School) and was initiated by two external actors responsible for entrepreneurship in school initiatives in the municipalities of Örebro and Västerås. See http://www.nelis.se.

REFERENCES

Ahl, H.J. (2002), *The Making of the Female Entrepreneur, A Discourse Analysis of Research Texts on Women's Entrepreneurship*, Doctoral thesis, Jönköping International Business School.

Audretsch D.B. and Thurik, R. (2001), *Linking Entrepreneurship to Growth*, Paris: OECD.

Backström-Widjeskog, B. (2010), 'Teachers' thoughts on entrepreneurship education', in Skogen, K. and Sjøvoll, J. (eds), *Creativity and Innovation: Preconditions for Entrepreneurial Action*, Trondheim: Tapir Academic Press.

Berger, P.L. and Luckmann, T. (1966/1991), *The Social Construction of Reality*, London: Anchor Books.

Berglund, K. (2007), Jakten på entreprenörer – Om öppningar och låsningar i entreprenörskapsdiskursen ('The hunt for the entrepreneurs – about openings and closures in the entrepreneurship discourse'), Doctoral Dissertation No. 39, Västerås: Mälardalen University.

Berglund, K. and Holmgren, C. (2007), *Entreprenörskap & skolan – vad är det lärare berättar att de gör när de gör entreprenörskap i skolan?* ('Entrepreneurship & school – what do teachers do when they do entrepreneurship in schools'), FSF 2007: 17.

Berglund, K. and Holmgren, C.A. (2008), 'What do teachers do when they do entrepreneurship education? . . . and how can we ask about it?' *International Journal of Business and Globalisation*, 2 (4): 354–372.

Berglund, K. and Holmgren, C.A. (2012), 'Entrepreneurship education in policy and practice', *International Journal of Entrepreneurial Venturing* (forthcoming).

Berglund, K. and Johansson, A.W. (2007), 'The entrepreneurship discourse – outlined from diverse constructions of entrepreneurship on the academic scene', *Journal of Enterprising Communities: People and Places in the Global Economy*, 1 (1): 77–102.

Burr, V. (1995), *An Introduction to Social Constructionism*, London: Routledge.

Czarniawska, B., and Sevón, G. (eds) (1996), *Translating Organizational Change*, Berlin: de Gruyter.

European Commission (2002), *Final Report of the Expert Group on Education and Training for Entrepreneurship Education*, Brussels: European Commission.

European Commission (2004), *Action Plan for Entrepreneurship*, Brussels: European Commission.
Finn-upp (2010a), *Finn-upp*, available at http://www.finnupp.se/finnupp.php (accessed 17 April 2010).
Finn-upp (2010b), *Finn-upp*, available at http://www.finnupp.se/index..php (accessed 17 April 2010).
Foucault, M. (1980), 'Truth and power', in *Power/Knowledge. Selected Interviews and Other Writings 1972–77*, Hemel Hempstead: Harvester Wheatsheaf.
Foucault, M. (1991), 'Governmentality', in Burchel, G., Gordon, C. and Miller P. (eds) *The Foucault Effect, Studies in Governmentality*, Hemel Hempstead: Harvester Wheatsheaf, pp. 87–104.
Foucault, M. (1993), *Diskursens ordning* ('The order of discourse'), Stockholm: Brutus Östlings bokförlag.
Gibb, A.A. (2008), 'Entrepreneurship and enterprise education in schools and colleges: Insights from UK practise', *International Journal of Entrepreneurship Education*, **6**.
Government Offices of Sweden (2009), *Strategi för entreprenörskap inom utbildningsområdet* ('Strategy for entrepreneurship within the educational system'), Stockholm: Regeringskansliet.
Holmgren, C. (2004), *Skapa din framtid – en utvärdering av Open for Business* ('Create your future – an evaluation of Open for Business'), Örebro: FSF.
Holmgren, C. (2007), *Entreprenörskap i grund- och gymnasieskolor – En kvantitativ studie 2004 och 2006* ('Entrepreneurship in primary and secondary schools – a quantitative study 2004 and 2006'), Örebro: FSF.
Holmgren, C. (2010), *Översättningen av entreprenörskap till skolans praktik. En processtudie av projektet Entreprenöriellt lärande i Västra Götaland* ('The translation of entrepreneurship into school practise. A process study of the Entrepreneurial Learning project in Västra Götaland County'), Stockholm: Entreprenörskapsforum.
Ingenjörsamfundet (2010), *Finn-upp*, available at http://www.ingenjorsamfundet.se/Om-oss/Finn-upp (accessed 17 April 2010).
Johannisson, B. (2010), 'The agony of the Swedish school when confronted by entrepreneurship', in Skogen, K. and Sjøvoll, J. (eds), *Creativity and Innovation: Preconditions for Entrepreneurial Action*, Trondheim: Tapir Academic Press.
Johannisson, B. and Madsén, T. (1997), *I entreprenörskapets tecken – en studie av skolning I förnyelse* ('In the name of entrepreneurship – a study of training for renewal'), Närings och handelsdepartementet, Ds 1997: 3, Stockholm: Fritzes.
Kirchhoff, B. (1994), *Entrepreneurship and Dynamic Capitalism: The Economics of Business Firm Formation and Growth*, Westport, Conn: Praeger.
Kirzner, I. (1982),'The theory of entrepreneurship in economic growth', in Kebt, C., Sexton, D. and Vesper K. (eds), *The Encyclopaedia of Entrepreneurship*, Englewood Cliffs, NJ: Prentice Hall, pp. 272–276.
Laclau, E. and Mouffe, C. (2001), *Hegemony and Socialist Strategy, Towards a Radical Democratic Politics*, New York: Verso.
Leffler, E. (2006), *Företagsamma elever – Diskurser kring entreprenörskap och företagsamhet i skolan* ('Proactive students – Discourses concerning entrepreneurship and enterprising in school'), Doctoral thesis in pedagogical work No. 8, Umeå: Umeå University.

Lundström, A. (ed.) (2005), *Creating Opportunities for Young Entrepreneurship – Nordic Examples and Experiences*, Örebro: FSF.

Mahieu. R. (2006), *Agents of Change and Policies of Scale – A Policy Study of Entrepreneurship and Enterprise in Education*, Doctoral thesis in pedagogical work No. 9, Umeå: Umeå University.

Nutek (1999), *Skolans entreprenörskaps bok* ('The book of entrepreneurship for schools'), Infonumber 044–1998, Stockholm: Nutek.

Nutek (2000), *För framtida företagsamhet – Ett nationellt handlingsprogram för ungt företagande* ('For future enterprising – A national action plan for young entrepreneurship'), Infonumber 062–2000, Stockholm: NUTEK.

Nutek (2004), *Projektplan Entreprenörskapsprogram 2005–2007* ('The Entrepreneurship programme project plan 2005–2007'), Stockholm: Nutek.

Ogbor, J.O. (2000), 'Mythicizing and reification in entrepreneurial discourse: Ideology critique of entrepreneurial studies', *Journal of Management Studies*, **37** (5): 605–635.

Peters, M.A. (2005), 'The new prudentialism in education: Actuarial rationality and the entrepreneurial self', *Educational Theory*, **55** (2): 123–137.

Peterson, M. and Westlund, C. (2007), *Så tänds eldsjälar – en introduktion till entreprenöriellt lärande* ('This is how genuine enthusiasts are inspired – an introduction to entrepreneurial learning'), Stockholm: Nutek.

Reynolds, P., Storey, D. and Westhead, P. (1994), 'Cross-national comparisons of the variation in new firm formation rates', *Regional Studies*, **28**, 443–456.

Rose, N. (1999), *Powers of Freedom – Reframing Political Thought*, Cambridge: Cambridge University Press.

Schumpeter, J.A. (1961), *The Theory of Economic Development*, Cambridge: Harvard University Press.

Seligman, M.E.P. (1975), *Helplessness: On Depression, Development, and Death*. A series of books in psychology. New York: W.H. Freeman/Times Books/Henry Holt & Co.

Swedish Government (2004), *Innovativa Sverige – en strategi för tillväxt genom förnyelse* ('Innovative Sweden – a strategy for growth through renewal'), Stockholm: Fritzes offentliga publikationer.

Swedish National Agency for Education (2011), *Curriculum for Compulsory School, Preclass and Leisure-time Centers 2011*, Stockholm: National Agency for Education.

10. Academic and non-academic education for societal entrepreneurship

Anders W. Johansson and Erik Rosell

PROLOGUE

[caption]If I think about what it really is that makes a person an entrepreneur, some abilities stand out as more obvious than others. One of those is to be committed and to burn for something. That is what creates the drive to do something. And in my view, this stems from your emotional life. Consequently, to listen to your emotions is necessary and in addition to be able to transform feelings like anger, irritation, joy and inspiration into seeing possibilities. As I see it, creativity is probably connected to all that. It's important to be trained in having a creative flow. That definitely doesn't happen when you are supposed to or must find something out.

To handle feelings (negative and positive) as opportunities is at the core of entrepreneurship education. This is what one of the teachers working within the organization SIP (the Swedish organization 'samhällsförändring i praktiken', in English: Societal Change in Practice) expresses above when reflecting upon the entrepreneurial approach he wants to promote among the students in the Folk High School education that he is involved in. In Chapter 8 Berglund explained how the entrepreneurial approach was made sense of in a preschool setting. Listen to your feelings and use your imagination were highlighted as pedagogical principles. In this chapter we will come back to these two principles as well as the third principle from Chapter 8 by Berglund – making friends – in the context of higher education, by comparing university and Folk High School education.

INTRODUCTION AND PROBLEM FORMULATION

The interest in entrepreneurship in the school system is discussed in Chapter 9 by Holmgren, mainly with reference to primary and secondary school. In Chapter 8 by Berglund the context is preschool education. In higher education, too, there is a growing interest in the value of entrepreneurship education (Olssen and Peters, 2005; Colette et al., 2005). This means that entrepreneurship education relates to all levels of education. Following the preceding chapters on lower education this chapter will discuss entrepreneurship in higher education.

Stevenson and Lundström (2005) in their global survey identify entrepreneurship education as one of six areas of entrepreneurship policy. In more and more countries entrepreneurship education is celebrated as a highway for future wealth creation undertaken by upcoming generations. However, there is a strong debate in pedagogy over what entrepreneurship education really means. Whether it is – or should be – a straightforward way of teaching youngsters how to start a new company or whether it is – or should refer to – a pedagogical philosophy that more generally aims at promoting entrepreneurial abilities such as collaboration, curiosity, joy, power of initiative and the taking of responsibility in an educational setting. Gibb (2005) argues that the emerging concept of an 'entrepreneurial university' calls for abandoning the dominant model of the entrepreneur being taught in favour of an appropriate model for entrepreneurial teaching. The former is portrayed as static, rational and focused on business management, while the latter is dynamic and much broader in scope, relating to life in general and to all sectors of society even if business remains an important context in the latter model. There is also an even more fundamental discussion in the entrepreneurship academy about whether we can actually teach students to be entrepreneurs (Fiet, 2001; Matlay, 2006; Hindle, 2007). This discussion concerns a lack of adequacy as to concepts, theory, pedagogy and context. The business school, teaching mainly management, might even be the wrong place for teaching students to be entrepreneurs.

As others have already stated, we might need to consider whether we educate about, for or in entrepreneurship (Taatila, 2010). The academy might be successful in transmitting scientific knowledge about entrepreneurship. It might even be successful in giving general advice and guidance to those who are already practising entrepreneurs, that is educating in entrepreneurship. Education for entrepreneurship, by contrast, implies a shift in focus from transmitting facts to training the kind of skills that are needed in order for students to become entrepreneurs. To educate for entrepreneurship in this way positions the teachers in the role of societal entrepreneurs, and more specifically in the role of promoting societal entrepreneurship, that is to encourage and release the entrepreneurial skills of the students. As pointed out by Ardalan (2008), allowing for students to develop such skills stands in opposition to the still very common academic conception that students lack knowledge that can be acquired through the transmission of general facts and theoretical models. The question is thus what the academy has to offer when it comes to educating for entrepreneurship. Is perhaps a non-academic educational environment more suitable when it comes to promoting an entrepreneurial approach among its students?

This chapter seeks to contribute to the ongoing discussion about what is actually possible to accomplish in higher education for entrepreneurship by comparing one educational program from the academy (a business school) with one related to the Swedish Folk High School movement. The business school has for ten years offered the education program 'Enterprising and Business Development' (EBD). This program uses a different pedagogical idea compared to other education programs at the business school, as it seeks to encourage a thematically and practically oriented learning. The Folk High School has since 2008 been offering a one-year education for societal entrepreneurship. The education program is performed in collaboration with an NPVO network organization called Societal Change in Practice (the SIP Network). Both the academic and the non-academic education seem to demonstrate capacity in terms of encouraging students to become entrepreneurs. Both programs have in common that the purpose is not to educate students how to start and run a company, but to encourage an entrepreneurial approach in a much broader sense. Both programs seek to promote enterprising people in all sectors of society and hence promote societal entrepreneurship as defined in this book.

As will be discussed in this chapter, there are several similarities between the EBD program and the Folk High School education program which relate to the different sector logics discussed in the introductory chapter. While the whole education system in Sweden is part of the public sector, business schools were originally closely connected to the private sector and its logic. The Folk High School tradition has its roots in the NPVO sector and the logic that characterizes this. The EBD program belongs to the business school domain, but with its broad approach to entrepreneurship the program seeks to embrace all three sectors. The Folk High School education program, while closely related to the NPVO sector, also encourages its students to start new firms in the private sector.

METHOD

We, the authors of this text, work in the academy as researchers. At the same time we are deeply involved as teachers in the EBD program. We thus represent reflecting practitioners (Schön, 1983) and self-ethnographers

(Alvesson, 2003), since educating for entrepreneurship is part of our own professional practice. Here we draw from our own direct involvement as teachers in the EBD program as well as from previously published papers about the education program, the latter written by teachers who have been involved in it before us. Further, our text is based on reflections written down by teachers involved in Folk High School education. In addition, there have been exchange activities between the contexts. Students from the Folk High School and staff from the SIP Network have been invited to activities in the EBD program and vice versa. Although not explicitly described in this text, the interactions have stimulated a dialogue over cultural differences that have created turbulence in the meetings between us, as well as similarities that we have perceived in our shared ambition to educate for entrepreneurship.

Doing 'self-ethnography' (Alvesson, 2003) means to struggle with closeness as well as closure. There is always a risk of portraying yourself in an overly positive way when you have yourself as study object. In our case we have a positive view of the EBD program that we are involved in and a rather critical view of the more traditional academic education. What has helped us to reflect at some distance on our own context is the exchange with the SIP Network. The critical view from SIP of all academic education (including the EBD program) has helped us to detach ourselves. We have been able to see limitations in the EBD program by comparing to the SIP Network and it has also stimulated our reflection on the limits of the latter and made us reconsider some of the values of academic training even in its traditional forms.

The exchange activities between the programs are part of a more extensive interactive research project that explores the organizing dimension of societal entrepreneurship in general, that is in other settings besides educational ones. One of the authors of this chapter has participated in the role of a doctoral student in several activities run by the SIP Network. He has often taken the initiative to discuss episodes from interaction related to the exchange activities, as questions were raised by students from both sides about the exchange. The other author has acted as a supervisor taking a minor part in the SIP Network activities. This way both authors have arrived at a mutual understanding and interpretation of these episodes. They both teach in the EBD program. The junior author is responsible for one of its semesters, while the senior author's major part is as supervisor for student project work. He has extensive previous experience both from teaching entrepreneurship at several universities and as an advisor for small firms. In this way, the overall interactive research project has given us additional insights from several perspectives into the practice, ambitions and organization of the SIP Network.

The text is structured in the following way. First, the EBD program is described, followed by the authors' reflections on some of the experiences and struggles involved in introducing and sustaining this program. After that, the SIP Network and its Folk High School education 'societal entre-preneurs' are described. This is followed by statements about the educa-tion from some of the teachers involved in the program, which further characterize their education program, accompanied by reflections from the authors. The chapter ends with author reflections on the similarities as well as the tensions between the two contexts and a concluding discus-sion about the role of entrepreneurship teachers as promoters of societal entrepreneurship.

THE EBD PROGRAM. EDUCATING FOR ENTREPRENEURSHIP IN THE ACADEMY

The EBD program was launched in the year 2000 at Växjö University, now Linnaeus University. The ambition was to create an alternative to the existing education program in business administration by emphasizing an entrepreneurial approach. Inspiration was found in the small business programs that had existed earlier and that were known for their close col-laboration with the small businesses in the region (compare Johannisson, 1991). Teachers in entrepreneurship also expressed a frustration with the fact that entrepreneurship as a subject was introduced late in the existing program in business administration. The ambition was instead to create a new three-year study program where an entrepreneurial approach could be developed over a longer period of time. The combination of theory, practice and personal experience was seen as important, and the program was developed with the aim of making all three kinds of knowledge avail-able to the students. The concept of enterprising was used to broaden the scope of the education and include both the traditional market-oriented view and an understanding of entrepreneurship as something that is performed in the everyday life of individuals. It was concluded that the program should focus on action, the creation of alternatives, and the ability of the students to simultaneously connect and relate to resources in the learning environment. Instead of describing the world as it is, the ambi-tion was to promote experimentation and the students' practicing of their own (Jonsson and Jonsson, 2002). A team was formed of teachers that represented different disciplines – business administration, law, informa-tion science, social psychology and economics. This team manifested one basic idea behind the program, namely that it should be cross-disciplinary. Managers were invited to form an advisory board that helped to formulate the expectations on students' skills, knowledge areas and attitudes. They also helped to describe a future target role for the student, that of a project leader (Kans, 2009).

The Basic Principles of the EBD Program

Initially, four basic principles were formulated in order to simplify the development of the program and to communicate its basic idea to new teachers. These principles were influenced by the process view of entre- preneurship as expressed by Hjorth and Johannisson (1998), which since then has been elaborated on by many others, not least Steyaert (2007), with the concept of entrepreneuring. It was also influenced by a wide range of pedagogical scholars, among them Freire (1970). Today when almost every one of the initial team of teachers working with the program has been replaced, those principles are still built into the structure of the program:

1. *Learning takes place in the space that is created between the student, the university and a partner organization.* From the very first weeks of the education the students work in teams of usually three students, each of which has a partner organization. The ambition is that each group has the same partner organization for at least two semesters. A longer time period together with the same partner organization is beneficial in several ways. It could even be seen as necessary in order for the stu- dents to obtain a rich and deep understanding of the organizational culture of their partner organization and its environment.
2. *Learning is stimulated by the investigation of themes.* The world that we are preparing our students for does not present itself as the disciplines that the academy is divided into. The ambition with the EBD program is to encourage a theme approach. These themes follow logically the life cycle of an organization. The program starts with themes con- nected to the generation of ideas and the creation of projects. Then follows a theme related to managing and developing an existing organization. Finally, themes related to renewal and international- ization follow. In every theme the idea is that the students create or take part in a relevant project related to the current theme together with their partner organization. Each theme is built up by all the academic disciplines included in the program (social psychology, law, informatics, economics, and business administration).
3. *The learning process is steered through the formulation and design of tasks and examination forms.* The examination activities in the program can be divided into two kinds. There are discipline

examinations, which are examinations related to one of the many disciplines that build up a theme. The only grades the students can obtain on these kinds of examinations are 'pass' or 'failure'. The most demanding and time-consuming are the theme examinations. Here the students work in groups of two or three with a project that they themselves formulate together with members of their partner organization and with teachers from the university. Workshops at the university and close contacts with the partner organization are important processes. More credits are assigned to a completed theme examination. This is the only kind of examination where the students can obtain the grade 'pass with distinction'. This is an important signal telling the students that this is where they show that they can formulate relevant questions, search for and integrate relevant knowledge from different disciplines and integrate aspects into something which is relevant both as academic knowledge and for the partner organization.

4. *Learning is an ongoing process.* The theme-based structure creates a different organization of the learning process. One common way is for students to take discipline-based courses in a pre-planned sequence. With the theme structure follows a different approach. The program begins with an overall and process-based picture of an organization. With every theme the disciplines return and contribute some more knowledge. Thus, each discipline follows the students throughout the three years. This means that as a teacher in the EBD program you have three years to communicate a message that you normally finish off within a couple of months. One important idea is to promote learning by stimulating self-reflections over how the learning process is organized on an individual level. Thus, not only the question 'what is learnt' is considered to be important, but equally important is the question 'how do I learn?' The ambition is to make the students' own development into one important subject in the program. Every student gets a handbook containing the schedule and the examination tasks. Based on this overview the students are supposed to plan and continually reflect upon their own learning process, that is how much time they devote to the different tasks. From the first day the message to the students is that they are responsible for their own learning process. The ambition is that the students will gradually understand that they are not passive recipients of knowledge, whether it comes from teachers of the university or the partner organization. They themselves are responsible for creating knowledge. They are also responsible for making the knowledge-creating process happen, as there is nobody else who will organize the process for them.

Struggling for the Possibility to do Things in a Different Way – Authors' Reflections as Teachers

The EBD program with its cohort of 40 students forms a tiny minority compared to the masses of students at the university campus. For both of us the program stands out as a movement in the margin of the formal academic education system. The EBD program appears as a reaction against a kind of education that relies heavily on de-contextualized theoretical knowledge. Academic education tends to ascribe authority to the teacher who instructs students to learn on the basis of questions that are either formulated by the teacher or in the course literature. It is too often based on a narrow empirical view of knowledge where facts are transmitted under the conviction that their meaning is already determined. This kind of education is weak on aspects such as how language is used depending on who is making an utterance and where and when the utterance is made. The knowledge is typically not related to different ethical and political standpoints.

The EBD program within the academic context represents a movement towards leaving room for the students to evaluate, investigate and test that which is presented to them and to suggest questions, problems and solutions. It also to a higher degree than traditional programs encourages students to be sensitive to the social psychological aspects of the learning process, for example by promoting teamwork and stimulating reflections on the relationship between individual and group. In this way there is much room for an entrepreneurial approach as this is conceptualized by preschool teachers (see Chapter 8 by Berglund) in the formal learning process. The students are encouraged to use their common sense, since what is useful and relevant for partner organizations cannot be found in textbooks. The interaction with the partner organization thus requires imagination and following gut feelings. Tensions within the academic context, however, make it difficult to go the whole way to emphasize friendships, feelings and imagination even if these elements are part of the underlying philosophy. A focus on such a conceptualization of an entrepreneurial approach is in the academic context easily recognized as 'fudgy', that is as something which is anything but academic. Subjectivity is invited instead of objectivity, which is still a paramount paradigm for many business school teachers. At times the EBD program has been contested by some of our colleagues who consider the program to be fraudulent, vague and obscure as well as requiring too many resources. As we see it, these reactions have to do with the situation described in this section, namely that the EBD program is developed and performed in a cultural context that is not fully used to or comfortable with the kind of pedagogy that it is based upon. The program has also been met with positive words from other colleagues within the business school, from students and from representatives of the partner organizations that are involved in the program. It has also passed formal evaluations with positive outcomes.

The staff in the program also have to cope with a formal organizational structure that in some ways prevents the teachers from accomplishing their ambitions and ideals. First, the formal role of the university teacher as an objective evaluator of students' work privileges a distant and instrumental relationship between student and teacher. To go beyond this role is not what most teachers want or feel comfortable with. For the senior of us authors it seems to be easier compared to the junior. This may be an effect of the hierarchical structure of a university, where those further down on the hierarchical ladder need to be more careful, while the seniors can be more courageous. It can also be related to the common situation that those who are lower down in the hierarchy often have a larger share of teaching as compared to research. This has been the situation for the junior author, who at times has experienced that the effort of handling close relations to a large number of student groups and partner organizations has been too time-consuming and demanding. Building and handling relationships takes time and energy. The workload easily becomes too heavy. In such situations creating distance is simply a way to cope with the situation. Additionally, we have realized that a close relationship that involves friendship and feelings potentially puts the neutrality and objectivity of the university teacher as evaluator at risk and hence the rights of the students to be treated in a fair and equal way.

The EBD program cuts across the borders between academic disciplines. Explaining the logic of the program to staff and students has been an important task for the group of teachers involved in the EBD program, especially for new academic colleagues who enter the program. They often cannot rely entirely on their previous teaching experiences, as they also need to understand how their contribution to a specific theme is supposed to interact with the contribution from other disciplines. The integration of separate academic disciplines into themes is an intricate commitment-building process. It consumes time and energy as it requires close cooperation between staff from separate institutions with academic traditions and routines that sometimes differ. As a consequence the workload of the individual teacher in the EBD program tends to grow high. Still, the program is not given more resources compared to other programs. This could explain why quite a few teachers who have been teaching in the program have left it and sometimes even left the university altogether. The extra effort must be compensated by extraordinary motivation and a whole-hearted belief in the pedagogical idea of the program. For us this involvement is double-edged. On one hand EBD gives us a lot of inspiration and professional satisfaction, but on the other hand it drains our energy. The latter is to a large extent due to the in-built antagonism that we experience between the traditional academic discipline orientation and the ambition articulated in this chapter to educate for entrepreneurship. Higher education leads to specialized education, while education for entrepreneurship calls for an integrated perspective where there is also space for personal development.

The struggles described in this section relate differently to the two of us authors. We both share the basic values behind the program. However, the risk of being in the margin is probably higher for the more junior of us, as the more senior is at the end of his career and therefore less concerned about the risks. These different positions in our careers have, on the other hand, helped us both to reflect upon what we are doing and why. As the senior of us has been advisor to small firms for many years as a private consultant, the philosophy of the EBD program is quite familiar. The students in the EBD program in many ways work as consultants/advisors to their partner organizations while at the same time being recognized as students. The junior author has his educational and teaching background in the area of management control. Prior to experiencing the EBD program, he mainly taught in courses in cost accounting and management/financial accounting. When he started to work with the EBD program he was not used to the kind of pedagogy that the program is based upon. He was more used to an educational situation where students are trained in standardized techniques that they must master before they start practising in real life situations. The junior author is also less experienced when it comes to other professional positions than that of a university teacher/researcher. As employed by the university he has been prepared for the practice of teaching. In his experience, courses in university pedagogy and informal talk between teachers are centred on how to handle students in a classroom setting. There is little focus on an educational setting that also involves partner organizations from other parts of society. The so-called third stream of activities involving interacting with the surrounding community is often understood as something reserved for research activities. The senior author, on the other hand, has vast experience from other professional positions. This difference has stimulated discussions between the two of us, where the junior author told about his experiences and the senior author could integrate them with his previous experiences from other contexts.

THE SIP NETWORK. EDUCATING FOR ENTREPRENEURSHIP IN THE FOLK HIGH SCHOOL

As an organization, the SIP Network emerged from a group of young people having fun together playing computer games. The activities were developed over time as the participants started to interpret their experiences together. New people became involved, and a network of inter-related non-profit/voluntary organizations was created which made it possible to communicate the interest of the participants to others in the local community (citizens as well as the local administration). Later, members of the network took a step towards formalizing the kind of learning that they practised when they started to collaborate with the Folk High School movement. The members of the SIP Network underline how well the values and ideals of the two collaborating organizations resonate with one another. The first Folk High Schools emerged in Scandinavia in the middle of the nineteenth century. The development of these schools was closely related to the social movements of the time, such as the temperance, the labour and the non-conformist movements. Today the Folk High Schools are funded by, but still separated from, the state government. The purpose of the governmental funding is that it should support activities that contribute to and develop democracy, increase the possibility for citizens to influence their own life situation and stimulate the commitment and the willingness to partake in the development of society through political, cultural, leisure and labour union engagement. Students need to be 18 years or older to study at a Folk High School, which makes it an alternative or complement to academic education.

The one-year education program 'Societal Entrepreneurs' was offered for the first time in the autumn of 2008. It was financed for three years by governmental funding to the local Folk High School that the SIP Network had started to collaborate with. The course was advertised and offered to anyone who wanted to run a project, start a business or organize an event. The course was tailor-made to each individual. Students could either come to the education with their own ideas, looking for support to realize them, or they could participate in existing assignments and develop their own ideas during the course. The aim of the course was to provide possibilities for personal development. Mandatory literature was a book about 'personal entrepreneurship written by two young entrepreneurs (Olsson and Frödin, 2007). Both have academic degrees, but the book is inspirational and non-academic in its language. The content of the course was organized around different themes, such as information processing, societal issues, leadership, networking, personal development, digital communication, marketing, project management, business and enterprising and creativity. The themes were all developed out of the experiences that staff from the SIP Network had gathered when developing their own network organization. In that sense the education was an extension of the kind of attitudes and values that had been important to the group of friends when they organized and developed their own interests. Values related to 'getting things done', 'inspiring others and be inspired', 'believing in yourself and that everything is possible', 'being positive and supportive', 'stimulating the passion that you have' and 'daring to fail – try again – and succeed' were communicated to the students in every theme. All these themes are articulated in Olsson and Frödin (2007) and internalized by the SIP Network. The concept of personal entrepreneurship as presented in the book communicates these ideas in an inspirational way and is likewise practised by the teachers. With a focus on getting things started while at the same time feeling good and having fun, the message is that everybody is responsible for realizing their own ideas ('you can't wait for somebody else to do it') and that everybody can mobilize the resources needed. In this way the perspective on entrepreneurship is inclusive in the sense that everyone can be (and should be) an entrepreneur. The focus on change and development is central. Flexibility is encouraged. You should be prepared to change yourself and the taken-for-granted beliefs that you currently have. The message is that everyone can design their own future. What is needed is determination and belief (you get what you choose to focus upon) and the right attitude and emotions.

The education program began with a period where the students and the SIP staff got to know each other personally. This was done through various social events. One important activity was that the students all got the opportunity to perform their own lectures to the rest of the class on subjects that they were particularly interested in. Just to mention a few examples, students have lectured on the Brazilian dance Capoeira, how to make a tattoo, medieval games, or the design of a chair included in the product range of a small business. The lectures often included a section where all participants had to try on their own. This kind of event reflects one important ambition of the education, namely that the SIP Network performed self-organized experiential learning: the themes and subjects were ideally generated by the participants themselves and later developed in the concrete form of a project during the education. One member of the staff expresses this ambition when she says: 'I wanted a class full of teachers; I did not want to be the teacher. I wanted to take care of all the knowledge and experiences that all these students brought with them.' Another expression of this ambition is more physical. The education administrators sit together with the students in one open office. They do their work in the same room as the students and they often interact the whole working day with the students. They eat together and have coffee together. There is a minimum of separation and distance between the staff of the SIP Network and the students. This low distance in relation to the students was also experienced by the senior of us authors when giving a guest lecture. The culture prescribes that you easily become friends, and soon afterwards I was contacted by one of the students for his project work.

The different events in the program were often performed in collaboration with other organizations in society. The Folk High School was an important collaborator. Collaboration was also developed with other organizations in the surrounding community, for example other associations with a social mission. The students made field trips, and members of the associations were invited to present themselves and their organizations at the SIP Network. The students also had periods of internship where they visited and worked together with another organization for a couple of weeks.

Over the last ten years a great many people have passed through the SIP Network, working in their different projects, sometimes as employees and sometimes in their leisure time. Those contacts are often sustained over time, and later they could be invited to create or take part in events in the education program. In this way the network of contacts and relations that constructs the SIP Network as an organization was successively presented to the students during the program. This network reaches all sectors of society, the business sector as well as the public and civil sectors. As stated in the course presentation, the ambition was to involve the whole person and the whole of society and everything that is happening there in the educational room that is created during the year. It is a clearly articulated aim of the SIP Network to change society and it is certainly an ambitious aim, which eventually may cause resentment from someone who experiences this aim not to have been reached individually or collectively. For others it resonates well, so for this reason the term 'societal entrepreneurship' is used by the SIP Network when they present the education.

There is, however, another way to make sense of the connection between entrepreneurship and society. A follow-up after the first year of the education showed that many students were fascinated by the fact that they had worked together during the year despite their different backgrounds and interests. As stated by one student: 'Everybody is so different, and still we have been able to cooperate. That is our strength!' This turned out to be a common theme that a number of students reflected upon when asked what they felt the education had contributed with. It was also a theme that was somewhat surprising, as it was not an explicitly stated goal of the education. This theme can be seen as one important result of the activities and projects that the SIP Network performs. One result of bringing together people that are different in terms of, for example, age, cultural background and interests to perform collaborative and practical work in groups is that cultural differences can be worked through and overcome. This is another illustration of the meaning of 'societal entrepreneurship'.

ATTITUDE AND PERSONAL DEVELOPMENT – AS VIEWED BY STAFF IN THE SIP NETWORK

In order to further elaborate on the thinking behind the program we will now turn to statements made by four teachers from the SIP Network as to how they assess and understand their education. We asked the staff from the SIP Network to write down their reflections and we have selected a few of their statements in order to further characterize their education program.

About personal development:

> We could have called the course personal entrepreneurship or personal development. The course where you acquire self-confidence and get a better self-esteem, but no one would have applied for that course as it sounds very scary. When we start talking about personal development many are shivering. What we actually do is that we almost exclusively work with personal development throughout a whole year without our students being aware of that and without their conscious choice, because we know that this is what is needed. This is what we ourselves need.

To us, the statement above reflects one of the most central ideologies that the SIP teachers bring into the course. We have seen this message coming through to the students as something they seem to make into their own conviction. To us as academic scholars the message appears as an ideology. It is not explicitly critically reflected upon in terms of how this eventually could have less positive side-effects in, for example, putting too high a pressure on individual students to develop themselves. It is also a message that the SIP Network seems to be careful not to confront the students too directly with when they advertise the education, as this might make some students afraid. Taking this reflection further, we can see the SIP Network as being a part of a higher education that needs to reproduce the kind of institutional stress on performativity which Olssen and Peters (2005) relate to the discourses of 'new public management'. This means that what appears to us as an ideology of personal development is part of a more general discourse of governmentality (compare Chapter 9 by Holmgren).

About the attitude of the student:

> All get coaching on an individual level. If you are uncertain about what you want you will be able to reflect upon that here. From the student is required positive thinking, to dare to look ahead, to dare to make decisions, to be generous about yourself, to aspire to development, to be receptive. In fact I don't think you can be educated in societal entrepreneurship. But you can get tools to work better as a societal entrepreneur. There are certain things you can learn like tools, models, networking etc. But to take a second step, a personal driving force and personal qualities are needed.

This statement underlines that students need to take responsibility for their own development. They are pushed, but at the same time provided a great deal of space for reflections and of support. In the academic contexts, students are expected to take responsibility for their own learning; and if they do not, it is up to them. In the SIP Network the social pressure is higher, but the personal support is also more intensive.

About equipping:

> What we can do is to get a hold of different aspects of how to view societal entrepreneurship, how to interpret this concept, how to inspire people to dare to take initiatives, to dare to be drifty, to dare to realize ideas, to dare to test ideas. We try to break with the routine patterns that people carry with them. It is something of a rehabilitating period here to break with the classical way of thinking nine to five, routines that have always existed and always will. We try to think more like: 'OK, this is your driving force; we will find a solution after that'. Not that we are looking for the most profitable thing to do. We are not teachers, we are more like inspirers and coordinators for all the resources we can find around us in society and use as impulses in the course.

The key concern that comes out of this statement is about change and the courage that is needed in order to change things. There is content in the course, but what is considered to be the most important is not to pass on knowledge, but to challenge the students to come out of the learning process as people who dare to make things differently. The inspirers and coordinators of the SIP Network want to meet the students where they are, and from that find out how they can be encouraged to become entrepreneurs.

On purpose:

> For me it is a requirement to have the experience of being an entrepreneur if you should teach entrepreneurship. It is also so that entrepreneurship is not something that is taught at the academic level, but what is taught is business administration or other types of disciplines and this is nothing I know very much about. But if you talk about entrepreneurship in itself I think experience

is required. If you talk more about feelings, personal qualities and how you are as a person I think it is important that the person who teaches or tries to encourage the other person has made this experience herself. As the course in societal entrepreneurship is a course which not only has its focus on business firms we have tried to involve teachers both with experience from business firms as project leaders and other people engaged in different societal matters in the civic sector so that you get different role models.

One approach to the question whether it is possible to educate for entrepreneurship is: Could you educate people to become creative, competitive, to use their feeling to create, to get new ideas and see opportunities? It is not easy to EDUCATE in this! Yes, you can tell and inform people about how it is and how it should be. The student is sitting there obediently and listening, taking notes and is nodding in agreement. And when they leave the place someone might have a fancy that 'now I have become more like an entrepreneur because now I know!' but then I think they fool themselves. In fact I don't believe you can educate someone to become an entrepreneur. But instead I think you can stimulate a person to develop as a person and to go in a positive direction with regard to different key personal qualities.

The statements above are clearly critical towards academic education. The message is that while the SIP Network actually educates entrepreneurs, the academic institution does something else. When we talked with SIP teachers about this they confirmed that this was what they thought. In order to be able to teach students to become entrepreneurs, the teacher needs to be entrepreneurial him- or herself, they thought. The academic teacher is typically seen as someone who has neither the experience nor the attitude of an entrepreneur and therefore cannot teach students to become entrepreneurs. Further, the teacher from the SIP Network thinks it is more or less impossible to educate for entrepreneurship. Students can be inspired to develop as individuals and that is all. This is how the entrepreneurial potential is released, in their thinking. Here we come back to the ideology of the SIP Network on personal development and personal entrepreneurship. The idea is that everyone has the potential and the key for personal development within him or her. You can choose to open yourself or you can choose not to. If you choose to open yourself to being developed you need others for the development to take place, but it all starts from within.

PROMOTING SOCIETAL ENTREPRENEURSHIP IN THE ACADEMY AND IN THE FOLK HIGH SCHOOL – A COMPARISON BETWEEN CONTEXTS

The EBD program has existed for ten years and so has the SIP Network. As authors we have three years' experience of working together with the

SIP Network. In the following we will discuss how these two contexts can be compared in terms of educating for entrepreneurship and promoting societal entrepreneurship.

Similarities between the Two Contexts – Promoting in the Same Way

One important part of the pedagogical idea of both contexts is to promote experiential learning. In the SIP Network the dominating logic or organization of the education is based on the students' own practical work. In the EBD program one ambition is to allow the students to experiment with the models and information that they read about and gather. The ambition to 'start by doing' is also illustrated by the decision to make the students become involved with a partner organization from the very first weeks of the education. Both contexts work with themes instead of disciplines. This reflects a belief that 'enterprising' involves and integrates many subjects at the same time, and that the ability to make a whole out of parts is crucial. To organize the education around many small projects is in both contexts seen as a suitable way to educate for entrepreneurship. This is related to the theme orientation described above. A project typically involves many perspectives and/or disciplines at the same time. It also captures the meaning of entrepreneurship as the term is understood by the two contexts, that is, that entrepreneurship is about projecting something, about having a vision and realizing this vision together with others.

As illustrated above, the SIP Network places personal development at the core of their education. This is what it is all about, according to the staff. This idea is also visible in the EBD program, most explicitly in the decision to include social psychology as one important discipline in the program. One of the ideas of social psychology is to encourage the students to reflect about themselves in relation to the group and in relation to society. Both contexts express the understanding that the everyday life of the students is an important ground for learning. This is the base for the kinds of results that are later on measured as signs of entrepreneurship, for example the creation of a new business venture. This understanding is expressed in an ambition to allow the students' own voices to be heard and to tailor the education after their personalities and interests. The SIP Network follows this through in a quite extreme way. Here the students as individuals are seen as the building blocks of the education. The education becomes whatever the students of that year choose to engage in. In the academic context there has been a great deal of struggle over the years to keep up the ambition not to standardize the education. This ambition was initially stated in the following way by two of the founders of the EBD program; 'our task as educators are, as we see it, to stimulate the learning process by creating a supporting curriculum and a learning environment advocating that learning can be done in different ways. That is, an individual way of learning depending on each individual's conditions, preferences and abilities developed at the moment' (Jonsson and Jonsson, 2002: 4). Finally, the relationship to other organizations in society could in both contexts be seen as dialogical, that is the surrounding society is not present only as an object to study but rather contributes in an interactive way to the realization of the education. In the SIP Network the education is performed in and to some extent by the community. The students ideally contribute to the community through their own projects. The ambition by the EBD program is to create bridges so that the students can pass on their knowledge to the partner organizations. The partners in their turn pass on their knowledge to the students and ideally also to the whole program through guest lectures and participation in workshops.

Tensions between the Two Contexts – Promoting in Different Ways

Even if many similarities between the EBD program and the Folk High School education have been pointed out, it is obvious that there are differences and tensions as well. At a rhetorical level, from the perspective of the staff of the SIP Network, the academic fascination with theory even as applied by the EBD program appears as less useful knowledge. Our counter argument is that training in abstract thinking is required in order to get access to certain parts of society. The access that follows from training in abstract thinking is arguably not only due to the capacity for such thinking in itself, as it is also due to the kind of legitimization that academic education offers in different parts of society. On the other hand, those trained in abstract thinking might also be excluded from parts of society where the kind of practical knowledge that the SIP Network promotes is a key to access. This tension has a great deal to do with in what sphere of society the education is developed and performed.

While the business school stems from the private sector and economics, the SIP Network, in the same way as the Folk High School movement in Scandinavia, has been developed in and stems from what Habermas (1996) calls 'the public sphere', which includes the associations and social movements in society that can be located in the NPVO sector. Here, citizens come together and discuss their private interests and problems. Their experiences can be thematized, dramatized and furnished with possible solutions. They can also be communicated to a wider audience. There is a strong focus on participation, as the active, committed and engaged citizen is sought after. The public sphere is in this way anchored in the life-world of the individual and represents a space in society where its existing structures, values and norms could be interpreted and contested in a relatively free way (ibid.: 329–387). In such an educational context it is relatively easy to build social relationships between individuals which are based on friendship and mutual interests. This in turn creates a fertile ground for promoting the kind of entrepreneurial approach that is conceptualized in Chapter 8 by Berglund. Focusing on 'making friends', 'listening to your feelings' and 'using your imagination' seems to require a certain kind of personal and informal intimacy that, in our experience, is hard to fully reproduce within the institution of higher education (as discussed in previous sections).

The business school, on the other hand, is closely linked to economics, where anonymous actors exchange goods and services. The EBD program is developed within a strong academic culture where scientific knowledge is traditionally privileged and where practical knowledge, as Hayek (1945) puts it, is sometimes even viewed with a mixture of distrust and contempt. Within this academic context the EBD program could be seen as an attempt to bring practical knowledge and theoretical knowledge closer together. This is done by stimulating the students to relate theoretical knowledge to the practical circumstances of a concrete project in a partner organization. This is seen by the teachers involved in the EBD program to promote the entrepreneurial approach of the students, not primarily by training them in solving predefined problems analytically, but rather by enhancing their ability to find, understand, frame and formulate problems, which is to make sense of complex situations (Schön, 1983; see also Weick, 1995).

The staff of the SIP Network see a risk with academic and theoretical knowledge of being less fruitful and useful. As academic teachers we see a risk with being too ideological about the issue of personal development. There are limits for personal development as well, which is not really a part of the message from the SIP Network. Theoretical and critical thinking helps not to take the ideologically-driven idea that anyone can become anything they want to too far, and to foster more realistic expectations of what is possible to attain. 'Making friends', 'listening to your feelings' and 'using your imagination', as discussed in Chapter 8 by Berglund, questioning taken-for-granted assumptions and thus balancing a strong emphasis on the personal development of the individual with the more social and interactive dimensions of entrepreneuring. Therefore this pedagogy could be a guiding star for the SIP program as well as for the EBD program.

CONCLUSION

The SIP Network stands out as a genuinely social space where the entre-preneurial approach of the student is promoted in an intimate way by focusing on personal development and the kind of practical knowledge that more or less immediately leads to action. The academic context, on the other hand, puts greater emphasis on conscious reflection as it is practised by students involved in the EBD program. Action based on more thorough and theoretically driven reflection is likely to be practic-ally useful in situations where immediate action will not be possible or useful. Both education programs described in this text are however, when regarded in their own context, examples of how the idea of entrepreneur-ship education has been translated into a kind of progressive pedagogy, rather than a means for creating economic growth (compare Chapters 8 by Berglund and 9 by Holmgren). In both contexts, the ambition is to encourage students to be(come) enterprising, regardless whether this is expressed in terms of starting new firms, becoming project leaders in a large corporation or being involved within the public or civic sector. It is a context where the efforts are directed to educating for, instead of about, entrepreneurship. In both contexts the efforts to build upon the potentials of the students aim at stimulating their commitment and willingness to partake in the development of society. In this sense our role as educators for entrepreneurship in the academy as well as in the Folk High School puts us, together with our students, in the role of promoters of societal entrepreneurship.

REFERENCES

Alvesson, M. (2003), 'Methodology for close-up studies: struggling with closeness and closure', Higher Education, **46** (2), 167–193.
Ardalan, K. (2008), 'The philosophical foundation of the lecture-versus-case con-troversy: its implications for course goals, objectives, and contents', *International Journal of Social Economics*, **35** (1/2), 15–34.
Berglund, K. and C. Holmgren (2008), 'What do teachers do when they do entre-preneurship education? . . . and how can we ask about it?', *International Journal of Business and Globalisation*, **2** (4), 354–372.
Colette, H., F. Hill and C. Leitch (2005), 'Entrepreneurship education and train-ing: can entrepreneurship be taught? Part I', *Education + Training*, **47** (2), 98–111.
Fiet, J.O. (2001), 'The theoretical side of teaching entrepreneurship theory', *Journal of Business Venturing*, **16** (1), 101–117.
Freire, P. (1970/1996), Pedagogy of the Oppressed, London: Penguin Books.
Gibb, A.A. (2005), 'Towards the Entrepreneurial University. Entrepreneurship

education as a lever for change'. NCGE Policy paper series, available at www. ncge.org.uk.

Habermas, J. (1996), *Between Facts and Norms: Contributions to a Discourse Theory of Law and Democracy*, Cambridge, MA: The MIT Press.

Hayek, F.A. (1945), 'The use of knowledge in society', *The American Economic Review*, **35** (4), 519–530.

Hindle, K. (2007), 'Teaching entrepreneurship at university; from the wrong building to the right philosophy', in A. Fayolle, *Handbook of Research in Entrepreneurship Education, Volume 1. A General Perspective*, Cheltenham, UK and Northampton, MA, USA: Edward Elgar Publishing, pp. 104–126.

Hjorth, D. and B. Johannisson (1998), 'Entreprenörskap som skapelseprocess och ideologi' (Entrepreneurship as process of creation and ideology), in B. Czarniawska (ed.), *Organisationsteori på svenska*. Malmö: Liber, pp. 86–104.

Johannisson, B. (1991), 'University training for entrepreneurship: Swedish approaches', *Entrepreneurship & Regional Development*, **3** (1), 67–82.

Jonsson, C. and T. Jonsson (2002), 'Entrepreneurial learning – an informed way of learning. The case of enterprising and business development', paper presented at the 12th Conference on Small Business Research in Kuopio, Finland.

Kans, L. (2009), 'Enterprising and business development – undervisning på annat vis', in K. Jonnergård and R.G. Larsson (eds), *Från barkbröd till ciabatta-kreativitet och kontroll inom ekonomistyrning*, Växjö: Växjö University Press, pp. 41–55.

Matlay, H. (2006), 'Researching entrepreneurship and education. Part 2: What is entrepreneurship education and does it matter?', *Education + Training*, **48** (8/9), 704–718.

Olssen, M. and M.A. Peters (2005), 'Neoliberalism, higher education and the knowledge economy: from the free market to knowledge capitalism', *Journal of Higher Education Policy*, **20** (3), 313–345.

Olsson, S. and M. Frödin (2007), *Personligt entreprenörskap. Att få saker att hända (Personal entrepreneurship. Getting things done)*, Gdansk: Universe Imagine Publishing.

Schön, D (1983), *The Reflective Practitioner: How Professionals Think in Action*, New York: Basic Books.

Stevenson, L. and A. Lundström (2005), 'Entrepreneurship policy for the future: Best practice components', in R.E. Horst, S. King-Kauanui and S, Duffy (eds), *Keystones of Entrepreneurship Knowledge*, Malden, MA: Blackwell Publishing.

Steyaert, C. (2007), '"Entrepreneuring" as a conceptual attractor? A review of process theories in 20 years of entrepreneurship studies', Entrepreneurship and Regional Development, **19** (6), 453–477.

Taatila, V.P. (2010), 'Learning entrepreneurship in higher education', *Education + Training*, **52** (1), 48–61.

Weick, K.E. (1995), *Sensemaking in Organizations*, Thousand Oaks, CA: Sage.

11. Conclusions

Karin Berglund, Bengt Johannisson and Birgitta Schwartz

THE LESSONS WE WANT TO SHARE

In the Swedish context societal entrepreneuring appears in many forms, besides social enterprise, for example as the intermediating function in small-firm settings, as art and experience production and as education. Three themes – *positioning*, *penetrating* and *promoting* – have been used to organize our encounters with these different forms. This thematic structure should, however, only be considered as a starting point for further reflexivity, thus inviting a prolonged research journey. Three further possible themes or issues have then caught our attention. The first issue concerns for what reason and in what way societal entrepreneurship can supplement the basic social contract between the citizen and the state, which in Sweden has been produced culturally but has also become enforced by a strong public sector. The outcome would be people with enhanced self-confidence who acknowledge their own capabilities and use them together with others to *co-create the conditions that organize their everyday life* and thus practise entrepreneuring. The second emerging issue recognizes the *divide*, not only between different sectors, but also *between the private sphere and the public sphere* and how this divide is bridged in societal entrepreneuring. On one hand, we have associated societal entrepreneuring with cross-sectorial (public) efforts to make up for deficiencies in the public and private sectors. On the other hand, we have argued that only by engaging themselves personally, as authentic beings, that is, as private persons, will people make societal entrepreneuring materialize. The third new issue elaborates on the second one by addressing *the role and responsibility of us as researchers* in social value creation, which we relate to societal entrepreneuring as part of our knowledge creation process.

Dealing with these issues in this final chapter we only provide modest further conceptualization, which is, however, supported by accounts from the preceding chapters. We will first introduce the notion of 'organizing context' as a mental construct and practice produced by and feeding societal entrepreneuring. Our argument is that in the Swedish context community building appears as a way to make the most of the individual/collective duality that prevails in the country. Then we explore the public/private contrast and elaborate upon how this is bridged by, for example, recognizing the crucial role of the NPVO sector in societal entrepreneuring. The private/public divide reveals how the contract, referred to as 'state individualism' in Chapter 1, develops into collective efforts in the organizing contexts where private concerns are turned into public issues to be dealt with. Hence, in societal entrepreneuring – taking form as a collective activity – the contract of individualism is renegotiated when actors come together to reconstruct what is missing and what is not functioning in parts of Swedish society. The final subsection deals with the necessity of, and forms for, researchers (also) acting as responsible citizens when inquiring into societal entrepreneuring.

SOCIETAL ENTREPRENEURING AS PROVIDING ORGANIZING CONTEXTS

Positioning societal entrepreneuring evokes the concepts of 'habitat' and 'community', which in turn communicate a sense of physical place and its importance for human agency. In the Swedish context this practical and emotional commitment to place is important to most people, including entrepreneurs. What is more, strong popular movements organize civic society in Sweden, see Chapter 1. Further, an individualistic culture can be questioned from our empirical accounts of societal entrepreneuring presented throughout this book in the chapters illustrating strong collective activity. Societal entrepreneuring deals with this paradoxical situation by, on one hand, inviting collective movements and activity and, on the other, upholding the contract of individualism. Our cases do not, for instance, raise any debate about reformulating either the Swedish social security system or the tax system.

In the introductory chapter we referred to Tönnies' proposed duality Gemeinschaft/community versus Gesellschaft/corporation (Tönnies 1965). Gemeinschaft is an ideal social construct characterized by strong, bonding ties, empirically appearing in rural communities, while Gesellschaft is ideally dominated by weak bridging ties and appears in urban settings. Accordingly, in an original study of societal entrepreneuring as local mobilization for new firms and jobs, Johannisson and Nilsson (1989) addressed the instigator of the change process as a 'community entrepreneur'. The Gemeinschaft/Gesellschaft duality may be used for reflecting upon the transition from historical to modern times, but it needs to be reconsidered in contemporary post-modern times; see for example Johansson (2009). Brint (2001) in his review of the original use of the Gemeinschaft concept identifies a number of generic features that release it from the original association with closed (physical) communities with common beliefs and ways of life. Nevertheless, Brint (2001: 8) defines communities as 'aggregates of people who share common activities and/ or beliefs and who are bound together *principally* by relations of affect, loyalty, common values, and/or personal concern (i.e. interest in the personalities and life events of one (another)' (*italics* in original). He also states that community members are, on one hand, expected to be open to new (personal) relations but are, on the other, emotionally and morally tied to existing ones. This is well illustrated in the Macken case in Chapter 3. While new social rescue operations are incessantly started in Macken, communal relations confirm that the responsibility for those already launched is strongly felt. When Fredrik, the social entrepreneur and CEO, was relieved from his formal obligations in order to focus on new venture development, he was not delivered from the informal obligations to those he had once enabled to overcome penury. However, as experienced in the Moon House venture (reported in Chapter 7), these expectations on total commitment from an active and driving entrepreneur may as well hinder involvement and co-creation in the first place.

Searching for communities where not only sectorial boundaries are crossed, but also those between the public and privates spheres, the 'industrial-district' phenomenon comes to mind. Such localities are well-known empirical settings for intertwined commercial and societal entre-preneuring as a collective phenomenon that is historically, culturally and socially embedded; see Becattini et al. (2009) for a general review and Johannisson (2009a) for an empirical report from Sweden. These com-munities are certainly built for trading on tradition and homogeneity with respect to both activities and values. The local forces for change appear as centripetal rather than centrifugal, which means that they enforce existing ways of enacting business and social life. Using the notion of 'heterarchy' as an analytical device Grabher (2001) demonstrates that large metro-politan areas may accommodate networked clusters in industries (such as advertising) which are, in contrast, based on heterogeneity but still appear as communities as defined above by Brint. In such turbulent places and industries history, of course, matters less than in rural areas with traditional manufacturing industries. Focusing on societal rather than on business entrepreneuring suggests that the coexistence of different sectors may provide the heterogeneity and creative tensions that stimulate change. This seems to be the general lesson from the comparative study of social ventures in Chapter 2 and is clearly observed in Vimmerby as the domicile for Astrid Lindgren's World (ALW) (Chapter 4) and in Macken as a social enterprise (Chapter 3).

When studying (societal) entrepreneuring we need a concept that depicts a community which can accommodate both centripetal forces that build commitment to basic values and practices and centrifugal pressures that turn change into a natural state. This fuzzy zone between, on one hand, interrelated individual and organizational agents that make the community, and the (enacted) environment, on the other, we address as an *organizing context* (OC), to which we ascribe a number of characteristics; see Johannisson (2009; 2011). It makes evident, for example, that any kind of entrepreneuring is a collective phenomenon; compare Chapter 7. The empirically used concept 'entrepreneurial approach' in Chapter 8, referring to how preschool teachers view entrepreneuring as a relational matter to create a sense of security in terms of making friends, listening to one's feelings and practising imagination, also points out these collective features. See also Chapters 9 and 10.

We thus see the OC as an *interactively enacted shared reality*, which, being historically and culturally embedded, manifests and reforms itself by way of face-to-face exchange. Elsewhere entrepreneuring has generally been associated as creative organizing with personal networking (Johannisson 2000). By participating in everyday local life the members of the OC gain the overview needed to trade on the variety of opportunities and resources that the OC produces as a collective. Presumably, this shared worldview and existence produces the ambition to include disadvantaged and marginalized groups. The OC thus offers its members 'ontological security' (Giddens 1991), that is a sense of meaning. Typically, the languages used in public discourse and to guide concrete action coincide in the OC, rooting the context deeply in everyday local life. This makes it possible to reflect upon as well as negotiate the conceptions of entrepreneuring to raise the awareness of how we can view each other in an OC (see Berglund and Johansson's (2007) discussion on processes of conscientization for regional development to occur). The self-confidence created opens up 'potential spaces' (Winnicott 1971) that the OC member can use to acknowledge her/his own creativity and practise playfulness.

Just as the OC itself is constituted by diversity with respect to social interaction/networking, it provides an arena that triggers, amplifies and supports societal (social) venturing. Sometimes the organizing context appears as an organization, as in the case of Macken, whose business centre provides a supportive context of new ventures triggered by marginalized people. On the other hand, Macken itself draws on the town of Växjö with its social-business network and municipal administration. Embeddedness is obviously a multi-layered phenomenon. In Chapter 5

Andersson and Johansson present municipal intermediaries as societal entrepreneurs and contributors to the making of towns into organizing contexts for venturing. The making of an organizing context may be spontaneous and emergent as well as intentional and designed. The latter approach does not mean that the contexts emerge faster or provide a richer context. The integration of the event park Astrid Lindgren's World into the small town of Vimmerby as a spatial/legal unit demonstrates the hardships and time – 30 years in the ALW case! – it may take to orchestrate contrasting forces into supportive action. Tillmar's review of 30 cases of societal entrepreneuring in Chapter 2 also demonstrates how advanced collaboration is needed in order to make social ventures take off.

The organizing context as a qualification of the community is thus applicable to both urban and rural settings, to heterogeneous as well as homogenous places, to both arenas for face-to-face interaction and for digitalized interaction. This makes the concept useful also in mental spaces, whatever their reach in physical and social space; see Hernes (2003). Thus mobilizations such as those organized by for example the Attac movement (Gawell 2006) and those that have re-created several Arab nations in 2011 represent community building and societal entrepreneuring. However, as pointed out by Illouz (2007), strong bonds in a digitalized world may be 'cold', since they do not include physical encounters.

Relaxing the time dimension, temporary gatherings may also be considered as communities/organizing contexts by themselves or as occasions for making latent communities manifest themselves in social events. Thus, for example, (international) trade fairs build such temporary communities for business exchange (Maskell et al. 2006) of special importance to small and medium-sized firms (Ramirez-Pasillas 2010), while conferences appear as temporary communities for learning (Hansen 2010). The attempts to bridge between different sectors and actors by intermediaries, as described in Chapter 5, can also be interpreted through this lens, while Chapter 6 on Fair Trade provides a number of contexts where temporary gatherings take place. The enactment of the Moon House project (see Chapter 7) seemed to happen in a loose network that occasionally condensed in order to mobilize attention, resources and legitimacy.

To sum up, we see several arguments for introducing the notion of 'organizing context' (OC) as a contributor to a further conceptualization of societal entrepreneuring. First, the OC appears as a networked structure with fuzzy boundaries in all spaces (physical, social and mental) and in time. Thereby it becomes a proper general habitat for societal entrepreneuring, since it aligns with our understanding of entrepreneuring as creative and boundary-spanning organizing. Second, the OC provides an organizing vehicle that encompasses not only the three sectors but also invites community members to instigate further initiatives in their own and their community's interest. Third, although family businesses in the private sector and dedicated professionals in the public sector may mobilize strong involvement that makes people transcend public and private lives, physical, social and mental proximities in an OC may amplify such forces. Such involvement presumably also means that the barrier between the public and private spheres in everyday life is torn down; compare Hirschman (1982). This brings us to the next section.

SOCIETAL ENTREPRENEURING AND THE PRIVATE/PUBLIC DIVIDE

The three sectors – public, private and NPVO – in Sweden are, as stated in Chapter 1 and illustrated throughout the book, characterized by following different institutional logics and the way these logics have been developed in relation to Swedish society, crafted by its history, culture and political system. The three sectors are obviously not equal in terms of number of employees. However, the actors in non-profit and voluntary organizations often highlight what kind of issues should be focused on in the debate to instigate and guide certain kinds of actions. This means that the members of the NPVO sector formulate societal issues and set the ground for dealing with them. In that sense this sector can be described metaphorically as 'the spice in the food', whose bulk of ingredients is thus provided by the two other sectors. Even if spices make up a small amount of the ingredients in a course, they give the food its taste and character. This analogy tells us that, even if the NPVO sector is small in relation to the other two sectors as regards employment statistics, many individuals engage in non-profit and voluntary organizations in their leisure time. The engagement of its members in OCs puts life into public debate and debate into (re)action. In their work they do not only debate and react to social issues, but they also try to solve the problems that are formulated. Concurrently, this may question existing values and norms in the other sectors.

What is of particular interest in this work, taking place at various locations in society, is that its members through their deep involvement dissolve the boundary between public and private life (see Hirschman 1982). Questions are being transformed from being of private concern to becoming, amplified by an organizing context, public issues that need to be dealt with. However, they are not public in the sense of being an issue on the parliamentary agenda, but a mission for members of an OC to solve. The responsibility of addressing invisible, or silenced, societal issues and formulating them into questions that need to be solved is part of the work in the organizational contexts described throughout the chapters of this book; the review of different initiatives by Tillmar in Chapter 2 illustrate this well. This emphasizes how actors in organizational contexts weave together not only sectors, but also life spheres, creating communities of shared worldviews on particular topics. Consequently, what the members of the OCs do in their leisure time is of importance, since activities relevant to societal entrepreneuring comprise not only what they do as employees during work hours, but also what is done in their spare time. Besides, the concerns that are brought up in societal entrepreneuring move from being private concerns to becoming public issues. Bringing in illustrations from, for example, the youth culture, Hjorth and Bjerke (2006) associate public entrepreneurship with transforming creative citizenship from private to public life by organizing different kinds of events. Their view on public entrepreneurship goes in line with how we faced the public/private in the chapters of this book, which adds complexity to the notion of sectors by putting our commitment and engagement as citizens in the limelight (see Hjorth and Bjerke 2006).

In the second theme of this book we learn that the notion of a dark versus a bright side of entrepreneurship actually collapsed where societal entrepreneuring takes place. As illustrated in Chapter 5, the intermediaries became translators between the municipality and small business owners. Focusing on the concept of intermediation, the authors make it clear how societal entrepreneuring can be seen as a process of creating nuanced views of different issues, making them dialogic and enactable. This is also made visible in Chapter 6, where the social entrepreneur, searching ways of how to make Fair Trade, finds herself squeezed in between dilemmas, which actually reveals that the world can either be seen as totally fair, or as totally unfair. Still, the work of societal entrepreneuring seems to be of the kind which creates a continuous move without being caught by an unattainable ideological dilemma. This is further reflected upon in Chapter 7, which brings forward how the entrepreneurship discourse tends to create polarized effects, disconnecting the entrepreneur from the collective efforts of entrepreneuring, and distancing mundane entrepreneuring from the continuous investments in spectacular events. The lesson to be learnt for members in OCs is that, when they succeed in solving an issue and it is turned into a 'success', they ought to be aware of the consequences of being depicted as 'heroes' or a 'successful venture', because it brings with it a downside that may disrupt the very practice of societal entrepreneuring. However, from all three chapters on this theme we also learn that where societal entrepreneuring takes place, the dark and bright sides are in some sense reflected upon, which makes some existing dichotomies collapse. Of course, not all dichotomies fall apart, and certainly new ones are being shaped in the new practices that societal entrepreneuring lays a basis for. But – for a brief moment – some parts of societal structures are reflected upon and enacted, reminding us about the inevitable process of societal entrepreneuring. It is about making a society – over and over again.

In the third theme of the book we followed how teachers, at the different levels in the school system, make sense of entrepreneurship. When they enact it and transform it into something else it unfolds potentiality. This, however, does not mean that societal entrepreneurship is promoted from behind a master's desk in a traditional view of knowledge input and output. The accounts of education give more of an insight into how the private life sphere becomes enmeshed in societal entrepreneuring, for example in Chapter 7, by way of parents leaving and picking up children at the preschool, taking part of the ideas of preschool teachers regarding their work on entrepreneurship. In Chapter 9 Holmgren illustrates how different actors – from the public, private and NPVO sectors – work together to create situations that facilitate teachers to experiment and develop their pedagogy. The same goes for Chapter 10 by Johansson and Rosell, which discusses how educating for societal entrepreneuring varies depending on whether it is carried out in the public (academic) sector or in the private and NPVO sectors. What they all have in common is the ambition to create conditions for students to be creative and take initiative (action) and to give ground for critical reflection. Nevertheless, the private sphere in many ways remains present, not only through the involvement of children and their parents. Promoting societal entrepreneuring can then be described as a process where actors from different sectors act together, creating a common language and shared practices, laying the ground for an OC that does not belong to one sector or the other, but becomes shared for all involved, irrespective of their sectorial residence.

Promoting societal entrepreneuring cannot only be related to education, but is discernible in many other chapters in the book. In Astrid Lindgren's World (ALW) (Chapter 3), for instance, the 'problem' of organizing ALW has shifted over time and is described in five phases, addressing not only different ways of bridging between the three sectors but also between actors' public and private lives. Accordingly, the crises that ALW experiences sometimes appear as a private-sphere challenge and at other times as a public challenge; sometimes, too, as both a private and public concern. There is also a dynamic aspect to consider. Private problems are continuously made public, because whether they are about water access, Fair Trade or educating students in a new way, they rely on people from different sectors to work together and come up with a solution. In contrast to the traditional view of commercial entrepreneurship, societal entrepreneurship can thus be seen as private/public nexus rather than an individual/opportunity nexus (Shane 2003).

Hence, boundaries between the (three) sectors are not the only ones crossed or intertwined, as discussed by Tillmar in Chapter 2 in the enactment of societal entrepreneurship. Those between the private and public spheres of life are enmeshed as well. Referring to both business and social entrepreneurs as existentially driven, it points towards how the venturing career absorbs them, making the creation of economic and social value become the very meaning of life. The existential commitment, as part of the private sphere and individuals' engagement and commitment, is also seen in the case in Chapter 3, where people entrepreneuring in the private sector who are employed in the public sector engage in the development of Macken in their leisure time. This also goes for the Moon House (in Chapter 7), which illustrates how powerful people in society have been fascinated by the idea of putting a small red cottage on the surface of the moon and have thus enrolled themselves as individuals, downplaying in their engagement their professional positions as, for example, politicians, county governors, CEOs or researchers. In Chapter 2 Tillmar argues that in the rural context the intertwining of the public and private sectors is a more common process. Business owners are engaged in associations in their leisure time, where with their personal engagement they act as both societal entrepreneurs and as sponsors. This is also seen in Chapter 4 by Johannisson and Sundin, portraying actors playing several roles in the local community as businessmen, and local politicians making their private spheres public by taking responsibility for ALW and caring for its survival due to their double loyalties, both to the business and the local community.

Moreover, it is well known that a great deal of work on introducing entrepreneurship education is carried out by fiery souls from all sectors in their spare time (for example Berglund and Holmgren 2007). This means that when they work with public issues in the private sphere (for example at the dinner table in someone's home) as well, their spare time is turned into a resource (voluntary work). In that sense, the private/public divide is no longer clear-cut. This is especially apparent in industrial districts where the family (business) is preserved, where the boundary between the private and public spheres becomes dissolved on different arenas, some private per se and some public. This boundary-crossing between different spheres also seems to be a remedy against the colonization of the private-sector logic. Recently (2012) the heirs of Astrid Lindgren announced that they want to regulate contractually, not ALW, but other operations that use the stories created by the great author. This concerns an amusement park in Stockholm, which is obviously lacking the strong social embedding that ALW has acquired in its small-town setting. The Gesellschaft setting in combination with weaker relations between the private and public spheres may explain why contractual ones replace personal trust relations.

Even if we have a state apparatus that is engaged in reformulating public problems, we have witnessed in this book how actors from different sectors have come together to solve public problems that have been silenced (for example the non-visible small business owners in Chapter 5) or reformulated (the notion of a new entrepreneurial pedagogy in Chapters 8, 9 and 10), or even problems that seem to lie outside everyone's responsibility (Macken in Chapter 3) or the seemingly new problems that have been invented, like the one described in Chapter 7 of putting a house on the moon to create cooperation in between sectors. However, these problems originate in private concerns rather than state interventions. Accordingly, societal entrepreneuring seems to be grounded in the logic of re-formulating private problems in a public terrain.

SOCIETAL ENTREPRENEURING: CREATING SOCIAL VALUE AND NEW ROLES FOR RESEARCHERS

Our ambition has been to create an understanding of how societal entrepreneuring mobilizes power among actors in different sectors, and how they together come up with innovative solutions to social problems, which are turned into communal opportunities. In these processes – here referred to as societal entrepreneuring – social value is created. As a concluding point of this anthology we want to elaborate somewhat on this issue. Our journey within the research project 'Organizing Societal Entrepreneurship in Sweden', as presented in this book, has revealed the presence of local capabilities to creatively organize favourable conditions for entrepreneuring in the name of society. Associating value creation with the form (the process here described as entrepreneuring) and not the content (the output) makes us stand out if compared with how 'social value creation' is usually made sense of. While many talk about 'social value' without further comments, social (as well as environmental) value is often juxtaposed to the economic bottom line. Austin et al. (2006) present a reverse definition, stressing that social value is what is not (economic) wealth for individuals and shareholders. However, rather than elaborating on a more precise definition they argue that 'the social demand for social value creation is enormous' (Austin et al. 2006, p. 18). We agree, but since the demand is enormous we must be aware what we subscribe to when we write about social value so as to protect this particular value from becoming eviscerated.

The recently published *Handbook of Research Methods on Social Entrepreneurship* edited by Richard Seymour (2012) provides a broad exposé of methods for studying social entrepreneurship. Moreover, Seymour makes an ambitious attempt to clarify what might be associated with social value in the kind of entrepreneuring that is constructed in line with the broad understanding of 'societal'. That is a kind of entrepreneuring – call it social or societal – that imbues society and is part of transforming its structures. After an extensive excursion into the varied landscape of proposed definitions Seymour, however, ends up in contrasting commercial and social entrepreneurship, associating the latter with collective and playful human activity with a focus on process rather than on outcome. This process view is in line with our own basic view, but we also want to move beyond such dichotomizations – an either/or as regards the commercial and the social (see Chapter 1).

We argue that the will to contribute with social value cannot be reserved to some and removed from others. This will is likewise important among small-business owners, high-tech companies, new social media ventures and bio-medical innovations, even though it may not be explicitly stated, but taken for granted as part of the process. We argue that empirical phenomena associated with entrepreneuring cannot be divided into either/or. On the contrary, from the perspective of societal entrepreneuring, we hope to provide a language for recognizing the taken-for-granted creation of social value in every venture, as well as making it clear that entrepreneurship cannot be isolated to particular forms or activities. Where there are human beings, there is entrepreneuring. Where there is entrepreneuring, social value is produced – in one way or another.

This way of stitching together entrepreneuring from the notion of social value, as well as from the view of entrepreneurial approach, as outlined in the third part of the book, goes in line with the introductory reasoning of bridging. We are not only interested in researching into how actors bridge or intertwine the three sectors described throughout the book. We also want to illustrate how the public-private divide is recreated. If societal entrepreneuring means to stitch together in novel ways, researching this practice means to be attentive to how this stitching is made creatively in everyday practices. Otherwise we may end up in reproducing (as a contrast to problematizing) the structures that actors have come together to change. This also reminds us that there is no grand solution, and that society will never be completed, but needs to be made over and over again, and again, and again.

Let us now, briefly, move back to Seymour, who concludes by proposing exchange theory as a conceptual basis (ibid. p. 36). Whereas we agree that commercial activity should be considered as a means of creating social value, we think that the exchange theory is insufficient for a comprehensive understanding of social value creation. Goods and services also have a user value, and communal relations are especially frequent in settings where societal entrepreneuring is practised. '[T]he norm in communal relationships is to give benefits in response to needs or to demonstrate general concern for the other person. . . . It does not create a specific debt or obligation to return a comparable benefit, as it does in an exchange relationship' (Clark and Mills 1993, p. 684). Besides, creating change does not necessarily mean that a better society is crafted out for all those concerned, as pointed out in Chapter 6. What we may retain from Seymour's arguments is that commercial activities appear as means to create social value that is subjective to both the provider and the beneficiary and thus includes expressive value. Such value production should be guided by basic human ideals such as equality and a belief in everybody's potentiality. Several chapters in the book have directly and indirectly reflected on the enactment of such a view. Chapter 3, for example, presenting the Macken initiative, illustrates processes that seek to create integration, equality and solidarity based in an enterprise that is constantly (re)shaped by the actors involved.

Discussing the notion of social value in relation to societal entrepreneuring, a question between the lines concerns the responsibility of researchers to search for methodologies that enable them to contribute to social value creation outside their own professional community. In the outset of this book we stated that interactive approaches are especially relevant when researching societal entrepreneuring. Now reflecting on how the research presented in this book was conducted, we want to conclude by stepping back and reflecting upon the methodological pillars of interactive research, which has more or less informed all of the cases provided in the nine chapters. We will start out by applying a classification of different knowledge (cognitive) interests that has been brought up by Habermas and been elaborated upon by Richard Normann (1977, p. 191–192). These constitute the guiding knowledge interests in an investigation according to Normann:

- *Technical*, which is based on a realism approach and has the ambition to generalize;
- *Practical (or hermeneutic)*, which is about providing interpretations of individuals' experiences as expressed in behaviours and speech acts;
- *Emancipatory/critical*, which aims at revealing power structures that empower those being oppressed;

- *Innovative*, which aims at imagining new ways of improving the world.

However, something is lacking here, namely, the ethical reflections of the researchers' decisions to address certain questions, the choice of methodological approaches, and also their moral responsibility in participating in changing what they find to be 'wrong' or even 'bad' in some sense for the society that we inhabit. We thus want to add a fifth knowledge interest:

- *Moral*, which invites, or rather requests, the researchers themselves to participate in the enactment of a more human world.

This anthology includes contributions that jointly reflect all these knowledge interests. As presented in Table 1.2 in the introductory Chapter 1, this often means that several chapters are guided by a research strategy that draws upon more than one knowledge interest. Considering our general belief in qualitative research, only one chapter reveals a touch of the technical knowledge interest. Tillmar's Chapter 2 reports from a comparative study of 30 social ventures, only to end up in an in-depth case analysis that bridges to an interpretative approach. Hermeneutic research ambitions are most visible in Schwartz's discussion on fair trade in Chapter 6 but the emancipatory/critical is obvious as well. The hermeneutic knowledge interest is also reflected in Andersson and Johansson's ethnographic study of intermediaries as practising societal entrepreneuring (Chapter 5). This research interest recurs in Chapter 7 in Berglund and Johansson's analysis of the leaders of the Moon House project and IKEA. The hermeneutic and moral research interests are reflected in Johansson and Rosell's Chapter 10 in their discussion of promoting entrepreneuring education at the university and the SIP Network in a Folk High School context. Berglund's report in Chapter 8 from preschools bridges the hermeneutic and emancipatory/critical knowledge interests. The latter interest dominates Holmgren's discourse analysis in Chapter 9 about the Swedish school policy on entrepreneuring. The innovative research interest is observable in Johannisson and Sundin's reflections in Chapter 4 on the emergence of Astrid Lindgren's World (ALW) as an attempt by the famous author Astrid Lindgren to protect children from untamed market forces. In Chapter 3 Johannisson employs the innovative but also the moral research interest in his engagement in the social enterprise Macken.

We associate innovative approaches, also in research, with bridging what has so far not been linked. Proposing new methodologies or imagining new worlds is, however, not enough for contributing to moral knowledge creation. Then the crossing of the boundary between the academic community and the many others who inhabit society, usually addressed as '(communities of) practice', becomes especially salient. The Scandinavian countries have a long tradition in action and interactive research approaches; see for example Nielsen and Svensson (2006). Interactive research aims at joint knowledge creation between academics and practitioners. In contemporary Sweden this is an ambition of great concern, and the responsibility of universities to actively engage in exchange with representatives of the surrounding society is regulated by law. A recent anthology reports from the Swedish arena how different disciplines deal with this challenge (Johannisson et al. 2008). In this book we have reported some innovative ambitions; see for example Chapter 8 where Berglund applies multi-site ethnography and Chapter 3 where Johannisson uses daily digital conversations as a method that interactively creates mutually reflected knowledge on the part of the practitioner and researcher. Moreover, Johansson and Rosell in Chapter 10 illustrate that education can be seen partly as a sacrificial practice, a kind of communal relationship where teachers and students come together to give benefits in response to needs. Their story demonstrates the general concern for the other person in a way that transgresses the view of relationships described by exchange theory.

Outside Scandinavia, for example in the Anglo-Saxon world, interactive approaches are practised far less. Often they then become dramatized, as in the recent publication by Andrew Van de Ven (2007). The title *Engaged Scholarship* conceals ambitions that have already for several decades been nurtured in Scandinavia as pillars of action and interactive research. In a traditionally pragmatic American way Van de Ven defines *engaged scholarship* as 'a participative form of research for obtaining the different perspectives of key stakeholders (researchers, users, clients, sponsors and practitioners) in studying complex problems. By involving others and leveraging their different kinds of knowledge, engaged scholarship can produce knowledge that is more penetrating and insightful than when scholars or practitioners work on the problems alone' (Van de Ven 2007: 9). Still, the importance of practical knowledge for making sense also in an academic context was long before presented in another national context, namely the Japanese context, by Nonaka and Takeuchi (1995).

'Engagement' as defined by Van de Ven has thus become almost taken for granted in much social research in Sweden, and, as this book also reveals, in entrepreneurship research as well. Further development therefore has to advance beyond traditional action/interactive research. Such research may, however, be considered as a forerunner to what we associate with practising a genuine moral knowledge interest. From a participatory action research project Berglund and Wigren (2012) discuss how new worlds were created in a Swedish think-and-do tank that aimed at introducing societal entrepreneuring in Swedish regions and municipalities. In this project the researchers were invited to be part of the process. Since the participants deliberately wished to move away from traditional understandings of entrepreneurship, the researchers, in their turn, invited the participants (including themselves) to work with pictures and artefacts to find new words of entrepreneuring in order to craft societal entrepreneuring worlds. This process took place over a period of one year and resulted in new words being formulated to embrace the notion of societal entrepreneuring as a spontaneous, fun, artistic and historic activity, but also as a problem-solving activity that acknowledges resources such as time and energy, in contrast to money, and that calls for an understanding of the effects of inclusion and exclusion in contemporary society. During this process it was stressed that politics was about power, and questions were raised among involved politicians whether they really exercised this power. At the end of the process the members started to reconcile themselves to the fact that social entrepreneurship was not a new 'thing' addressed by policy-makers, but an integral part of the making of society, which made them view themselves as committed and involved societal entrepreneurs with a responsibility to take action. They were no longer looking upon themselves as 'helpers' in promoting societal entrepreneuring in their municipalities, but as equal members in societal entrepreneuring. This reflects the even broader conviction that the authors of this book share: that all human beings contribute to the making of societal entrepreneurship.[1]

In *The Deliberative Practitioner* John Forester (1999) argues that the public planner must move beyond her professional role and acknowledge that she works in a setting with many stakeholders with different interests which are often in conflict. The planner must then look upon herself as an integral part of such a context and sensitively cope with the different views. This calls for what Forester addresses as 'moral improvisation', which reflects and feeds phronesis, the Aristotelian understanding of prudence, practical knowledge. Elsewhere Johannisson (2011) argues that phronesis is practised by any experienced entrepreneur, but in societal entrepreneuring the need for balancing technical and moral matters becomes emphasized.

Researchers are by definition professionals and may as well act as politicians. Accordingly, they participate as equals in social entrepreneuring and practise moral improvisation. Obviously, this adds another argument to those provided in Chapter 1 for adopting a contextualized approach to societal entrepreneuring.

Researchers thus do not only invite practitioners to a knowledge creation process, but researchers may also be invited by practitioners (as in the case of Rosell in Chapter 10, or as Berglund and Wigren (2012) were by the think-and-do tank). Alternatively, researchers invite themselves, as Johannisson did in the case of Macken in Chapter 3, Schwartz in the case of the Fair Trade company Oria in Chapter 6, or that Berglund did by following the Moon House project, which has been running for over ten years. In all these cases the researcher is enrolled in a position beyond that of the 'traditional researcher' who steps in to acquire knowledge and then steps out. While Johannisson has been involved in daily conversations with the actors of Macken, seeking knowledge, but also promoting reflection and action, Schwartz found herself in the role of legitimizing the entrepreneur and her growing Fair Trade business. Berglund, in the Moon House, has deliberately initiated entrepreneurial processes on the arena that the Moon House has already created. Her entering and becoming part in entrepreneuring both fuelled the enactment of the Moon House event and the knowledge creation process.

The division line between researcher and practitioner is thus dissolved at times, to be re-established again – by reflection and writing. Elsewhere we have introduced the notion of 'enactive research' (Johannisson 2005; 2011), which is especially relevant for research into societal entrepreneuring. Enactive research means that the researcher instigates an innovative process and practises auto-ethnography to make the eventing of the process comprehensible. This reflects an involvement that includes the researcher's active participation in the world of the practitioners. Such enactment on the part of the researcher is not always intentional. In Chapter 10 Johansson and Rosell report how the latter was rather seduced to take on the role as an interactive researcher.

We also associate the acknowledgement of a moral knowledge interest with what Chia and MacKay (2007) address as 'dwelling' in time and space(s), physical, social and mental; compare Chapter 1. Dwelling means being present in the context of the persons and activities making the research phenomenon that is going to be studied without any immediate need to instrumentally use the insight gained. Schwartz in her story about Oria tells about several occasions when she was 'hanging around' in order to get a general feeling of what was going on. The paying of such respect to the world of practice can be seen in Chapter 7, where one of the authors (Berglund) was involved in different arenas in the Moon House case long before the events reported had happened. In his study of Macken in Chapter 3 Johannisson has been dwelling in the spatial and social context of the societal venturing since 2005 and he has so far (2012) remained involved. Chapter 10 can be mentioned again, in which researchers and teachers are driven by the idea of creating a better education environment. This can be seen as a moral knowledge interest, which is enhanced by interacting with an organization outside of the university. Instead of dwelling in their own university environment, they have dwelled in the environment of Folk High School education. We argue accordingly that practising a moral knowledge interest means that the researcher acknowledges the responsibility to discursively provide guidance towards a better world and in addition shares the responsibility to enact the crossing of boundaries, between the three sectors as well as between the private and public spheres.

NOTE

1. We thank our colleague Senada Bahto at Linnaeus University for making this position, taken-for-granted by us, visible.

REFERENCES

Austin, J., H. Stevenson and J. Wei-Skillern (2006), 'Social and commercial entrepreneurship: same, different or both?', *Entrepreneurship Theory and Practice*, January, 1–22.

Becattini, G., M. Bellandi and L. De Propris (eds) (2009), *A Handbook of Industrial Districts*, Cheltenham, UK and Northampton, MA, USA: Edward Elgar Publishing.

Berglund, K. and A.W. Johansson (2007), 'Entrepreneurship, discourses and conscientization in processes of regional development', *Journal of Entrepreneurship and Regional Development*, **19** (6), 499–525.

Berglund, K. and C. Wigren (2012), 'Using pictures and artefacts to disclose new wor(l)ds of entrepreneurship', forthcoming in *Action Research*.

Brint, S. (2001), 'Gemeinschaft revisited: A critique and reconstruction of the community concept', *Sociological Theory*, **19** (1), 1–23.

Chia, R. and B. MacKay (2007), 'Post-processual challenges for the emerging strategy-as-practice perspective: discovering strategy in the logic of practices', *Human Relations*, **60** (1), 217–242.

Clark, M.S. and J. Mills (1993), 'The difference between communal and exchange relationships: What it is and is not', *Personality and Social Psychology Bulletin*, **19**, 677–683.

Forester, J. (1999), *The Deliberative Practitioner. Encouraging Participatory Planning Processes*, Cambridge, MA: The MIT Press.

Gawell, M. (2006), *Activist Entrepreneurship. Attac'ing Norms and Disclosing Stories*, Stockholm: Stockholm University.

Giddens, A. (1991), *Modernity and Self-identity. Self and Society in the Late Modern Age*, Cambridge: Polity Press.

Grabher, G. (2001), 'Ecologies of creativity: the village, the group, and the heterarchic organisation of the British advertising industry', *Environment and Planning*, **33**, 351–374.

Hansen, N.J. (2010), *Conferences as Dramaturgical Learning Spaces*, Disseration, Danish School of Education, Copenhagen: Aarhus University.

Hernes, T. (2003), 'Organization as evolution of space', in B. Czarniawska and G. Sevón (eds) *Northern Light – Organization Theory in Scandinavia*, Malmö: Liber, pp. 267–289.

Hirschman, A-O. (1982), *Shifting Involvements. Private Interest and Public Action*, Oxford: Martin Robertson.

Hjorth, D. and B. Bjerke (2006), 'Public entrepreneurship: moving from social/ consumer to public/citizen', in C. Steyaert and D. Hjorth (eds), *Entrepreneurship as Social Change*, Cheltenham, UK and Northampton, MA, USA: Edward Elgar Publishing, pp. 97–120.

Illouz, E. (2007), *Cold Intimacies. The Making of Emotional Capitalism*, Cambridge: Polity Press.

Johannisson, B. (2000), 'Networking and entrepreneurial growth', in D. Sexton and H. Landström (eds) *Handbook of Entrepreneurship*, London: Blackwell, pp. 368–386.

Johannisson, B. (2003), 'Entrepreneurship as a collective phenomenon', in E. Genescà, D. Urbano, J. Capelleras, D. Guallarte and J. Vergès (eds), *Creación de Empresas – Entrepreneurship*, Barcelona: Servei de Publicacions de la Universitat Autònoma de Barcelona, pp. 87–109.

Johannisson, B. (2005), *Entreprenörskapets väsen* (*The Essence of Entrepreneurship*), Lund, Sweden: Studentlitteratur.

Johannisson, B. (2009), 'Networking and entrepreneurship in place', in M-A. Galindo, J. Guzman and D. Ribeiro (eds), *Entrepreneurship and Business – A Regional Perspective*. Berlin: Springer, pp. 137–162.

Johannisson, B. (2009a), 'Industrial districts in Scandinavia', in G. Becattini, M. Bellandi and L. De Propris (eds) *A Handbook of Industrial Districts*, Cheltenham, UK and Northampton, MA, USA: Edward Elgar Publishing, pp. 521–534.

Johannisson, B. (2011), 'Towards a practice theory of entrepreneuring', *Small Business Economics*, **36** (2), 135–150.

Johannisson, B. and A. Nilsson (1989), 'Community entrepreneurship – networking for local development', *Journal of Entrepreneurship and Regional Development*, **1** (1), 1–19.

Johannisson, B., K. Gunnarsson and T. Stjernberg (eds) (2008), *Gemensamt kunskapande* (*Joint Knowledge-creation*), Växjö: Växjö University Press.

Johansson, A.W. (2009), 'Regional development by means of broadened entrepreneurship', *European Planning Studies*, **17** (8), 1205–1222.

Maskell P., H. Bathelt and A. Malmberg (2006), 'Building global knowledge pipelines: The role of temporary clusters', *European Planning Studies*, **14**, 997–1013.

Nielsen, K.A. and L. Svensson (eds) (2006), *Action and Interactive Research. Beyond Practice and Theory*, Maastricht: Shaker Publishing.

Nonaka, I. and H. Takeuchi (1995), *The Knowledge-Creating Company*, Oxford: Oxford University Press.

Normann, R. (1977), *Management for Growth*, Chichester: Wiley.

Ramirez-Pasillas, M. (2010), 'International trade fairs as amplifiers of permanent and temporary proximities in clusters', *Journal of Entrepreneurship and Regional Development*, **22** (2), 155–187.

Seymour, R.D. (ed.) (2012), *Handbook of Research Methods on Social*

Entrepreneurship, Cheltenham, UK and Northampton, MA, USA: Edward Elgar Publishing.

Shane, S. (2003), *A General Theory of Entrepreneurship: The Individual-Opportunity Nexus*, Cheltenham, UK and Northampton, MA, USA: Edward Elgar Publishing.

Tönnies, F. (1965), *Community and Association*, London: Routledge & Kegan Paul.

Van de Ven, A.H. (2007), *Engaged Scholarship. A Guide for Organizational and Social Research*, New York: Oxford University Press.

Winnicott, D.W. (1971), *Playing and Reality*, London: Penguin, Harmondsworth.

Index